StartUp

Ken Beatty, Series Consultant

Lynn Bonesteel
Peter Clements
Jane Curtis
Linda L. Lane
Nancy Blodgett Matsunaga
Geneva Tesh

StartUp 8

Pearson, 221 River Street, Hoboken, NJ 07030

Staff credits: The people who made up the StartUp team representing editorial, production, and design are Gregory Bartz, Peter Benson, Magdalena Berkowska, Stephanie Callahan, Jennifer Castro, Tracey Munz Cataldo, Dave Dickey, Gina DiLillo, Irene Frankel, Christopher Leonowicz, Bridget McLaughlin, Kamila Michalak, Laurie Neaman, Katherine Sullivan, Claire Van Poperin, Joseph Vella, Peter West, and Autumn Westphal.

Cover credit: Front cover: Javier Osores/EyeEm/Getty Images. Back cover: Klaus Vedfelt/Getty Images (Level 1); Alexandre Moreau/ Getty Images (Level 2); Matteo Colombo/Getty Images (Level 3); Javier Osores/EyeEm/Getty Images (Level 4); Liyao Xie/Getty Images (Level 5); Ezra Bailey/Getty Images (Level 6); guvendemir/Getty Images (Level 7); Yusuke Shimazu/EyeEm/Getty Images (Level 8); tovovan/Shutterstock (icons)

Text composition: emc design ltd.

Library of Congress cataloging-in-publication data on file.

Photo credits: See page 168

Printed in the United States of America

ISBN-10: 0-13-736028-2
ISBN-13: 978-0-13-736028-4

2 2022

ISBN-10: 0-13-733182-7 (with Online Practice)
ISBN-13: 978-0-13-733182-6 (with Online Practice)

2 2022

ACKNOWLEDGMENTS

We would like to thank the following people for their insightful and helpful comments and suggestions.

Maria Alam, Extension Program-Escuela Americana, San Salvador, El Salvador; **Milton Ascencio**, Universidad Don Bosco, Soyapango, El Salvador; **Raul Avalos**, CALUSAC, Guatemala City, Guatemala; **Adrian Barnes**, Instituto Chileno Norteericano, Santiago, Chile; **Laura Bello**, Centro de Idiomas Xalapa, Universidad Veracruzana, Xalapa, México; **Isabela Villas Boas**, Casa Thomas Jefferson, Brasília, Brazil; **Jeisson Alonso Rodriguez Bonces**, Fort Dorchester High School, Bogotá, Colombia; **Juan Pablo Calderón Bravo**, Manpower English, Santiago, Chile; **Ellen J. Campbell**, RMIT, Ho Chi Minh City, Vietnam; **Vinicio Cancinos**, CALUSAC, Guatemala City, Guatemala; **Viviana Castilla**, Centro de Enseñanza de Lenguas Extranjeras UN, México; **Carlos Celis**, Cel.Lep Idiomas S.A., São Paulo, Brazil; **Bernal Cespedes**, ULACIT, Tournón, Costa Rica; **Carlos Eduardo Aguilar Cortes**, Universidad de los Andes, Bogotá, Colombia; **Solange Lopes Vinagre Costa**, Senac-SP, São Paulo, Brazil; **Isabel Cubilla**, Panama Bilingüe, Panama City, Panama; **Victoria Dieste**, Alianza Cultural Uruguay-Estados Unidos, Montevideo, Uruguay; **Francisco Domerque**, Georgal Idiomas, México City, México; **Vern Eaton**, St. Giles International, Vancouver, Canada; **Maria Fajardo**, Extension Program-Escuela Americana, San Salvador, El Salvador; **Diana Elizabeth Leal Ffrench**, Let's Speak English, Cancún, México; **Rosario Giraldez**, Alianza Cultural Uruguay-Estados Unidos, Montevideo, Uruguay; **Lourdes Patricia Rodríguez Gómez**, Instituto Tecnológico de Chihuahua, Chihuahua, México; **Elva Elizabeth Martínez de González**, Extension Program-Escuela Americana, San Salvador, El Salvador; **Gabriela Guel**, Centro de Idiomas de la Normal Superior, Monterrey, México; **Ana Raquel Fiorani Horta**, SENAC, Ribeirão Preto, Brazil; **Carol Hutchinson**, Heartland International English School, Winnipeg, Canada; **Deyanira Solís Juárez**, Centro de Idiomas de la Normal Superior, Monterrey, México; **Miriam de Käppel**, Colegio Bilingüe El Prado, Guatemala City, Guatemala; **Ikuko Kashiwabara**, Osaka Electro-Communication University, Neyagawa, Japan; **Steve Kirk**, Nippon Medical School, Tokyo, Japan; **Jill Landry**, GEOS Languages Plus, Ottawa, Canada; **Tiffany MacDonald**, East Coast School of Languages, Halifax, Canada; **Angélica Chávez Escobar Martínez**, Universidad de León, León, Guanajuato, México; **Renata Martinez**, CALUSAC, Guatemala City, Guatemala; **Maria Alejandra Mora**, Keiser International Language Institute, San Marcos, Carazo, Nicaragua; **Alexander Chapetón Morales**, Abraham Lincoln School, Bogotá, Colombia; **José Luis Castro Moreno**, Universidad de León, León, Guanajuato, México; **Yukari Naganuma**, Eikyojuku for English Teachers, Tokyo, Japan; **Erina Ogawa**, Daito Bunka University, Tokyo, Japan; **Carolina Zepeda Ortega**, Let's Speak English, Cancún, México; **Lynn Passmore**, Vancouver International College, Vancouver, Canada; **Noelle Peach**, EC English, Vancouver, Canada; **Ana-Marija Petrunic**, George Brown College, Toronto, Canada; **Romina Planas**, Centro Cultural Paraguayo Americano, Asunción, Paraguay; **Sara Elizabeth Portela**, Centro Cultural Paraguayo Americano, Asunción, Paraguay; **Ana Carolina González Ramírez**, Universidad de Costa Rica, San José, Costa Rica; **Luz Rey**, Centro Colombo Americano, Bogota, Colombia; **Octavio Garduno Ruiz**, AIPT Service S.C., Coyoacán, México; **Amado Sacalxot**, Colegio Lehnsen Americas, Guatemala City, Guatemala; **Deyvis Sanchez**, Instituto Cultural Dominico-Americano, Santo Domingo, Dominican Republic; **Lucy Slon**, JFK Adult Centre, Montreal, Canada; **Scott Stulberg**, University of Regina, Regina, Canada; **Maria Teresa Suarez**, Colegios APCE, San Salvador, El Salvador; **Daniel Valderrama**, Centro Colombo Americano, Bogotá, Colombia; **Kris Vicca**, Feng Chia University, Taichung, Taiwan; **Sairy Matos Villanueva**, Centro de Actualización del Magisterio, Chetumal, Q.R., México; **Edith Espino Villarreal**, Universidad Tecnológica de Panama, El Dorado, Panama

LEARNING OBJECTIVES

WELCOME UNIT

Unit	Vocabulary	Language Choices	Conversation / Speaking	Listening
1 Do you accept the challenge? **page 5**	• Words related to performance	• Noun clauses as subjects, objects, and complements • More ways to express future time • Preparatory subjects: *it*, *here*, and *there*	• Talk about performance • Talk about challenges • Discuss world problems **Conversation Skill** Make suggestions	• Listen to a podcast about 30-day challenges **Listening Skill** Listen for rhetorical questions
2 Are you a member? **page 17**	• Words related to stereotypes	• Passive voice: agent versus no agent • Causative verbs • Active versus passive reporting	• Talk about stereotypes • Talk about fandom • Discuss bias **Conversation Skill** Use hyperbole	• Listen to a podcast about fandom **Listening Skill** Listen for phrases that guide a conversation
3 How do you explain that? **page 29**	• Words related to mysteries	• Modals for speculation about the past • Modals for expectation • Passive modals	• Talk about famous mysteries • Talk about personal mysteries • Discuss urban legends **Conversation Skill** Keep listeners' attention	• Listen to a podcast about mysterious experiences **Listening Skill** Listen for emphasis
4 Is it art? **page 41**	• Words related to street art	• Substitution with *so* and *not* • Phrasal verbs • Past perfect and past perfect continuous with the simple past	• Talk about street art • Talk about AI and art • Discuss the benefits of improvisation **Conversation Skill** Ask for an opinion	• Listen to a podcast about AI and art **Listening Skill** Listen for signal phrases in conclusions
5 Say that again? **page 53**	• Words related to communication	• The subjunctive • Embedded *yes/no* questions • Embedded *Wh-* questions	• Talk about diplomatic language • Talk about cultural differences • Discuss the origin of slang **Conversation Skill** Communicate diplomatically	• Listen to a podcast about the importance of silence in communication **Listening Skill** Listen for contrasts

Pronunciation	Video Talk / Discussion	Reading	Writing	Problem Solving
• Final intonation in rhetorical questions	• Listen to or watch a talk about solving world problems **Note-taking Skill** Create a matrix chart **Discussion Skill** Ask follow-up questions	• Read about viral challenges **Reading Skill** Check-Underline-Question	• Write a narrative essay **Writing Skill** Vary sentence construction	• Consider ways in which people can reduce stress
• Stress in causative verb phrases	• Listen to or watch a talk about bias **Note-taking Skill** Use abbreviations and symbols **Discussion Skill** Build on ideas	• Read about virtual friendships **Reading Skill** Identify key information	• Write a compare and contrast essay **Writing Skill** Use transition words	• Consider ways in which people can be more critical about news they encounter
• Reduction of modal perfects	• Listen to or watch a talk about urban legends **Note-taking Skill** Use mapping **Discussion Skill** Acknowledge ideas	• Read about life's mysteries **Reading Skill** Respond to the writer	• Write a plot summary **Writing Skill** Build excitement	• Consider how people might be convinced to review current scientific evidence
• Stress in phrasal verbs	• Listen to or watch a talk about improvisation **Note-taking Skill** Use an outline **Discussion Skill** Say "yes" to keep a conversation going	• Read about a famous festival **Reading Skill** Summarize paragraphs	• Write a descriptive essay **Writing Skill** Use different tenses	• Consider ways to ensure that the sale and resale of art is fair to everyone involved
• Contrastive stress	• Listen to or watch a talk about slang **Note-taking Skill** Know what to write **Discussion Skill** Speculate	• Read about communicating with aliens **Reading Skill** Recognize word choices	• Write a rhetorical analysis **Writing Skill** Vary placement of transitions	• Consider whether the group of origin affects a word's inclusion in the dictionary

Unit	Vocabulary	Language Choices	Conversation / Speaking	Listening
6 What are they hiding? **page 65**	• Words related to financial crime	• Restrictive and non-restrictive relative clauses • Relative clauses after prepositions and quantity expressions • Reducing relative clauses to phrases	• Talk about financial crime • Talk about a system of government • Discuss power in society **Conversation Skill** Show interest with interjections	• Listen to a podcast about a system of government **Listening Skill** Recognize arguments
7 So you think we should break up? **page 77**	• Words related to persuasion	• Negative gerunds and infinitives • Perfect gerunds and infinitives • Reported speech	• Talk about the art of persuasion • Talk about a breakup • Discuss monopolies **Conversation Skill** Negotiate	• Listen to a podcast about breakups **Listening Skill** Recognize stress on key words
8 Get it? **page 89**	• Words related to humor	• Reduced adverb time clauses • Cause and effect in participial phrases • Participial adjectives and nouns as adjectives	• Talk about humor • Talk about laughter • Discuss the art of joke telling **Conversation Skill** Express concern	• Listen to a podcast about the science of humor **Listening Skill** Recognize pauses
9 Can we talk about this? **page 101**	• Words related to conflict	• Implied conditionals • Inverted conditionals • *Hope* and *wish*	• Talk about conflict • Talk about how to deal with conflict • Discuss conflict in narratives **Conversation Skill** Repair communication breakdowns	• Listen to a podcast about conflict **Listening Skill** Listen for signal words
10 How do you feel? **page 113**	• Words related to emotions	• Articles • *Too* and *enough* • Adverbs	• Talk about emotions • Talk about sadness • Discuss happiness **Conversation Skill** Show empathy	• Listen to a podcast about sadness **Listening Skill** Listen for questions

Pronunciation	Video Talk / Discussion	Reading	Writing	Problem Solving
• Dropped vowels	• Listen to or watch a talk about power in society **Note-taking Skill** Note the main points **Discussion Skill** Explore alternative viewpoints	• Read about a public crisis **Reading Skill** Process information	• Write a letter of advice **Writing Skill** Speak directly to the reader	• Consider ways in which individuals and governments might fight corruption
• Stress in pronouns and auxiliary verbs	• Listen to or watch a talk about monopolies **Note-taking Skill** Take notes in different colors **Discussion Skill** Signpost	• Read about the global plastic crisis **Reading Skill** Scan for data	• Write an argumentative essay **Writing Skill** Use conjunctions and conjunctive adverbs strategically	• Consider what types of questions might help couples decide if they are suited to marry each other
• Pausing with participial phrases	• Listen to or watch a talk about the art of joke telling **Note-taking Skill** Make lists **Discussion Skill** Take feedback well	• Read about the funniest jokes **Reading Skill** Use a KWL chart	• Write an opinion essay **Writing Skill** Use parallel structure with paired conjunctions	• Consider ways in which consumers could make more intelligent choices about the advertising they encounter
• Intonation in parenthetical expressions	• Listen to or watch a talk about conflict in narratives **Note-taking Skill** Prioritize important information **Discussion Skill** Invite others to participate	• Read about action movies **Reading Skill** Use informal tones	• Write a process essay **Writing Skill** Determine your audience	• Consider different ways of responding to conflicts
• Intensifiers and emphatic stress	• Listen to or watch a talk about happiness **Note-taking Skill** Use charts for organization **Discussion Skill** Tell an anecdote	• Read about the pursuit of happiness **Reading Skill** Visualize a story	• Write an analytical essay **Writing Skill** Use a formal style	• Consider how you might convince people with fixed mindset traits to adopt growth mindset traits

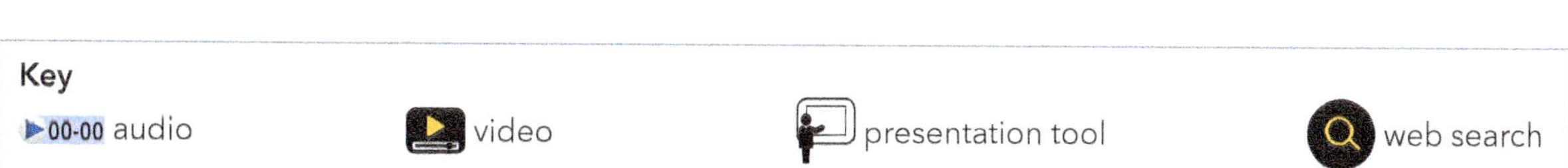

TO THE TEACHER

Welcome to *StartUp*

StartUp is an innovative eight-level, general American English course for adults and young adults who want to make their way in the world and need English to do it. The course takes students from CEFR A1 to C1 and enables teachers and students to track their progress in detail against the Global Scale of English (GSE) Learning Objectives.

StartUp Level	GSE Range	CEFR	Description
1	22-33	A1	Beginner
2	30-37	A2	High beginner
3	34-43	A2+	Low intermediate
4	41-51	B1	Intermediate

StartUp Level	GSE Range	CEFR	Description
5	49-58	B1+	High intermediate
6	56-66	B2	Upper intermediate
7	64-75	B2+	Low advanced
8	73-84	C1	Advanced

English for 21st-century learners

StartUp helps your students develop the spoken and written language they need to communicate in their personal, academic, and work lives. In each lesson, you help students build the collaborative and critical thinking skills so essential for success in the 21st century. *StartUp* allows students to learn the language in ways that work for them: anytime, anywhere. The Pearson Practice English App allows students to access their English practice on the go. Additionally, students have all the audio and video files at their fingertips in the app and on the Pearson English Portal.

Motivating and relevant learning

StartUp creates an immersive learning experience with a rich blend of multimedia videos and interactive activities; podcasts, interviews, and other audio texts for listening practice; humorous, engaging conversations with an international cast of characters for modeling conversation skills; high-interest video talks beginning at Level 5; media project videos in Levels 1-4; presentation skills videos in Levels 5-6; and problem-solving challenges in Levels 7-8 for end-of-unit skills consolidation.

Personalized, flexible teaching

The unit structure and the wealth of support materials give you options to personalize the class to best meet your students' needs. *StartUp* gives you the freedom to focus on different strands and skills; for example, you can spend more class time on listening and speaking. You can choose to teach traditionally or flip the learning. You can teach sections of the lesson in the order you prefer. And you can use the ideas in the Teacher's Edition to help you extend and differentiate instruction, particularly for mixed-ability students and for large and small classes.

Access at your fingertips

StartUp provides students with everything they need to extend their learning to their mobile device. The app empowers students to take charge of their learning outside of class, allowing them to practice English whenever and wherever they want, online or offline. The app provides practice of vocabulary, grammar, listening, and conversation. Students can go to any lesson by scanning a QR code on their Student Book page or through the app menu. The app also provides students with access to all the audio and video files from the course.

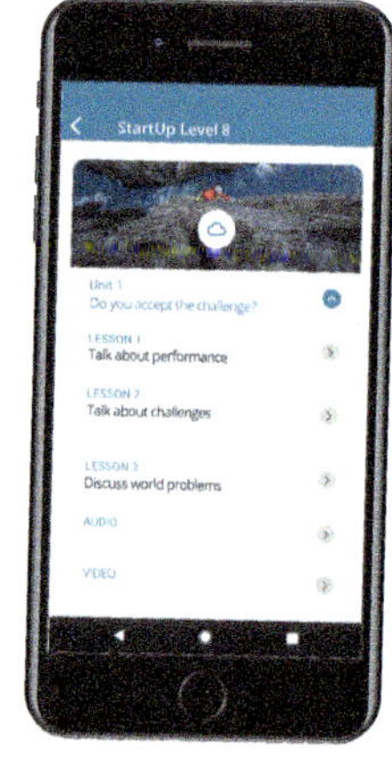

Components

For the Teacher

StartUp provides everything you need to plan, teach, monitor progress, and assess learning.

The ***StartUp* presentation tool** allows you to

- zoom in on the page to focus the class's attention
- launch the vocabulary flashcard decks from the page
- use tools, like a highlighter, to emphasize specific text
- play all the audio texts and videos from the page
- pop up interactive grammar activities
- move easily to and from any cross-referenced pages

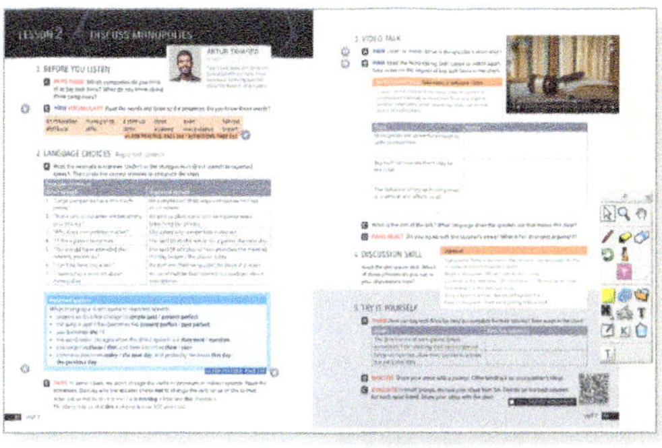

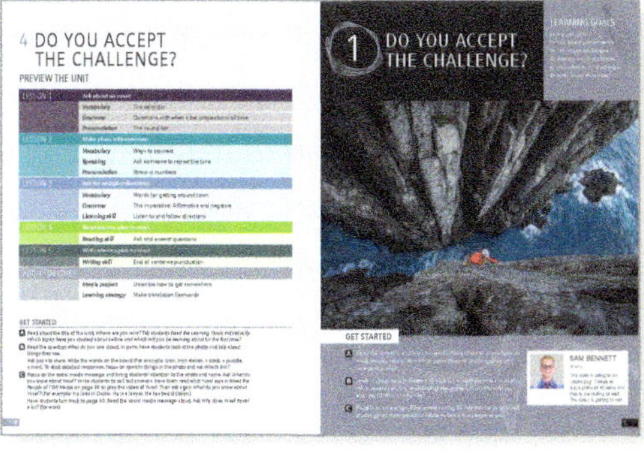

The interleaved **Teacher's Edition** includes

- an access code to the mobile app online resources
- language and culture notes
- teaching tips to help you improve your teaching practice
- *look for* notes to help assess students' performance
- answer keys on the facing page of the notes
- and more!

Teacher's online resources on the Teacher's Portal, include the following, plus video-conferencing integration with easy-to-use class scheduling:

- Teaching with StartUp videos
- Teaching StartUp online resources
- Teacher Methodology Handbook
- A unit walkthrough
- Test Generator assessment software
- Teacher's Edition notes
- rubrics for speaking and writing
- hundreds of reproducible worksheets
- answer keys for all practice
- audio and video scripts
- the GSE Teacher Mapping Booklet
- the GSE Toolkit

For the Student

***StartUp* Student's Book and eBook**

The eBook enables students to complete grammar activities and play audio and videos directly from the page.

***StartUp* Mobile app** for anytime, anywhere on-the-go practice

- Vocabulary, grammar, and listening activities
- All audio and video files
- Access from the app menu or QR codes on the lesson page

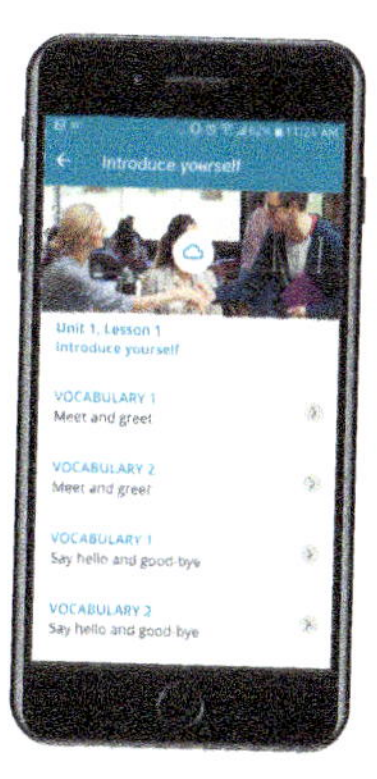

***StartUp* Online Practice** (optional) for more formal online practice

- Grammar practice and access to all Grammar Coach videos
- Vocabulary practice, including games and flashcards
- Feedback that guides students to the correct answer
- Speaking and pronunciation practice, with access to all Pronunciation Coach videos
- Summative assessments that measure students' mastery of all content
- A gradebook that records scores on practice and assessments and helps both teachers and students monitor progress and plan further practice

***StartUp* Workbook** (optional) for more formal traditional practice

- Practice of vocabulary, grammar, reading, and writing
- Self-assessments of grammar and vocabulary

WELCOME UNIT

1 IN THE CLASSROOM

A Get to know your classmates

Talk to your classmates. Find someone who matches each prompt. Write his or her first name on the line. Then ask follow-up questions.

- enjoys shopping ___________
- loves scary movies ___________
- is afraid of heights ___________
- can draw ___________
- has traveled to another country ___________
- is very athletic ___________

A: Excuse me, do you enjoy shopping?
B: Yes, I do! My name is Hana. H-A-N-A.
A: Thanks! What kinds of things do you like to buy?

B Strategies for class and business discussions

Here are some examples of strategies that will help you overcome challenges in discussions with classmates or colleagues. Complete the tips with problems from the box.

~~doesn't participate~~	goes off topic	speaks too softly
speaks too quickly	speaks too much	interrupts others

☐ 1. If someone doesn't participate, invite him or her to join in by saying things like…
- "What do you think, Diego?"
- "We haven't heard from Chiyo yet. What do you think about…?"

☐ 2. If someone ___________, get him or her back on track by saying things like…
- "Let's return to what Lanh was saying."
- "That's a good point, but let's get back to the main issue."

☐ 3. If someone is impatient and frequently ___________, you can say…
- "Wait your turn, please. You'll have a chance to talk in a moment."
- "Hold on. Let Malik finish what he's saying."

☐ 4. If someone ___________ and others don't have the opportunity to speak, you can politely interrupt by saying…
- "Thank you, Noor. Now let's hear what other people have to say."
- "That's an interesting idea. What do you think about that, Jae-jin?"

☐ 5. If someone ___________, ask him or her to slow down by saying…
- "Would you mind slowing down?"
- "Could you say that a little more slowly, please?"

☐ 6. If someone ___________, and others have trouble understanding what is being said, get him or her to speak up by saying…
- "Would you mind speaking up a little?"
- "I'm afraid we can't hear what you're saying."

C
▶00-01 **Listen. Check (✓) the strategies from 1B that you hear.**

D
DISCUSS **In groups, discuss the strategies in 1B. Which ones are the most / least useful? Say why.**

2 LEARN ABOUT YOUR BOOK

1. Look at pages iv–vii. What information is on those pages? ______________________
2. How many units are in the book? ______________
3. How many lessons are in each unit? ____________
4. Look at Language Choices on page 6. Where is the practice? ______________________
5. Look at the QR code [QR code] at the bottom of page 7. What does it mean? ______________________

   ____
6. Look at the ■ I CAN STATEMENT at the bottom of page 7. What does it tell you? ______________

   ____
7. Look at this icon [search icon] on page 13. What does it mean?

   ____

   ____

3 LEARN ABOUT YOUR APP

1. Look inside the front cover. Where can you go to download the Pearson Practice English App for *StartUp*? ______________________
2. Where are the instructions for registering for the app? ______________________

   ____
3. Look at the picture of the app. What do you see?

   ____
4. Look at the picture again. Fill in the blanks with the numbers 1-3.
   a. Number _____ shows the practice activities.
   b. Number _____ shows the video files.
   c. Number _____ shows the audio files.
5. Look at the picture again. What does [cloud icon] mean? ______________________
6. Look at the QR code on page 7 again. What happens when you scan the code?

   ____

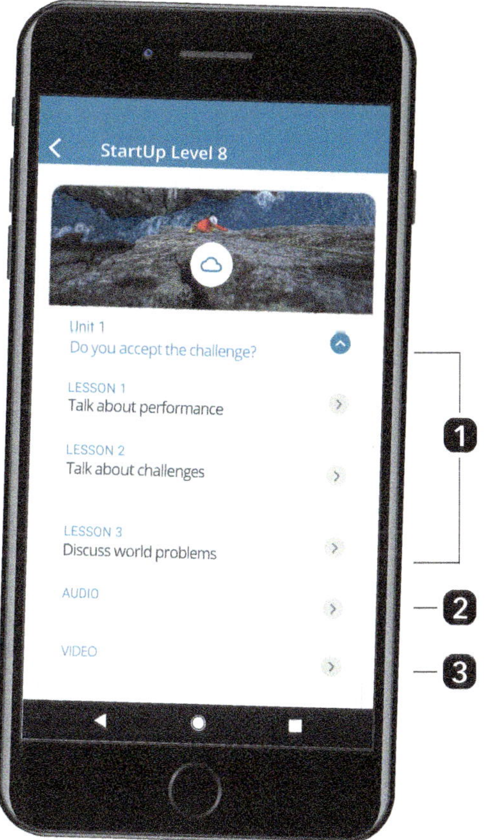

MEET THE PEOPLE OF TSW MEDIA

To find out more, listen to the introductions!

TSW Media is a big company with big ideas. It has offices all over the world. It works with international clients to help them market their products and services.

SAM BENNETT

Editorial intern

▶00-02 Hello! My name is Sam Bennett. I'm an editorial intern in the New York office.

IRIS LIN

Lawyer

▶00-05 Hello. My name is Iris Lin. I'm a native of Beijing, China. I'm a lawyer.

CAMILA RIVAS

Production coordinator

▶00-03 Hi, everyone! I'm Camila Rivas. I live in Santiago, Chile, where I work as a production coordinator.

ARTUR TAVARES

Sales rep

▶00-06 Hi, everybody. My name is Artur Tavares. I'm a sales rep from São Paulo, Brazil.

EDGAR VELA

Creative director

▶00-04 Hi there. I'm Edgar Vela. I'm a creative director, and I live and work in Lima, Peru.

ARIYA SUKSUAY

Office manager

▶00-07 Hi! I'm Ariya Suksuay. I was born in Thailand, but now I live in New York. I work as an office manager.

Every year, TSW sponsors a competition for employees to get mentoring and coaching to improve their public speaking skills. Here are three of the winners!

ADRIANA LOPEZ

▶00-08 Hi. My name is Adriana Lopez. I work in the technology department in the Quito office.

KENDRICK SCOTT

▶00-09 Hey! I'm Kendrick Scott, and I'm a designer in the Vancouver office.

DAVID CRUZ

▶00-10 Hi. My name is David Cruz. I'm from Florida, but I've lived and worked in Singapore for the past six years. I'm an advertising manager.

1 DO YOU ACCEPT THE CHALLENGE?

LEARNING GOALS

In this unit, you

- talk about performance
- talk about challenges
- discuss world problems
- read about viral challenges
- write a narrative essay

GET STARTED

A Read the unit title and learning goals. What kinds of challenges do most people face in life? What other kinds of challenges do you face personally?

B Look at the photo. It shows a climber on a rockface over the ocean. What would you find challenging about this activity? Would you ever do it? Why or why not?

C Read Sam's message. Why would having friends visit be considered challenging? How does that relate to Sam's busy week at work?

SAM BENNETT

@SamB

This week is going to be challenging. There's so much going on at work, and friends are visiting as well. The stress is getting to me!

LESSON 1 TALK ABOUT PERFORMANCE

1 VOCABULARY Words related to performance

A Look at the infographic. What qualities do you think are the most important for success at work?

B ▶01-01 Read and listen. Do you know the words in bold?

QUALITIES EMPLOYERS WANT

1 Drive
These employees show **initiative**. They are **high achievers** who set goals and meet them. They require limited **oversight**.

2 Dependability
Supervisors rely on **dependable** employees to follow through. They have a strong **track record** for completing tasks on time.

3 A Positive Attitude
Upbeat employees create a positive work environment. People with this personality **trait** face challenges with enthusiasm. They **acknowledge** their mistakes and view them as opportunities for growth.

4 Teamwork
Team players have strong **collaboration** skills. From a **brainstorming** session through job completion, they always put the company first. They give credit to the group effort.

5 Flexibility
Employers value workers with a broad **skill set** who are able to complete a variety of assignments. Flexible employees easily adapt to change, and can handle pressure as they **juggle** multiple tasks.

>> FOR PRACTICE, PAGE 125 / DEFINITIONS, PAGE 155

2 LANGUAGE CHOICES Noun clauses as subjects, objects, and complements

A Read the example sentences. Underline the noun clauses. Then circle the correct answers in the chart.

Noun clauses are dependent clauses that function as nouns.

Use	Example sentences
Object of sentence	1. I'd say (that) you have a good track record.
Object of preposition	2. Collaboration is an important part of what we do.
Subject of sentence	3. That you met all your goals this quarter is remarkable. 4. What impresses me most is your ability to juggle multiple tasks.
Subject complement	5. The problem with this review is that it focuses on only one skill set.
Adjective complement	6. I'm not surprised (that) you've set ambitious goals.

Noun clauses as subjects, objects, and complements

- We can add extra emphasis to a noun clause by making it the **subject / object** of the sentence.
- A noun clause can function as the object of certain verbs or **nouns / prepositions**.
- A subject complement provides more information about the subject and usually follows a form of ***be* / *have***.
- When a noun clause follows certain adjectives, it functions as an adjective complement. The adjective complement gives information about the **adjective / noun clause**.

>> FOR PRACTICE, PAGE 125

B Read the sentence. Identify the three noun clauses and describe their functions.

Our director says what's most important is that we maintain open lines of communication.

3 CONVERSATION SKILL

A ▶01-04 Read the conversation skill. Listen. Notice the words the speakers use to make suggestions. Complete the sentences that you hear.

1. ______________ write down questions as you're listening?
2. _________________________ replacing this green background with a lighter color?
3. _________________________ you send the agenda for the next meeting in advance.

Make suggestions

Use expressions like these to make polite suggestions:

Could you...?	*Have you considered...?*
How about...?	*What if...?*
If I were you, I'd...	*Why not...?*
It might be better if...	

B PAIRS Student A: Identify a problem. Student B: Respond with a suggestion. Use an expression from the conversation skill box.

4 CONVERSATION

A ▶01-05 Listen. What do María and Sam talk about?

B ▶01-05 Listen again. Complete the chart with information from Sam's performance review.

Accomplishments	
Problems	
Challenges	

C ▶01-06 Listen. Complete the conversation.

María: You always fully complete your assigned work. That's important. But ______________ you have a tendency to work alone. ______________ think of some ways to better engage with the team? Collaboration is an important part of what we do here.

Sam: OK. I hear what you're saying. I'll try to think of some ideas.

María: That's great. And actually, that leads me to my next point. Overall, I'm looking for ______________ on your part. As one of your new challenges, I'd like you to identify ways that ______________ to upcoming projects and discuss them with me.

5 TRY IT YOURSELF

A THINK Imagine that you are the manager of an electronics store, a restaurant, or a customer service call center, and that one of your staff members has a performance problem at work. What is the problem? What are two possible solutions to the problem? What advice or feedback would you offer? Take notes.

B ROLE PLAY Student A: As a manager, give feedback and suggestions to your staff member during a performance review. Student B: Respond. Use the conversation in 4C as a model.

☐ I CAN TALK ABOUT PERFORMANCE.

LESSON 2 TALK ABOUT CHALLENGES

SAM BENNETT

@SamB

Just started a 30-day challenge. I'm limiting social media to 15 minutes a day.

1 BEFORE YOU LISTEN

A PAIRS THINK What do you know about 30-day challenges?

B ▶01-07 VOCABULARY Read and listen. Do you know the words in bold?

Journal I March 2021 Logout

My 30-Day Chocolate Challenge

Day 1: Today marks day 1 of 30 days without chocolate. **For one reason or another**, I've put off my no-chocolate challenge. But no more excuses. Today's the day I **take the plunge**.

Day 5: Am I counting the days? Yes! This is not easy but day 30 is circled on my calendar. **The end is in sight**.

Day 9: I feel like I'm starting to **build momentum**. Life without chocolate is getting a little easier.

Day 15: Things **aren't going my way** today. It's one problem after another. But there's no stopping now.

Day 23: Feeling more confident. I might **raise the bar** on my next challenge and go from no-chocolate to sugar-free.

Day 29: Unbelievable! I almost had a **setback**! There were double chocolate cupcakes in the office today, but I didn't have one bite. Luckily, I resisted the **temptation**.

Day 30: I did it! Thirty days without chocolate. And I found time to **map out** my next challenge.

>> FOR PRACTICE, PAGE 126 / DEFINITIONS, PAGE 155

2 LANGUAGE CHOICES More ways to express future time

A Read the example sentences. Then circle the correct answers in the chart.

In addition to *will* and *be going to*, there are several other ways to express future time.

Example sentences

1. I can't talk right now. I**'m about to go** to my yoga class.
2. There's no way I can give up caffeine. I**'m not about to try** that challenge.
3. I**'m on the brink of collapsing**. / I**'m on the verge of collapsing**.
4. Things **are bound to change**. It can't stay this way forever.
5. This challenge **is due to end** soon. My next challenge **isn't due to start** until next month.
6. All employees **are to attend** a meeting this afternoon. You **are not to arrive** late.

More ways to express future time

- *About to*, *on the brink of*, and *on the verge of* are about the **near** / **distant** future.
- *Not about to* means **prepared** / **unwilling**.
- If something is *bound to happen*, it is **likely** / **unlikely**.
- If something is *due to happen*, it is **expected** / **unplanned**.
- Use *be to* for **friendly suggestions** / **official instructions**.
- Use *be not to* when something is **unexpected** / **prohibited**.

>> FOR PRACTICE, PAGE 126

B Rewrite the sentences using other ways to express the future. Explain how your sentences modified the meaning or changed the emphasis.

Runa is going to start training for a marathon soon. The marathon will take place on May 20.

3 PRONUNCIATION

A ▶01-09 Listen. Read the pronunciation note.

B ▶01-10 Listen. Notice the final intonation. Then listen and repeat.

1. Do you ever want to sleep again? You have to cut back on caffeine.
2. What do you have to lose? You should give it a shot.

Final intonation in rhetorical questions

Rhetorical questions usually end with falling intonation. Pitch usually rises on the last important word and then falls to the end of the question. Final falling intonation is common in both rhetorical *Wh-* questions and in rhetorical *yes/no* questions.

C ▶01-11 Listen. If the question ends with falling intonation, draw a ↘. If it ends with rising intonation, draw a ↗.

How do you want to change your life? ____ Do you want to limit social media? ____ Do you want a healthier lifestyle? ____ Do you want a better job? ____ Oh, but before we start, could someone turn off the lights? ____

4 LISTENING

A ▶01-12 Listen. What is the topic of the podcast?

B ▶01-12 Read the Listening Skill. Listen again for rhetorical questions. Complete the chart.

LISTENING SKILL Listen for rhetorical questions

Speakers sometimes ask rhetorical questions to focus listeners' attention on organization or on a specific point. For example:

Are you ready for a change?
What's the point of this example?
Where do we go from here?

Rhetorical questions	Purpose
So, what is a 30-day challenge, and why should you consider doing one?	to introduce the topic of the podcast
	to focus on why people do 30-day challenges
	to focus on tips for completing a 30-day challenge

C ▶01-12 Listen again. Answer the questions.

1. How do people decide what they will do for their 30-day challenge?
2. Why is 30 days a good length of time for a challenge?
3. What are some examples of 30-day challenges?
4. If someone wanted to plan a 30-day challenge, what tips would you recommend?

D PAIRS REACT Which of the examples mentioned in the podcast seem easy? Which seem difficult? Why?

5 TRY IT YOURSELF

A THINK Create a 30-day challenge for yourself. What is your motivation for doing this challenge? What can you do to prepare for it? Take notes.

B DISCUSS In small groups, discuss your ideas from 5A.

C EVALUATE Keep a daily journal of your 30-day challenge. At the end of 30 days, read your journal and take notes on the following: the outcome of your challenge, reasons for the outcome, and ideas for your next challenge. Report to the class.

☐ I CAN TALK ABOUT CHALLENGES.

LESSON 3 DISCUSS WORLD PROBLEMS

SAM BENNETT
@SamB

Just read an article about a man who invented a way to create water out of nothing! Amazing what people can do when they put their minds to it.

1 BEFORE YOU LISTEN

A PAIRS THINK Can you think of any recent inventions that solve a problem in any of the following fields: education, the environment, healthcare, transportation?

B ▶01-13 VOCABULARY Read the words and listen to the sentences. Do you know these words?

a monumental effort	specialist expertise	a spin-off	vulnerable
galvanize	a breakthrough	crowdsourcing	a norm
an innovation	renewable energy	a small-scale initiative	tangible

>> FOR PRACTICE, PAGE 127 / DEFINITIONS, PAGE 155

2 LANGUAGE CHOICES Preparatory subjects: *it*, *here*, and *there*

A Read the example sentences. Then complete the chart with *it*, *here*, and *there*.

Example sentences

1. **It** seems impossible to solve that problem. **It** will take a lot of effort.
2. **It** turned out that the winner was disqualified.
3. **It** takes a lot of time and effort to galvanize people.
4. **Here**'s some information about crowdsourcing. **It**'s really interesting.
5. **Here** are your registration forms. **It** takes only a few minutes to complete them.
6. **There**'s a lot more interest in renewable energy now than **there** used to be.

We use *it*, *here*, and *there* as preparatory subjects. In sentences with *it*, the real subject is often an infinitive or *that*-clause. In sentences with *here* and *there*, the real subject usually comes after the verb.

Preparatory subjects: *it*, *here*, and *there*

- Use ______________ + *takes* to talk about what is needed in order to finish something.
- Use ______________ + *be* + a noun to show that something exists.
- Use ______________ + *be* + a noun when giving or presenting something to someone.
- Use ______________ + *be* / *seem* + an adjective to describe something.
- Use ______________ + *turn out* to express a result.
- Always use a singular verb with ______________ .
- With ______________ and ______________ , the verb agrees with the noun that follows.

>> FOR PRACTICE, PAGE 127

B PAIRS *Here* is used in a lot of idiomatic expressions. Read the following sentences. Discuss the meaning of each.

Here you go. / Here you are.
Here goes.
Here I am!
Here's to you.
Here's the thing…

3 VIDEO TALK

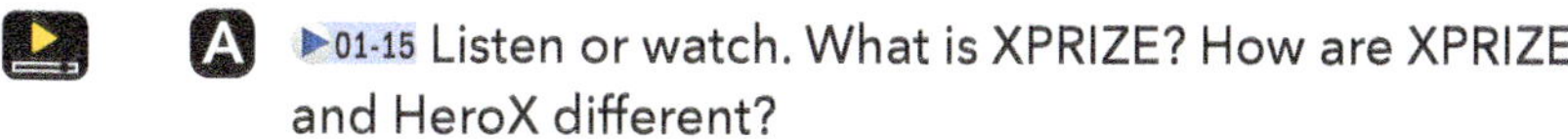

A ▶01-15 Listen or watch. What is XPRIZE? How are XPRIZE and HeroX different?

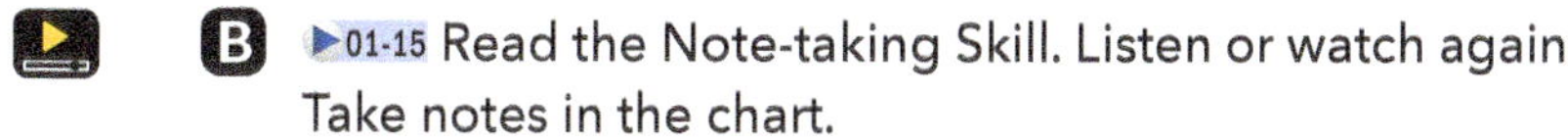

B ▶01-15 Read the Note-taking Skill. Listen or watch again. Take notes in the chart.

NOTE-TAKING SKILL Create a matrix chart

Matrix note taking is a way of organizing notes into a chart format. To create a matrix chart, place the main topics in columns at the top of your chart, and place questions in the left-hand column. This encourages you to be concise, helps you to identify relationships among concepts, and allows you to notice gaps in your notes.

Questions	XPRIZE	HeroX
What is it?		
Who participates?		
What are some example challenges and solutions?		

C What is the speaker's purpose? Explain your answer.

D PAIRS REACT Do you think these types of challenges are a good idea? Why or why not?

4 DISCUSSION SKILL

Read the discussion skill. Do you use follow-up questions in your discussions now?

Ask follow-up questions

You can help others develop their ideas and opinions in more detail by asking follow-up questions. Useful follow-up questions begin with *Why* or *How*. These prompt thoughtful answers from the speaker and require further justification or explanation of the person's ideas.

5 TRY IT YOURSELF

A THINK What global problems should we be addressing in this age? What challenges would you create, and what incentives would you offer? Take notes.

B DISCUSS In small groups, discuss your ideas from 5A. Ask follow-up questions.

C EVALUATE Decide who has the best idea for a challenge. Work together to write a description of that challenge. Remember to mention the specific problem, solution required, and the prize offered. Present your challenge to the class.

☐ I CAN DISCUSS WORLD PROBLEMS.

LESSON 4 READ ABOUT VIRAL CHALLENGES

SAM BENNETT

@SamB

Interesting read. I did a viral challenge back in college. It was a hot dog eating contest. I got so sick I'll never eat another hot dog—ever!

1 BEFORE YOU READ

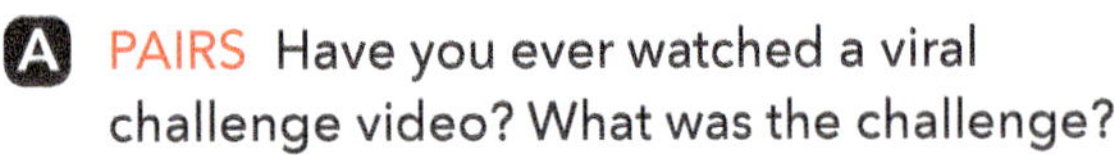

A PAIRS Have you ever watched a viral challenge video? What was the challenge?

B ▶01-16 VOCABULARY Read and listen. Do you know these words?

innocuous	in the wake of	alluring	hardwired	bragging rights	daredevil antics
blindfold	beg the question	be predisposed to	inhibition	kudos	inherent

>> FOR DEFINITIONS, PAGE 156

2 READ

A PREVIEW Look at the title and photo. Predict the information that will appear in the article.

B ▶01-17 Read and listen to the article. Explain the title.

A RISKY COMBINATION: THE YOUNG PERSON'S BRAIN AND THE LURE OF VIRAL CHALLENGES

Love them or hate them, viral challenges have been all over social media in recent years. These online dares are often harmless fun. Take the Ice Bucket challenge, which involved people throwing buckets of ice water over their heads in the name of charity.

Some viral challenges, however, are less innocuous. The Laundry Pod challenge encouraged participants to eat (yes, eat) a capsule of laundry detergent. This landed dozens of people in the emergency room. In another challenge, people imitated events in the popular film *Bird Box* by doing everyday activities blindfolded. Predictably, this resulted in injuries and at least one auto accident.

In the wake of these incidents, social media companies decided that they had a responsibility to keep users from harm and banned dangerous challenges. However, the popularity of these challenges begs the question: What made them so alluring in the first place? The answer could be human nature. Or, in particular, "young" human nature.

Viral challenge participants are usually between 13 and 25 years old. This is no surprise. The key component of these videos is often risk, and some evidence suggests that young brains are predisposed to taking risks. Various neuroscientific studies have found that teens and young adults may be hardwired to make poor judgment calls. This trait simply reflects their stage of cognitive development.

The pre-frontal cortex of the brain plays an important role in the inhibition of risk-taking behavior. This area analyzes potential risk and gives the all-clear to proceed with an action. However, the pre-frontal cortex does not fully develop until the age of 25, meaning that young people do not have the same capacity as adults when it comes to analyzing risk.

Furthermore, research suggests that most young people have a reward-seeking brain. That is, they are more sensitive to the rewards associated with a goal or challenge than adults are. The bragging rights, the kudos, and the "likes" that can be gained for completing such daredevil antics seem to outweigh the dangers for many young people. Of all the benefits of >>

social media, the chance of social recognition is seen as particularly attractive.

Beyond the science, there may be other elements involved in making viral challenges popular. One is a fear of missing out on the latest trends. Many young people are constantly connected to social media. Disconnecting can cause anxiety and a feeling that they might miss something important. Some studies report that this social anxiety is one of the main causes of social media addiction among young people. Their constant online presence means more exposure to viral challenges and perhaps a stronger desire to participate.

Whether the main factor compelling young people to take part in these challenges is social or cognitive, findings suggest that it is inherent. They have a built-in tendency towards risk-taking, and risky viral challenges merely add fuel to the fire.

3 CHECK YOUR UNDERSTANDING

A Answer the questions, according to the article.

1. What are three reasons that teens take part in viral challenges?
2. What does having a "reward-seeking brain" mean?
3. How might social media use lead to participation in viral challenges?

B CLOSE READING **Reread lines 55-59 in the article. Then circle the correct answers.**

1. In the phrase, "…, findings suggest that it is inherent," what does the word *it* refer to?
   a. whether taking part in challenges is social or cognitive
   b. taking part in these challenges
   c. challenges in general
2. Which sentence means "…risky viral challenges merely add fuel to the fire"?
   a. Viral challenges make teenagers take risks they wouldn't take otherwise.
   b. Viral challenges make teenagers take even more dangerous risks.
   c. Teenagers already have a problem with risk-taking–viral challenges make this worse.

C Read the Reading Skill. Then reread the article and follow the steps in the box.

D PAIRS **Summarize the article in 3-5 sentences.**

READING SKILL Check-Underline-Question

Evaluating our existing knowledge of a topic helps us focus on new information, understand what we have learned, and identify what else we wish to know about a topic. As you read, follow these steps:

1. Put a checkmark next to the information that you already knew.
2. Underline any information that is new and useful.
3. Write three questions about the topic.

4 MAKE IT PERSONAL

Find out more about the social media ban on viral challenges. 

A THINK **Do you agree with social media bans on viral challenges? What other kinds of content do you think should be banned? Why? Complete the chart.**

Type of content	Reason

B GROUPS **Discuss your ideas from 4A. Give reasons to support your ideas.**

C EVALUATE **In the same groups, use your ideas from 4A to draft a fair use policy for users uploading content to a social media video network. Present your policy to the class.**

Users must not upload videos that include graphic violence.

☐ I CAN READ ABOUT VIRAL CHALLENGES.

LESSON 5 WRITE A NARRATIVE ESSAY

SAM BENNETT

@SamB

Sometimes we choose challenges, and sometimes they just happen to us. Builds character either way.

1 BEFORE YOU WRITE

A Read about narrative essays.

A narrative essay tells a story in a formal, structured way. It typically has a five-paragraph structure with an introduction, three body paragraphs, and a conclusion. Narrative essays can cover a wide range of topics, which are often personal in nature. They are often required as part of a college admissions application.

B Read the model. What challenge does the writer describe? Was she able to overcome it?

October 10

As a professional pianist, the biggest challenge I ever faced was my fear of public performance. I encountered this fear early on, around the time I turned 12 years old. It was a dual challenge: besides the stage fright itself, I had to overcome the shame of being afraid of something that was supposed to be easy and fun for me.

I had been playing the piano since I was 4 years old. I was a high achiever even then, and I practiced hard every day. I also enjoyed composing music, which I started early, writing my first piece for piano when I was 7. I performed often, encouraged by my parents and my teachers, and I remember the amazing feeling of being up on a stage, looking out at the proud faces of my parents, and the thrill of having a room full of people applaud just for me.

But then something changed. As I got older, I started experiencing anxiety attacks before performances. My hands would shake, and I couldn't breathe easily. I had to make a monumental effort just to get up on stage. Of course, this affected my ability to play, but even worse was the feeling that I was terrified when I was supposed to love performing. What was the matter with me? Of course, I understand now that performance anxiety is a very common issue. But at the time, I felt very alone in my fear, and it made me feel ashamed.

When I finished high school, I wanted to audition for music colleges. I would need to perform in front of panels of judges—professional musicians who held the keys to my future. I needed to find a way to overcome my fear. So I worked with a therapist to learn some techniques to manage my anxiety. I started meditating to help my mind focus and stay calm. And I practiced breathing techniques before every performance. All of these approaches helped me get through my auditions successfully.

Today, I still experience stage fright. But now I have the tools to manage it. Acknowledging the fear was a critical first step. Now, I try to look at the fear almost as a tangible thing, something outside of myself. Then I can put the fear away into a corner of my mind, and I can get on with the performance. I have come a long way. Music was always the thing I loved best, and my fears almost stopped me from following my dream. I am lucky and grateful that I found a way to overcome this challenge.

C PAIRS Discuss. What is the main idea of each paragraph?

D PAIRS Read the model again. Complete the chart.

THE CHALLENGE

Fear of ____________________

Before the challenge		Effects of the challenge		Coping with the challenge		Result
The writer played ____________ and ____________ music. She loved ____________.	→	The writer started getting ____________. She felt ____________.	→	The writer worked with ____________, started ____________, and learned ____________.	→	The writer overcame the challenge. She still experiences ____________ but has the ability to ____________.

2 FOCUS ON WRITING

Read the Writing Skill. Then reread the model. Underline four examples of short, simple sentences. Put an asterisk (*) at the beginning of four long, complex sentences.

WRITING SKILL Vary sentence construction

To make your writing interesting and engaging, vary your sentence construction. Use long, complex sentences to express complicated thoughts, and use short, simple sentences to make points stand out.

3 PLAN YOUR WRITING

A Think of a challenge that you had to face in your life. It can be a challenge you didn't expect, or one that you chose to take on. Create a chart like the one in 1D to organize your ideas.

B PAIRS Discuss your ideas.

I'm going to write about when I was a kid and moved to a new city.

Writing tip

In narrative essays, you want to show your unique qualities. Try to look past the surface of the question you are answering and think about how you were affected on a deeper level. For example, the model writer describes not only her fear but also her shame about feeling fear.

4 WRITE

Write a first draft of a narrative essay about the challenge you described in 3A. Remember to vary your sentence construction. Use the essay in 1B as a model.

5 AFTER YOUR FIRST DRAFT

A PEER REVIEW Read your partner's essay. Answer the questions.

- Is there a clear, five-paragraph structure?
- Is the challenge clearly stated in the introductory paragraph?
- Are the body paragraphs organized chronologically?
- Did the writer make clear whether or not the challenge was overcome, and how?
- Is there variety in the sentence constructions, and are they used effectively?

B REVISE Write another draft, based on the feedback you got from your partner.

C PROOFREAD Check the spelling, grammar, and punctuation in your essay. Then read it again for overall sense.

☐ I CAN WRITE A NARRATIVE ESSAY.

PUT IT TOGETHER

1 PROBLEM SOLVING

A CONSIDER THE PROBLEM Everyone experiences stress in some way. However, stress factors seem to affect age groups differently. Review the data and circle the correct answers.

Stress factors	Ages 18-29	Ages 40-49	Ages 65+
Conflict with family	28%	37%	35%
Conflict with friends	29%	10%	10%
Conflict with neighbors	6%	6%	4%
Excess responsibilities	65%	54%	46%
Financial problems	47%	52%	42%
Family health issues	24%	36%	53%
Personal health issues	22%	48%	60%

1. Excess responsibilities are most stressful for **18-29** / **40-49** / **65+** -year-olds.
2. Conflict with neighbors is the least stressful for **one** / **two** / **three** of the age groups.
3. Personal health issues are likely to be more stressful among older people because they have **fewer** / **more** / **no** health problems.

B THINK CRITICALLY **Why do different kinds of stress affect people to a greater or lesser extent at different ages? Discuss with a partner.**

C FIND A SOLUTION **Consider the data, the problem, and possible solutions in small groups.**

Step 1 **Brainstorm** Think of 3-5 ways people can reduce one type of stress found in the chart.

Step 2 **Evaluate** Choose the best solution. Consider the impact of age on the type of stress and how easy or difficult it would be to reduce it.

Step 3 **Present** Explain the best solution to the class. Refer to the data to support your ideas.

2 REFLECT AND PLAN

A Look back through the unit. Check (✓) the things you learned. Highlight the things you need to learn.

Speaking Objectives
- ☐ Talk about performance
- ☐ Talk about challenges
- ☐ Discuss world problems

Vocabulary
- ☐ Words related to performance

Conversation
- ☐ Make suggestions

Pronunciation
- ☐ Final intonation in rhetorical questions

Listening
- ☐ Listen for rhetorical questions

Note-taking
- ☐ Create a matrix chart

Language Choices
- ☐ Noun clauses as subjects, objects, and complements
- ☐ More ways to express future time
- ☐ Preparatory subjects: *it*, *here*, and *there*

Discussion
- ☐ Ask follow-up questions

Reading
- ☐ Check-Underline-Question

Writing
- ☐ Vary sentence construction

B What will you do to learn the things you highlighted?

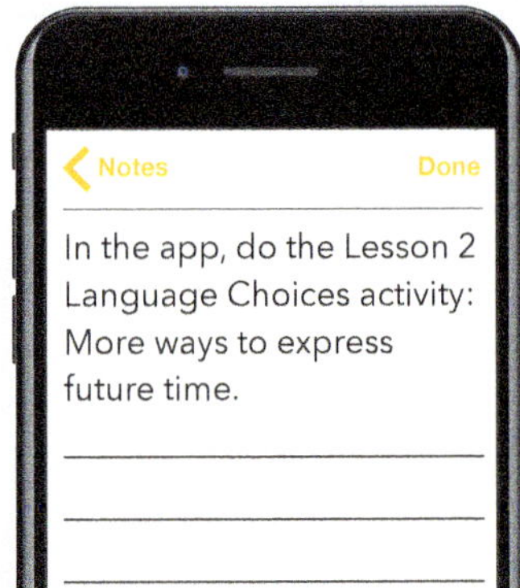

2 ARE YOU A MEMBER?

LEARNING GOALS

In this unit, you

- talk about stereotypes
- talk about fandom
- discuss bias
- read about virtual friendships
- write a compare and contrast essay

GET STARTED

A Read the unit title and learning goals. What social, academic, or work groups do you belong to? What do they mean to you?

B Look at the photo. It shows a group of people reacting to something. Where might these people be and what might they be feeling?

C Read Edgar's message. What does he mean when he says, "lean on others"? Can you think of an example of this from your own life?

EDGAR VELA

@EdgarV

Lucky to have my close group of friends. Life is much easier when you're part of a group. It's nice to lean on others for help sometimes.

LESSON 1 TALK ABOUT STEREOTYPES

EDGAR VELA
@EdgarV
Is it just me, or is the news media obsessed with millennials?

1 VOCABULARY Words related to stereotypes

A Read the comments on a blog post. What is your definition of a stereotype? How do these people feel about them?

B ▶02-01 Read and listen. Do you know the words in bold?

Blog | About | Destinations | Contact Logout

Comments on June 5 blog post "Stereotypes All Around"

Stereotypes are inherently dangerous and are often **debunked**. The **assumption** that all members of a group are identical is impossible to prove. And it's **absurd** to think that you can know how a person will think, feel, or act based solely on **preconceived** beliefs. —Kevin2786

Your blog post shows how **commonplace** stereotypes are, especially in the ads we see every day. They **perpetuate** the idea that women are responsible for housework. It's a **misconception** that women spend their days cleaning and doing laundry. It's unfair to **characterize** women in this way. —LunaM

LunaM, I think it's wrong for you to **sensationalize** this problem. I try to look at things **objectively**. Many ads do show women doing housework, but I've also seen similar ads with men. Still, housework isn't the only example of an inaccurate **generalization** of the roles of men and women. I'm a male nurse. I almost never see anyone like me in ads. Advertisers need to make some **drastic** changes. —NurseJoe234

>> FOR PRACTICE, PAGE 128 / DEFINITIONS, PAGE 156

2 LANGUAGE CHOICES Passive voice: agent versus no agent

A Read the example sentences. Underline the passive verb and circle the agent if there is one. Then complete the chart. Check (✓) all the rules that apply.

Example sentences

1. We are constantly surrounded by stereotypes.
2. By the time I heard about it, the criminal had already been caught.
3. Facebook was invented by Mark Zuckerberg.
4. The crime was being sensationalized by journalists.
5. Incorrect assumptions are always going to be made.
6. This problem should have been corrected long ago.

In a passive sentence, the agent is the person or thing that performs the action of the verb. In an active sentence, the agent is the subject. The agent is usually ***not*** included in a passive sentence, or it is written as a *by*-phrase after the verb.

Passive voice: agent versus no agent

Do not include a *by*-phrase in a passive sentence when the agent is ______ .

- ☐ unknown
- ☐ obvious or unimportant
- ☐ the name of an author, inventor, or artist
- ☐ to blame for a situation or problem
- ☐ an unexpected person or thing

>> FOR PRACTICE, PAGE 128

B PAIRS Passive voice sentences can usually be rewritten in the active voice with no change in meaning. Rewrite the example sentences from 2A in the active voice. Then discuss whether each sounds better in the active or passive voice.

3 CONVERSATION SKILL

▶02-04 Read the conversation skill. Listen. Notice the words the speakers use for hyperbole. Complete the sentences that you hear.

1. ____.
   They can lead to more serious problems like prejudice and discrimination.
2. She refuses to move from her apartment, and ____.
3. I'll never get a promotion. ____.
4. I want to be a movie star. ____.

Use hyperbole

Use hyperbole, or exaggerated statements, to show emphasis in a conversation. Hyperbole creates a humorous effect, which draws attention to your ideas and feelings. Listeners understand that hyperbole is an overstatement and should not be taken literally. For example:

They sensationalize absolutely everything.

I agree with you a thousand percent.

There are millions and millions of these stereotypes.

This weighs a ton!

It's totally, completely, and absolutely unfair.

It costs a fortune.

They're all trillionaires.

4 CONVERSATION

A ▶02-05 Listen. What do Edgar and Ariya talk about?

B ▶02-05 Listen again. Answer the questions.

1. Why is Edgar upset?
2. What are adulting classes? What are some likely subjects?
3. What does Edgar claim are the stereotypes? How does both he and Ariya refute them?

C ▶02-06 Listen. Complete the conversation.

Edgar: I'm so ____________________ about millennials! We're characterized as narcissistic, immature, unreliable, and selfish.

Ariya: OK.

Edgar: These generalizations are ______________ . Why do they always have to sensationalize ______________ everything?

Ariya: By "they" you mean the media, right?

Edgar: Yes. The ideas that millennials are lazy and that we refuse to grow up ____________________ articles like this.

5 TRY IT YOURSELF

A MAKE IT PERSONAL What is a common stereotype that you have encountered? How do you feel about it? Take notes in the chart.

Stereotype	How I feel about it

B PAIRS Share your ideas. Use expressions from the conversation skill box to emphasize your point of view and respond to your partner.

LESSON 2 TALK ABOUT FANDOM

EDGAR VELA

@EdgarV

The championship game is tonight. Fans will be going wild. #psyched

1 BEFORE YOU LISTEN

A PAIRS THINK Do you know anyone who is a huge fan of something, such as sports or music? Discuss.

B ▶02-07 VOCABULARY Read and listen. Do you know the words in bold?

Prep for Oct. 23 Interview with Sports Psychologist AJ Paluch – Questions to Ask

1. Is the love of sports **visceral**? In other words, is being a sports fan all about raw emotion?
2. Are there **telling** differences between soccer, basketball, hockey, and baseball fans?
3. What is **cathartic** healing? It involves the release of emotions, but how does it connect to sports?
4. Does being a fan affect **self-esteem**? Do sports fans **live vicariously**—do they feel like they're sharing the success of their heroes?
5. What is the **correlation** between watching sports and how we feel about ourselves?
6. Why do sports fans seem so happy when they're in a crowd? Is there a natural **inclination** for fans to be in groups? Do they create a **bond** with each other?
7. If sports fans develop **camaraderie** with other fans, do the positive feelings of group membership help them in negative situations where they experience **alienation**?
8. **Avid** sports fans are **hooked**. Are they like addicts?

>> FOR PRACTICE, PAGE 129 / DEFINITIONS, PAGE 156

2 LANGUAGE CHOICES Causative verbs

A Read the example sentences. Then match the verbs with the correct meanings in the chart.

Example sentences

1. They don't **allow** fans **to take** pictures during the performances.
2. Did you **let** your kids **stay up** and watch the game last night?
3. Even though she hates sports, I **got** my co-worker **to go** to the game with me.
4. The coach **makes** the players **work** hard.
5. I'll **have** my assistant **call** you with the details.
6. I can **help** you **find** tickets for the next game.
7. Does the app **require** you **to enter** a passcode?

A causative verb is one that indicates when a person or thing causes someone else to do something.

Causative verbs

____________ : assist someone with something		allow, let
____________ : convince or persuade someone to do something		get
____________ : ask or hire someone to do something for you		make, require
____________ : force someone to do something		help
____________ : give permission for someone to do something		have

>> FOR PRACTICE, PAGE 129

B Some causative verbs are followed by an object + base form, and others are followed by an object + infinitive. Reread the example sentences in 2A. List the verbs that follow each pattern.

3 PRONUNCIATION

A ▶02-09 Listen. Read the pronunciation note.

B ▶02-10 Listen. Notice the stress in the underlined phrases. Then listen and repeat.

1. Winning the tournament made the team **cheer** loudly.
2. Even though she's not a fan, she actually **helped** me find tickets.

Stress in causative verb phrases

The second verb in a causative verb phrase is usually stressed more than the causative verb. The object is also usually stressed if it is not a pronoun: *Watching sports makes my **heart race**.*

The causative verb may be stressed if the speaker wants to emphasize causative meaning: *I wanted to be there, but they **made** me leave.*

C ▶02-11 Listen. Mark the stressed verbs in the underlined phrases with a dot.

A: That game was close. It got me so nervous.

B: Me, too. But that first goal after halftime was cathartic. It helped me relax.

A: I noticed. Before that, you had your eyes covered. You've got to have faith.

B: Yeah. But our mistakes in the first half are what made me lose faith.

4 LISTENING

A ▶02-12 Listen. What is the topic of the podcast?

B ▶02-12 Read the Listening Skill. Listen again for phrases that guide a conversation. Write the name of the speaker.

LISTENING SKILL Listen for phrases that guide a conversation

Speakers sometimes use phrases to guide a conversation. They may do this to keep a conversation on topic, to switch to a new topic, to elicit specific information, or to stay within time limits. For example: *Let's start off with…; Now let's turn to…; Another important aspect is…; Moving on,…; On a related note,…; We'll come back to that later.*

1. Let's start off with… ______
2. We'll come back to that later. ______
3. Moving on,… ______
4. And on a related note,… ______

C ▶02-12 Listen again. Take notes in the chart.

Field of science	What science says
Psychology	
Sociology	
Physiology	

D PAIRS REACT Think about the fan you discussed in 1A. How can his or her actions be explained by research in psychology, sociology, and physiology?

5 TRY IT YOURSELF

A MAKE IT PERSONAL Look at your notes from 4C. What are you a big fan of? How does your passion affect how you act? Take notes.

B DISCUSS In pairs, discuss your notes from 5A.

C EVALUATE In small groups, make connections between your experience and the information presented in the podcast. Present your findings to the class.

☐ I CAN TALK ABOUT FANDOM.

LESSON 3 DISCUSS BIAS

EDGAR VELA

@EdgarV

This talk about bias on social media sounds interesting. I always see the same kinds of news articles in my social media feed!

1 BEFORE YOU LISTEN

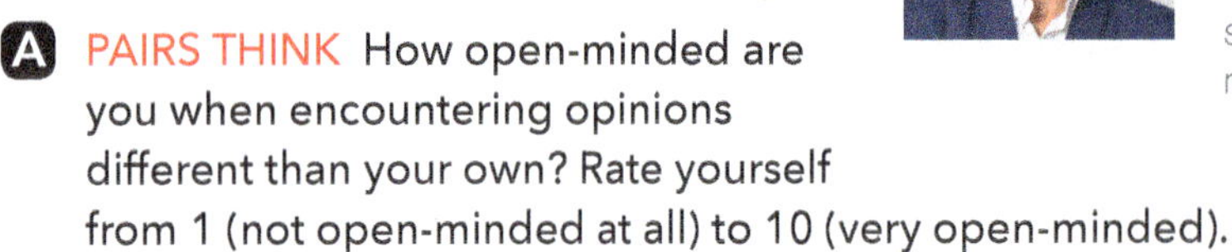

A PAIRS THINK How open-minded are you when encountering opinions different than your own? Rate yourself from 1 (not open-minded at all) to 10 (very open-minded). Discuss.

B ▶02-13 VOCABULARY Read the words and listen to the sentences. Do you know these words?

plagued with (something)	pay attention to (something)	ignorance
misinformation	an evolutionary trait	swayed into believing
filter	prioritize	a tendency
reinforce	exploited by (something)	

>> FOR PRACTICE, PAGE 130 / DEFINITIONS, PAGE 157

2 LANGUAGE CHOICES Active versus passive reporting

A Read the example sentences. Notice the different ways to report information. Label the example sentences *active* or *passive*. Then complete the rules in the chart with *Active* or *Passive*.

Example sentences

1. a. ___active___ Studies have shown that misinformation spreads quickly on social media.
   b. ________ It's been shown that misinformation spreads quickly on social media.
   c. ________ Misinformation has been shown to spread quickly on social media.
2. a. ________ Researchers at Harvard have found that negative headlines get more attention.
   b. ________ It has been found that negative headlines get more attention.
   c. ________ Negative headlines have been found to get more attention.
3. a. ________ They say social media content is filtered by algorithms.
   b. ________ It is said that social media content is filtered by algorithms.
   c. ________ Social media content is said to be filtered by algorithms.

Active versus passive reporting

- ____________ reporting creates distance between the speaker and the information being reported.
- ____________ reporting structures can hide the source of information if the source is obvious, unimportant, or unknown.
- ____________ reporting includes the source of information.

>> FOR PRACTICE, PAGE 130

B What reporting verbs are used in the example sentences in 2A? What other reporting verbs are commonly used in active and passive reporting structures? Make a list.

3 VIDEO TALK

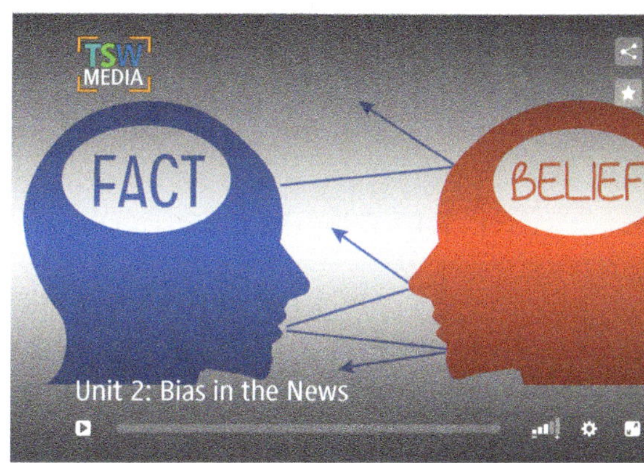

A ▶02-15 Listen or watch. What is the speaker's main message?

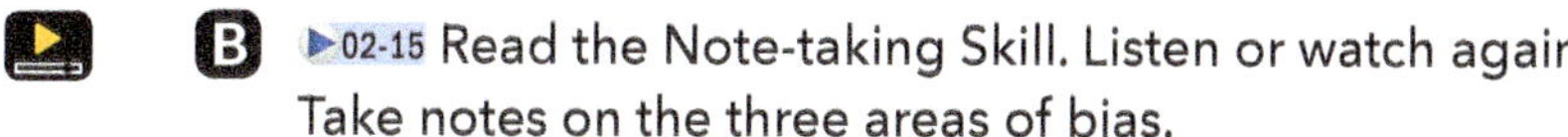

B ▶02-15 Read the Note-taking Skill. Listen or watch again. Take notes on the three areas of bias.

NOTE-TAKING SKILL Use abbreviations and symbols

Use abbreviations and symbols so you can take notes more quickly. You can use standard abbreviations that many people use, or you can make up your own by shortening words, leaving out letters, and using symbols. For example, use > to mean *more* and < to mean *less*.

Type of bias	Description / Examples
Bias in the machine	
Bias in society	
Bias in the brain	

C The speaker is trying to persuade the audience that social media is biased. Which persuasive techniques does he use?

D PAIRS REACT Do you feel that avoiding exposure to opinions that you disagree with is a bad thing? Explain.

4 DISCUSSION SKILL

Read the discussion skill. Which of these phrases do you use in your discussions now?

Build on ideas

Building on the contributions of others helps you to explore ideas further and consolidate opinions.

- Seek to clarify points by paraphrasing: *So, are you saying that…?; So, do you mean…?*
- Ask opinion-based questions to help others understand their stance: *So, do you think that…?*
- If others share an idea that supports your own views, use this as a springboard: *It's interesting (that) you say that because…*

5 TRY IT YOURSELF

A THINK Look at the chart in 3B. Consider examples of your own biases on social media in these three areas. Take notes.

B DISCUSS Share your ideas from 5A in small groups.

C EVALUATE Reconsider the open-mindedness rating you gave yourself in 1A. Would you change this rating based on information in the talk and your self-evaluation in 5A? Discuss.

☐ I CAN DISCUSS BIAS.

EDGAR VELA
@EdgarV

Dunbar's number doesn't sound right to me. I think we can maintain more than 150 friendships, and I have lots of great online relationships!

1 BEFORE YOU READ

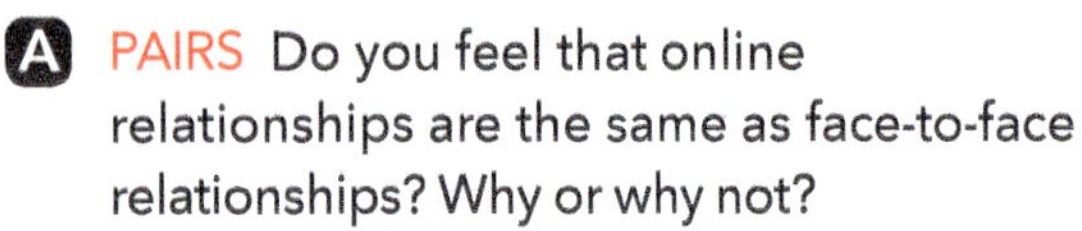

A PAIRS Do you feel that online relationships are the same as face-to-face relationships? Why or why not?

B ▶02-16 VOCABULARY Read and listen. Do you know these words?

popularize	a drop in the ocean	correlate	crucial	trigger
the advent of	intimate	an underlying issue	replicate	

>> FOR DEFINITIONS, PAGE 157

2 READ

A PREVIEW Read the title of the article. Why do you think we have more friends these days?

B ▶02-17 Read and listen to the article. Does the author feel that online relationships are better, worse, or the same as face-to-face relationships?

MODERN FRIENDSHIPS: IS MORE REALLY BETTER? BY KERRY M. KENDRICK

50–150 – people you hardly know
50–150
15–50
5–15
<5
15–50 – your good friends; may include ex-classmates or ex-colleagues
5–15 – your close friends; you care for them
<5 – your closest friends; your emotional support network

In the 1990s—the pre-social networking era—anthropologist Robin Dunbar estimated that the average person can maintain around 150 friendships. This figure, also known as "Dunbar's number," has been popularized since then, appearing in books and articles.

What has happened to this number since the advent of social media? While it is estimated that the average social media user has 150 friends, it is also estimated that the average person has seven social media accounts. Friendships these days are not restricted to real-life interactions, nor are they restricted to one social media platform. So Dunbar's number might sound like a drop in the ocean to social media users who have friend counts in the thousands.

But evidence suggests that quantity doesn't necessarily mean quality. In Dunbar's initial research, friendships were broken down into types. The average person had around fifty good friendships, fifteen close friendships, and an intimate support group that usually consisted of just five people. Current research has shown that although our average number of total friendships has increased, the number of close and intimate friendships we maintain has stayed roughly the same. We may acquire more online friends, but a majority of these will probably be casual acquaintances. Online friendships may be commonplace, but research suggests they are no substitute for the real thing.

Why don't the online friendships we build become more intimate? It's possible they don't satisfy us—not in the same way that real friendships do. Researchers found that our number of real-life friends directly correlates with our well-being—the more friends you have in real life, the happier you are. However, they found no evidence that the size of our online friendships has the same effect. Even if our virtual friendship >>

network grows far beyond Dunbar's number, it's still our real-life friendships that mean the most to us. The underlying issue making these virtual relationships seem less fulfilling could be emotional distance. Researchers found that people are happier and laugh 50% more frequently during face-to-face interactions as compared to online interactions. The emotional touch of face-to-face interaction, such as responses like genuine laughter, is very important. Further research has shown that physical touch, like hugging, is also crucial for building social bonds. Video calls can bridge the gap to an extent, but it isn't possible to fully replicate physical bonding in a virtual world.

Overall, research suggests that online relationships can't fully meet the social and emotional needs of most adults. They fail to reproduce the emotional and physical intimacy of real-life friendships, and they don't trigger the same feelings of well-being as real-world relationships do. Social networks may evolve to accommodate our relationship needs, but for now they are inadequate. Social media isn't the place for close friendships; the real world is.

3 CHECK YOUR UNDERSTANDING

A Answer the questions, according to the article.

1. How have our friendships changed since the arrival of social media?
2. What is the relationship between online friendships and well-being?
3. What is meant by emotional distance, and how does it affect friendships?
4. What overall impact does the lack of intimacy have on our online relationships?

B CLOSE READING **Reread lines 25-27 and 29-32 in the article. Then circle the correct answers.**

1. Why does the writer use *could be* in line 27?
   a. She doesn't believe that emotional distance is the underlying issue.
   b. She is emphasizing that emotional distance is one possible explanation.
   c. She is suggesting that there is limited evidence for this idea.
2. In line 31, what does the phrase *bridge the gap* mean?
   a. diminish the difference between online and real-life friendships
   b. help people develop their online friendships
   c. reproduce the same conditions in online and real-world interactions

C Read the Reading Skill. Go back to paragraph 3 in the article and follow the steps in the box. Allow yourself 2 minutes. Use your notes to explain Dunbar's number to a partner.

READING SKILL Identify key information

Identifying the most important information in a text helps you stay focused and read more efficiently. Follow these steps:

1. Circle the main idea of the paragraph.
2. Underline words or phrases that relate to the main idea.
3. Underline content words, which are words that carry meaning. These are typically nouns, verbs, and adjectives.

D PAIRS Summarize the article in 3-5 sentences.

Find out how Robin Dunbar decided on the number 150.

4 MAKE IT PERSONAL

A THINK Look at the graph in the article. How accurate is Dunbar's number when related to your own friendships? How do you communicate with each group of friends? What kinds of activities do you do together? Take notes for each group.

B PAIRS Describe your friendship network. Are they similar or different? Do you think the Dunbar number has changed? How? Why?

C EVALUATE Determine the Dunbar number for your class. Calculate the average number of friendships in your networks.

☐ I CAN READ ABOUT VIRTUAL FRIENDSHIPS.

LESSON 5 WRITE A COMPARE AND CONTRAST ESSAY

EDGAR VELA

@EdgarV

I try to listen to both sides when it comes to politics, but never with sports. Go Bears!

1 BEFORE YOU WRITE

A Read about compare and contrast essays.

A compare and contrast essay compares two things or ideas to analyze the similarities and differences between them. A good essay goes beyond a simple list to make a larger statement about the topic. For example, the essay might draw a conclusion about which idea is preferable, or it might propose suggestions for how to integrate the benefits of both.

B Read the model. Why does the writer think the difference between sports and politics is important?

THE GAME OF POLITICS

How much do sports fans have in common with political partisans (people loyal to one political party)? Quite a lot, it seems. Listening to political discourse today can be like listening to two sports fans angrily debating whose team is better. But how far can we take this comparison? While there are commonalities between sports fans and political partisans, there are also some key differences. And it is those differences that may help us to create a more cohesive political future.

Everyone knows that sports fans sometimes get a little overexcited. In fact, the word *fan* comes from the word *fanatic*, meaning someone who shows excessive enthusiasm for something. Sports fans will be loyal to their team no matter what, in large part because their loyalty has often developed out of regional pride or family relationships. This also means fans are unlikely to change loyalties over the course of their lifetime. Sometimes their sense of self is so tied up with their home team that they may even act negatively toward other teams in order to show their own superiority.

Similarly, political partisans feel "team" loyalty and will often have strong negative feelings toward their rivals. A recent study revealed that 41% of partisans believe that winning an election is more important than achieving policy goals. We can easily see how people develop these attitudes. As with sports fans, people often develop political affiliations through their family or their region. And furthermore, like sports fans, partisans tend to have their self-esteem tied up with the success of their party. Politicians feed into the "my team / your team" mentality because the more divisive they act, the more motivated people become to vote. This creates a cycle that is hard to break.

Nonetheless, disrupting this cycle is not impossible. A sport is still just a game, after all, whereas politics has an effect on people's everyday lives. While at the end of a sports game, the fans all go home, at the end of an election, the winner takes office. And if this person enacts policies to benefit people, voters who opposed the candidate might change their minds and vote differently next time. Furthermore, unlike in sports, in politics we do sometimes see a person's loyalty changing—either because the party has changed or because the person himself or herself has.

The way towards change, then, is to enable people to understand and to focus on how policy affects them in their everyday lives. Ultimately, although sports fans and political partisans have much in common, it is the differences between them where our hope for the future lies.

C PAIRS How is the essay organized? What is the main idea of each paragraph?

D PAIRS Read the model again. Complete the diagram.

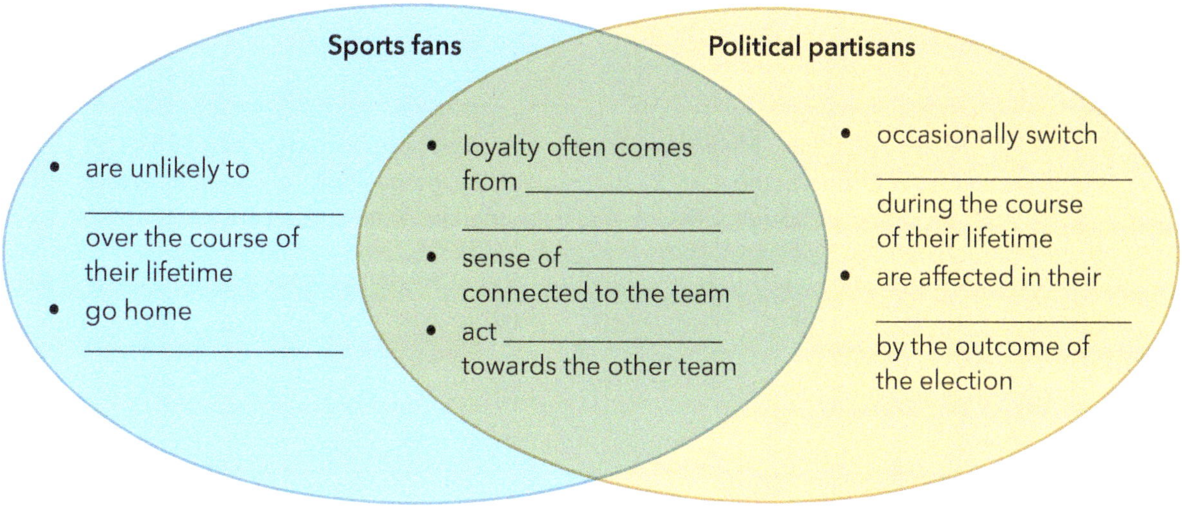

Sports fans

- are unlikely to _______________ over the course of their lifetime
- go home _______________

Sports fans and Political partisans

- loyalty often comes from _______________ _______________
- sense of _______________ connected to the team
- act _______________ towards the other team

Political partisans

- occasionally switch _______________ during the course of their lifetime
- are affected in their _______________ by the outcome of the election

2 FOCUS ON WRITING

Read the Writing Skill. Then reread the model. Underline the transition words for comparison or contrast.

> **WRITING SKILL Use transition words**
>
> To create smooth connections between your ideas, use transition words. Some transition words for comparison are *similarly, as with,* and *like*. Some transition words that show contrast are *whereas, while, unlike,* and *although*.

3 PLAN YOUR WRITING

A Think of two different groups of people that you can compare (for example, online friends versus in-person friends, in-laws versus parents, or entertainers versus politicians). Create a diagram like the one in 1D to brainstorm the similarities and differences between the groups.

B PAIRS Discuss your ideas.

I think I'll write about vegetarians versus meat-eaters.

4 WRITE

Write a first draft of a compare and contrast essay about the two groups you described in 3A. Remember to use transition words. Use the essay in 1B as a model.

> **Writing tip**
>
> Get it all out. When writing your first draft, more is better. Your first draft provides all the raw material, which you can then shape and refine. So it's best to get all of your ideas onto the page. Then you can move things around or cut things out as needed.

5 AFTER YOUR FIRST DRAFT

A PEER REVIEW Read your partner's essay.

- Does the introduction clearly state which groups are being compared?
- Does the essay give equal attention to both of these groups?
- Are both similarities and differences between the groups identified and discussed?
- Does the essay use transition words effectively?
- Does the essay draw some kind of conclusion that goes beyond a simple list?

B REVISE Write another draft based on the feedback you got from your partner.

C PROOFREAD Check the spelling, grammar, and punctuation in your essay. Then read it again for overall sense.

☐ I CAN WRITE A COMPARE AND CONTRAST ESSAY.

1 PROBLEM SOLVING

A CONSIDER THE PROBLEM Millennials are a group of people born between 1981 and 1996 and reaching adulthood in the early 21st century. They increasingly rely on online news rather than more reliable print sources. Review the data and circle the correct answers.

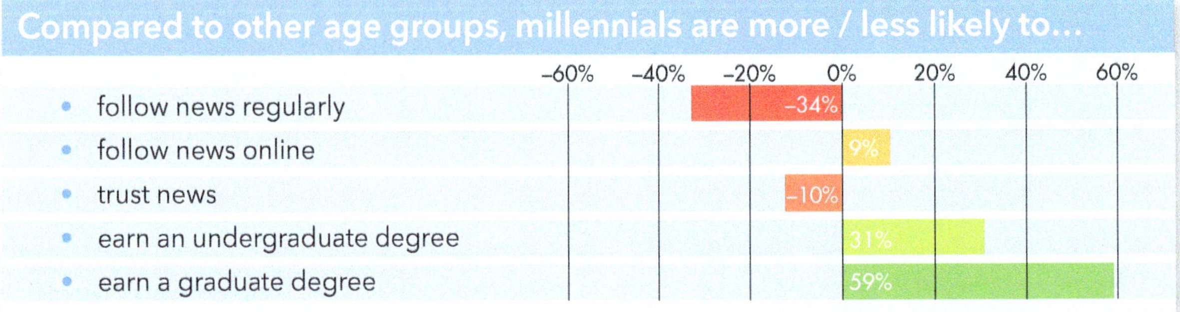

1. Compared to older adults, millennials have **the same amount of** / **less** / **more** education.
2. Millennials **do not trust** / **are less trusting of** / **are more trusting of** the news.
3. **All adults** / **Millennials** / **Older adults** are more likely to follow the news online because they grew up with the internet.

B THINK CRITICALLY Are millennials' ideas more likely to be shaped by inaccurate or fake news? Why or why not? Discuss the impact that this may have.

C FIND A SOLUTION Consider the data, the problem, and possible solutions in small groups.

Step 1 **Brainstorm** Think of 3-5 ways people can be more critical about news they read online.

Step 2 **Evaluate** Consider an example of online information that needs to be challenged and how your approach could help people to think more critically about it.

Step 3 **Present** Explain the best solution to the class.

2 REFLECT AND PLAN

A Look back through the unit. Check (✓) the things you learned. Highlight the things you need to learn.

Speaking Objectives
- ☐ Talk about stereotypes
- ☐ Talk about fandom
- ☐ Discuss bias

Vocabulary
- ☐ Words related to stereotypes

Conversation
- ☐ Use hyperbole

Pronunciation
- ☐ Stress in causative verb phrases

Listening
- ☐ Listen for phrases that guide a conversation

Note-taking
- ☐ Use abbreviations and symbols

Language Choices
- ☐ Passive voice: agent versus no agent
- ☐ Causative verbs
- ☐ Active versus passive reporting

Discussion
- ☐ Build on ideas

Reading
- ☐ Identify key information

Writing
- ☐ Use transition words

B What will you do to learn the things you highlighted?

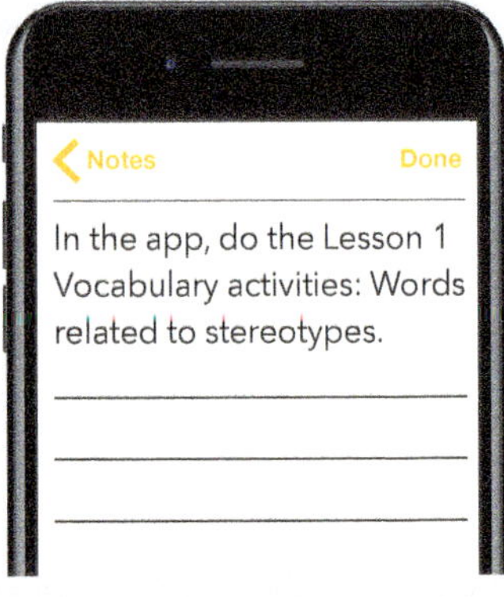

3 HOW DO YOU EXPLAIN THAT?

LEARNING GOALS

In this unit, you

- talk about famous mysteries
- talk about personal mysteries
- discuss urban legends
- read about life's mysteries
- write a plot summary

GET STARTED

A Read the unit title and learning goals. The world is full of mysteries. How do they sometimes make life more exciting?

B Look at the photo. It shows someone about to enter a large maze. If you were standing there, would you enter the maze? What would need to be at the center of the maze to make you enter it?

C Read Artur's message. What kind of treasure might he be looking for?

ARTUR TAVARES

@ArturT

I love reading stories about lost treasure. And now that I've learned how to scuba dive, I'm going to look for some treasure myself!

LESSON 1 TALK ABOUT FAMOUS MYSTERIES

ARTUR TAVARES
@ArturT
Just visited the Pyramids of Giza. What an incredible place! So full of mystery.

1 VOCABULARY Words related to mysteries

A What are some examples of mysterious places around the world?

B ▶03-01 Read and listen. Do you know the words in bold?

MYSTERIES AND HISTORIES Home | Online Viewing | Live TV Schedule | Specials

THE GREAT PYRAMID: FROM BAFFLING MYSTERIES TO INCREDIBLE BREAKTHROUGHS

For thousands of centuries, the Great Pyramid of Giza has been **shrouded** in mystery. From its **gargantuan** size to its secret chambers, it has been a source of **fascination** for archaeologists and travelers alike. This monument remains an **enigma** today, but researchers have uncovered **evidence** in hidden caves and **scrolls** that has unlocked many secrets. Join us as we follow their path from initial **hunches** to **conclusive** proof in a documentary that will **intrigue** and entertain you.

Check out our **trivia** and fun facts about pyramids around the world!

>> FOR PRACTICE, PAGE 131 / DEFINITIONS, PAGE 157

2 LANGUAGE CHOICES Modals for speculation about the past

A Read the example sentences. Underline the modals for speculation about the past. Then put the words from the box into the correct groups.

To make speculations about the past, use modal + *have* + past participle.

Example sentences

1. The empty space at the base of the tomb could have been part of the building's structure, or it might have been a secret chamber.
2. Some researchers believe the tomb may have belonged to a princess.
3. Archaeologists spent so much money on the project that it had to have been important.
4. Masa threw those files in the trash, so he must not have wanted them.
5. Those statues are gargantuan. It couldn't have been easy to construct them.
6. Explorers can't have discovered a new pyramid. If they had, it would be all over the news.

Modals for speculation about the past

can't have · could have · couldn't have · had to have · ~~may have~~
~~may not have~~ · might have · might not have · must have · must not have

50% certain something happened	50% certain something did *not* happen
may have	may not have
> 90% certain something happened	**> 90% certain something did *not* happen**

>> FOR PRACTICE, PAGE 131

B *Could* has different meanings. What does *could have* mean in the following sentences?

Researchers could have solved the mystery years ago, but they didn't have enough funding.

The discovery was more exciting than anyone could have imagined.

3 CONVERSATION SKILL

A ▶03-04 Read the conversation skill. Listen. Notice the words the speakers use to keep listeners' attention. Complete the sentences that you hear.

1. And _______________ . Khufu's mummified body might be there.
2. And _______________ of the mystery.
3. _______________ . It may be the face of Khafre.

B PAIRS Retell a mysterious story that you heard from a family member or friend when you were a child. Use an expression from the conversation skill box.

Keep listeners' attention

Use expressions like these to create interest during a conversation and to keep listeners focused on what you're saying:

That's just the beginning.
You're not going to believe this.
It gets better.
Wait. There's more.
Guess what.
Here's the best part.

4 CONVERSATION

A ▶03-05 Listen. What do Ariya and Artur talk about?

B ▶03-05 Listen again. Answer the questions.

1. What evidence did researchers use to prove that the workers at the Great Pyramid were not slaves?
2. What are two reasons why the floodwaters of the Nile were important in the construction of the Great Pyramid?
3. Why does Artur say that Merer's diary is better than a photo?

C ▶03-06 Listen. Complete the conversation.

Ariya: _______________ . You mentioned the massive blocks of stone used in the construction of the Great Pyramid. I _______________ by those massive blocks of stone, too. I wanted to know where they came from.

Artur: What did you find out?

Ariya: _______________ of stone arrived at the Giza Plateau by boat. Some was from locations close to the building site, but some came from _______________ .

5 TRY IT YOURSELF

A THINK What is a famous mystery that you have read about or seen on television? Take notes in the chart.

Mystery	Possible explanations from research

B PAIRS Share your mysteries and their possible explanations. Use the conversation in 4C as a model.

☐ I CAN TALK ABOUT FAMOUS MYSTERIES.

LESSON 2 TALK ABOUT PERSONAL MYSTERIES

ARTUR TAVARES
@ArturT
My flight was delayed. Mechanical difficulties. Had a feeling that something bad was going to happen.

1 BEFORE YOU LISTEN

A PAIRS THINK What do you know about paranormal experiences? Have you had an experience that can't be explained by science?

B ▶03-07 VOCABULARY Read and listen. Do you know the words in bold?

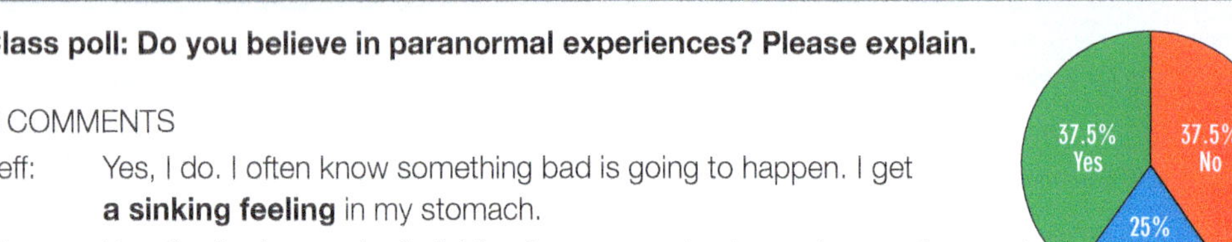

Class poll: Do you believe in paranormal experiences? Please explain.

8 COMMENTS

Jeff: Yes, I do. I often know something bad is going to happen. I get **a sinking feeling** in my stomach.
Max: Yes. I've had several **mind-blowing** supernatural experiences. I **swear**!
Dana: I'm not sure that I believe in paranormal experiences. I'm **skeptical**.
Zheng: No, I don't. But if a friend said he had an experience like this, I'd **take his word for it**.
Rose: No way. I **don't buy it**. **The odds** are there's a scientific explanation for almost everything.
Alexa: I had an experience once, but I thought it was **a gag**. Now I'm not so sure.
Ying: Yes. I saw a woman in a dream. The next day, I met someone who was her **spitting image**.
Ibrahim: Nope—don't believe it. The whole idea of paranormal experiences is **bogus**.

>> FOR PRACTICE, PAGE 132 / DEFINITIONS, PAGE 157

2 LANGUAGE CHOICES Modals for expectation

A Read the example sentences. Underline the modals and verbs used to show expectation. Then read rules in the chart. Are they true (*T*) or false (*F*)? Correct the false rules.

Example sentences

1. The ghost tour should be an interesting experience, and it shouldn't take more than a few hours.
2. Yuan should have been here an hour ago. He ought to have texted that he's running late.
3. I'm sure you didn't really see a ghost. There ought to be a logical explanation for what you saw.
4. There's supposed to be a fascinating UFO museum in Roswell, New Mexico.
5. There wasn't supposed to be anyone else in the house, but we thought we heard voices.
6. The movie was supposed to have been mind-blowing, but I thought it was boring.
7. There are supposed to be ghosts living there, but I don't really buy it.

Modals for expectation

____ • Use *should* and *ought to* to indicate expectation about the present or future. They cannot be used in the past.
____ • Use *shouldn't* or *isn't / aren't supposed to* to indicate something will not likely happen.
____ • Use *was / were supposed to* for expectations and obligations that were likely fulfilled.
____ • Use *supposed to*, ***not*** *should* or *ought to*, for situations that people claim to be true.

>> FOR PRACTICE, PAGE 132

B Read the sentences. How is *supposed to* used? Is there a difference in meaning?

There was supposed to be a ghost living in that house.
There was supposed to have been a ghost living in that house.

3 PRONUNCIATION

A ▶03-09 Listen. Read the pronunciation note.

B ▶03-10 Listen. Notice the reduced pronunciations in the underlined phrases. Then listen and repeat.

1. I should have run when I heard the noise, but I wasn't afraid at all.
2. I'd like to believe Ari, but his story was bogus and couldn't have happened.

Reduction of modal perfects

In modal perfects, the auxiliary *have* is reduced to /əv/ or /ə/ and joins closely to the preceding modal, and the past participle of the verb often receives the heaviest stress: *They should have* /ʃʊdə/ *been there.* In negative modal perfects, the negative modal also receives stress: *It couldn't have* /kʊdəntəv/ *happened*. The final *t* of negative modals may also be dropped. *It couldn't have* /kʊdənə/ *happened.*

C ▶03-11 Listen. Mark the stressed syllable in the underlined phrases with a dot.

A: The footsteps I heard upstairs couldn't have been my neighbors'. They weren't home yet.
B: They might have arrived when you weren't paying attention.
A: Then I should have heard them going upstairs. The stairs are very noisy.

4 LISTENING

A ▶03-12 Read the Listening Skill. Listen to part of the podcast. Underline the emphasized information.

It reminded me of a family camping trip when I was 7. I was looking at the stars when I noticed a strange object moving across the sky. I was sure it was a UFO–until my grandfather told me it was a communications satellite. I understand the appeal of mysteries, but I prefer scientific explanations.

LISTENING SKILL Listen for emphasis

Speakers often change speed, volume, and pitch to help you follow a story. They will talk slower, louder, and higher to emphasize key information.

B ▶03-13 Listen to the entire podcast. What is the podcast about?

C ▶03-13 Listen again. Answer the questions.

1. What are Devon, Flora, and Rita's opinions about mysterious experiences?
2. What happened to Devon's father?
3. When was the first time that Flora and Rita talked to each other about their mysteries?
4. Does Mohamed change his point of view about mysterious experiences? How do you know?

D PAIRS REACT Which of the experiences in the podcast was most interesting for you? Why?

5 TRY IT YOURSELF

A THINK What is a mysterious experience you or someone close to you has had? Complete the chart.

What happened	Where it happened	When it happened	Who was involved

B DISCUSS In small groups, use your notes from 5A to tell your story.

C EVALUATE Are there similarities in your stories? Brainstorm possible explanations for the mysterious experiences.

☐ I CAN TALK ABOUT PERSONAL MYSTERIES.

LESSON 3 DISCUSS URBAN LEGENDS

ARTUR TAVARES
@ArturT
Anyone know anything about the origins of urban legends? Would love to know where these weird ideas come from.

1 BEFORE YOU LISTEN

A PAIRS THINK What are some famous legends, either from your home country or other parts of the world? Describe them.

B ▶03-14 VOCABULARY Read the words and listen to the sentences. Do you know these words?

thrive	perceive	a worst-case scenario	a cautionary tale
sanitation	a reflection	dissolve	roam the streets
armed with (a weapon)	play (something) up	plant	

>> FOR PRACTICE, PAGE 133 / DEFINITIONS, PAGE 158

2 LANGUAGE CHOICES Passive modals

A Read the example sentences with active and passive modals. Underline the passive modals. Then circle the correct answers in the chart.

Example sentences

1. a. Someone should stop that rumor before it becomes an urban legend.
   b. That rumor should be stopped before it becomes an urban legend.
2. a. You can find examples of urban legends everywhere.
   b. Examples of urban legends can be found everywhere.
3. a. Do I have to return this book soon?
   b. Does this book have to be returned soon?
4. a. Some high school kids might have started that rumor.
   b. That rumor might have been started by some high school kids.
5. a. Someone must have made that story up as a cautionary tale.
   b. That story must have been made up as a cautionary tale.
6. a. They couldn't have taken that story seriously.
   b. That story couldn't have been taken seriously.

Passive modals

- Use **active** / **passive** modals when the agent is not important or not known.
- The meaning of the modal is **the same** / **different** in active and passive sentences.
- A passive modal in the present tense is formed with modal + ***have*** / ***be*** + past participle.
- A passive modal in the past tense is formed with modal + ***has*** / ***have*** + *been* + past participle.

>> FOR PRACTICE, PAGE 133

B PAIRS Most modals have more than one meaning. In some cases, the past tense of the modal changes based on the meaning. Read the following sentences. They all occurred in the past. What is the difference in meaning between the modals in each pair?

That story is ridiculous! It **had to have been invented**.
New technology **had to be invented** in order to film that movie.

The project **couldn't have been completed** in only two days. That's impossible!
The project **couldn't be completed** in two days. We needed more time.

3 VIDEO TALK

A ▶03-16 Listen or watch. What is an urban legend?

B ▶03-16 Read the Note-taking Skill. Listen or watch again. Take notes in the chart.

NOTE-TAKING SKILL Use mapping

The mapping note-taking method is a visual way to organize your notes. List the main topic at the top, with sub-topics and details below. This method of note-taking helps you to easily distinguish between topics.

Main topic: ______________________________

Definition: ______________________________

Sub-topic 1: ____________	Sub-topic 2: ____________	Sub-topic 3: ____________
Details / Examples:	Details / Examples:	Details / Examples:

C How does the speaker feel about urban legends?

D PAIRS REACT Had you heard the urban legends mentioned in the video before? Do you think they're believable? Why or why not?

4 DISCUSSION SKILL

Read the discussion skill. Which of these phrases do you use in your discussions now?

Acknowledge ideas

It's important to acknowledge others' ideas and opinions so that they feel supported and that their views are respected. Use phrases like these to acknowledge someone's ideas:

I see where you're coming from…

I see what you mean…

I understand what you're getting at…

That could be true…

5 TRY IT YOURSELF

A THINK Read the urban legends. Then think of one you know. Choose one to discuss.

- You shouldn't eat the end of a banana as it might be full of spider eggs.
- We once picked up a hitchhiker, and he disappeared into thin air from the back seat.
- That restaurant genetically modifies chickens to produce more legs.

B DISCUSS Describe the urban legend you chose from 5A. Consider the following: Is the urban legend believable? Is there a moral? Does it reflect fears or changes in society? Does it, or could it, contain a half-truth?

C EVALUATE Work in small groups. Based on what you've learned about urban legends, create your own legend to share with the class. Use the questions in 5B as guidance. Then share your legend with other groups. Decide which urban legend sounds most plausible.

☐ I CAN DISCUSS URBAN LEGENDS.

LESSON 4 READ ABOUT LIFE'S MYSTERIES

ARTUR TAVARES

@ArturT

Too bad humans didn't evolve to have more limbs. I wouldn't mind having another pair of arms. It might make texting faster!

1 BEFORE YOU READ

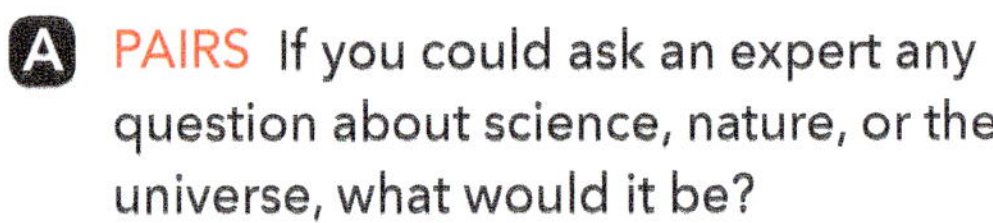

A PAIRS If you could ask an expert any question about science, nature, or the universe, what would it be?

B ▶03-17 VOCABULARY Read and listen. Do you know these words?

dim	a contour	an arthropod	advantageous	stability	consciousness
a neuron	an illusion	segmented	anatomy	plausible	

>> FOR DEFINITIONS, PAGE 158

2 READ

A PREVIEW Read the title and paragraph headings. What do you think the article will be about?

B ▶03-18 Read and listen to the article. Which of the questions could Paige answer conclusively?

Home | Logout  

ASK A BOOKWORM

Our librarian Paige Turner answers more of your curious questions.

Is it true that black makes you slim? If so, why?

Paige says: According to neuroscientists–yes. Black does make you look slimmer, or lighter colors make you look larger, depending on how you view it. The slimming properties of black are caused by an optical trick dubbed "the irradiation illusion" by Hermann von Helmholtz. Stare at the holes in the shape below, and you should notice that the white hole appears larger than the black one.

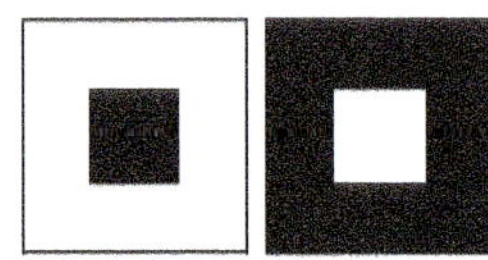

Helmholtz wasn't the first to notice this illusion. In the 1500s, the astronomer Galileo also witnessed a similar phenomenon when he realized that brighter planets in the night sky, like Venus, appeared larger than dimmer ones, like Jupiter. Since then, neuroscientists have discovered why this happens. They found that when we view light things on a dark background, our eyes become flooded with light-sensitive neurons. They suggest that this must be an evolutionary trait that helps us spot movement and danger at night. When we view dark things against a light background, the light-sensitive neurons narrow the contours of the black shape. This is why wearing black during the day creates the illusion of slimming.

Why aren't there any large animals with six or eight limbs?

Paige says: By large animals, I guess you mean mammals. Mammals are tetrapods, and many have four limbs. These animals are considered tetrapods because they all evolved from fish, even if some of them secondarily lost some or all of their limbs. On the other hand, the ancestors of today's arthropods (insects, arachnids, and crustaceans), who have more than four limbs, had segmented bodies with lots of limbs. There's not much more to it.

Is it possible for a mammal to evolve into a six-limbed creature? Well, anything is possible. However, having six legs wouldn't necessarily be advantageous for mammals. Their anatomy would have to change considerably to accommodate an extra pair of limbs. Controlling two more arms would also require more brain power. Crucially, there's the question of purpose. For insects, having six legs means more stability when crawling along walls and ceilings. Mammals don't need to perform similar actions so don't need the extra support.

>>

Why do we dream?

Paige says: There are a lot of plausible explanations for why we dream, although there's no definitive answer.

Many experts believe that dreaming is a form of memory processing and that it may help us convert information from our short-term to our long-term memories. There are many studies that have shown the importance of sleep for the consolidation of learning—the process that helps memories to become more stable and long-lasting. However, the role of dreaming in this consolidation process remains unclear.

Various theories explain dreaming as some form of preparatory process. One idea is that dreaming is a form of "threat simulation"—like a rehearsal for real-life dangers. Similarly, psychoanalysts believe that the purpose of dreaming might be to help us deal with complex experiences and emotions. Another theory, the theory of consciousness, suggests that dreaming helps us link three temporal dimensions in our minds—the past, present, and future. The belief is that dreaming facilitates information processing about past and present events, which in turn prepares us for future events.

While there are lots of theories out there about dreaming, none of them are conclusive. What do you think? Why do we dream?

3 CHECK YOUR UNDERSTANDING

A Answer the questions, according to the article.

1. Why do black objects appear slimmer on a light background?
2. How were the bodies of mammals and insects affected by their evolutionary ancestors?
3. What is the main reason why Paige thinks it is unlikely for mammals to develop extra limbs?
4. According to experts, how might dreaming help us?

B CLOSE READING **Reread lines 7-13 in the article. Then circle the correct answers.**

1. The phrase *depending on how you view it* suggests that the irradiation illusion ___ .
   a. can only be observed by certain people
   b. can be explained in two different ways
   c. demonstrates two different phenomena
2. The best definition for the word *dubbed* is to give something ___ .
   a. a formal, scientific name
   b. a name that describes it in some way
   c. a name that is not widely accepted by others

C Read the Reading Skill. Then reread the article. What further questions would you ask Paige about each topic?

D PAIRS **Summarize the article in 3-5 sentences.**

READING SKILL Respond to the writer

As you read, stop after each paragraph and respond to the writer with comments or questions. This helps you to relate to the text on a more personal level and to retain information better.

4 MAKE IT PERSONAL

Search online for an answer to your question from 1A. 

A THINK **Choose one question from the list and think of a possible answer. Take notes.**

- Why does the sunlight sometimes make us sneeze?
- What would be the most expensive way to fill a shoebox?
- What's the worst that could happen if the internet were to go down for the day?

B GROUPS **Discuss your ideas from 4A. Give reasons to support your answers.**

C EVALUATE **Choose the best possible answer from 4B and share it with the class. Try to make your explanation as believable as possible. As a class, vote on the most likely and most creative explanation.**

☐ I CAN READ ABOUT LIFE'S MYSTERIES.

LESSON 5 WRITE A PLOT SUMMARY

ARTUR TAVARES
@ArturT
Mystery books make for great travel reading. I just read this plot summary… think I'll pick up the book on my next trip.

1 BEFORE YOU WRITE

A Read about plot summaries.

A plot summary is a brief description of the sequence of events in a story (from a book, a movie, etc.). It includes the following major elements: exposition (how the story begins), developing or rising action, climax (the most exciting action or turning point in the story), falling action, and denouement (how the story ends). It includes the names of the main character(s) and the most important details of the storyline.

B Read the model. What happens during the climax of the book?

Home | Logout

A complex and thrilling mystery

The novel *Still Life* by Canadian crime writer Louise Penny is the thrilling start of a new mystery series featuring Chief Inspector Gamache. Set in the tiny fictional village of Three Pines, the book introduces us to a cast of characters who are interesting and complex—and have dark secrets to hide.

The novel opens with the revelation that Jane Neal, an elderly artist from the village, was killed while walking through the woods. On the surface, it looks as though the killing may have been a hunting accident. Inspector Gamache has come down from Montreal to investigate. We soon learn that Jane's art is about to be displayed for the first time at an exhibition in the town. Whether and how this fact is connected to the crime remains an enigma. But Inspector Gamache has a hunch that the killing was not, in fact, an accident.

As the plot thickens, we learn about Philippe, an angry teenager who may have been involved in the crime. He had gone into the woods on that morning, armed with a bow and arrow to hunt deer. Was it his arrow that accidentally killed Jane? All the evidence points in that direction, but Inspector Gamache doesn't buy it. There are other people who might have had motive to kill. There is Jane's niece, who was no longer on good terms with her aunt, and who believed she was inheriting her aunt's valuable house. Or Clara, Jane's best friend and an artist herself, who actually did inherit the house. Could it be Peter, Clara's husband, desperately jealous of Clara's relationship with Jane? Or Ben, an intriguing Englishman who seems to be in love with Clara? And finally, there is Ruth, a poet with a bad temper who has a secret she desperately needed to keep from Jane.

Almost any of the options seem plausible, and as the action builds toward the climax, we start to understand how Jane's art is at the center. It is her art that reveals the town's secrets and points the way toward her killer. Inspector Gamache, through his keen perceptions, gains insights into each of the town's characters, but it is ultimately one of the townspeople who figures out who did it—thereby endangering her own life. In a scene that has you on the edge of your seat, the murderer is about to strike again when wit and luck—and, of course, Inspector Gamache—come to the rescue just in time.

In the denouement, we once again see Jane's group of friends coming together and discussing how her art had revealed the secret. And together they start to realize how all of the signs had always pointed in that direction, if they had only been able to see them.

C PAIRS Discuss. Based on this summary, is this a book you would want to read? Why or why not?

D PAIRS Read the model again. Complete the plot diagram.

Book: *Still Life* by Louise Penny
Setting: a tiny ____________ village called Three Pines
Main characters: Jane Neal, Inspector Gamache

Exposition
- An elderly ____________ is found dead.
- Inspector Gamache is in town to ____________ .
- Jane's art was about to be ____________ ____________ .

Rising action
- The evidence points to ____________ having killed Jane in a(n) ____________ .
- Inspector Gamache has a(n) ____________ that it wasn't an accident.
- Many other characters have a(n) ____________ .

Climax
- Jane's ____________ is the key.
- A townsperson ____________ and puts her own life ____________ .

Falling action
- Inspector Gamache arrives just in time and catches the killer.

Denouement
- Jane's group of friends realize ____________ ____________ .

2 FOCUS ON WRITING

Read the Writing Skill. Then reread the model. Circle the suspenseful words and phrases. Underline the rhetorical questions and possibilities raised about the solution to the mystery.

WRITING SKILL Build excitement

A good plot summary will entice readers and create a desire to read the book. You can build excitement by using suspenseful words and phrases, such as *thrilling, intriguing*, or *on the edge of your seat.* You can also grab the reader's attention by asking rhetorical questions and raising possibilities, without revealing the answers.

3 PLAN YOUR WRITING

A Think of a mystery book or mystery movie that you know (you can also choose another genre, such as thriller or science fiction). Create a diagram like the one in 1D to identify the plot points.

B PAIRS Discuss your ideas.

I think I'll write about the movie Cold Pursuit.

4 WRITE

Write a first draft of a plot summary of the book or movie you described in 3A. Remember to use suspenseful words and phrases as well as rhetorical questions. Use the plot summary in 1B as a model.

Writing tip

Choose wisely. When writing a summary, you can't include every detail. You have to figure out which details are the most important in terms of the plot structure. Also, you may not want to give away the ending. And if you do, be sure to give people a "spoiler alert"!

5 AFTER YOUR FIRST DRAFT

A PEER REVIEW Read your partner's plot summary. Answer the questions.

- Does the introduction include the title and the author or director?
- Are the setting and main characters included?
- Is the summary organized by exposition, rising action, climax, falling action, and denouement?
- Does the summary use suspenseful, exciting words and rhetorical questions?
- Does the summary get you excited about the book or movie without revealing too much?

B REVISE Write another draft, based on the feedback you got from your partner.

C PROOFREAD Check the spelling, grammar, and punctuation in your plot summary. Then read it again for overall sense.

☐ I CAN WRITE A PLOT SUMMARY.

PUT IT TOGETHER

1 PROBLEM SOLVING

A CONSIDER THE PROBLEM **Some people reject evidence that they have not personally experienced. For example, despite mathematical and photographic evidence, some do not believe that the sun is at the center of the solar system. Review the data and answer the questions.**

340 BCE	Aristotle provides scientific reasoning that the earth is at the center of the solar system.
200 BCE	Aristarchus suggests that the sun is at the center of the solar system.
1630	Galileo Galilei uses a telescope to support Aristarchus' theory.
1688	Sir Isaac Newton invents a new telescope that shows the sun at the center.
1946	The first photograph of Earth is taken from space.
1961	The first human goes to space.
1969	The first humans go to the moon.
1990	Hubble Space Telescope is in orbit around the earth.
Since 2012	Satellites become common.

1. Who believed that the sun goes around the earth? ______
2. When did humans first explore space? ______
3. What instruments helped provide evidence for scientists? ______

B THINK CRITICALLY **What reasons do some people have for rejecting science? Discuss with a partner.**

C FIND A SOLUTION **Consider the data, the problem, and possible solutions in small groups.**

Step 1 **Brainstorm** Choose a current, debatable issue and think of 3-5 ways people could be convinced to adopt more scientific and/or critical thinking perspectives about it.

Step 2 **Evaluate** Choose the best solution. Consider how to go about changing people's minds using evidence and factual details.

Step 3 **Present** Explain the best solution to the class. Refer to the data to support your ideas.

2 REFLECT AND PLAN

A Look back through the unit. Check (✓) the things you learned. Highlight the things you need to learn.

Speaking Objectives
- ☐ Talk about famous mysteries
- ☐ Talk about personal mysteries
- ☐ Discuss urban legends

Vocabulary
- ☐ Words related to mysteries

Conversation
- ☐ Keep listeners' attention

Pronunciation
- ☐ Reduction of modal perfects

Listening
- ☐ Listen for emphasis

Note-taking
- ☐ Use mapping

Language Choices
- ☐ Modals for speculation about the past
- ☐ Modals for expectation
- ☐ Passive modals

Discussion
- ☐ Acknowledge ideas

Reading
- ☐ Respond to the writer

Writing
- ☐ Build excitement

B What will you do to learn the things you highlighted?

Notes Done

Review the Reading Skill: Respond to the writer.

______

______

______

______

4 IS IT ART?

LEARNING GOALS

In this unit, you
- talk about street art
- talk about AI and art
- discuss the benefits of improvisation
- read about a famous festival
- write a descriptive essay

GET STARTED

A Read the unit title and learning goals. Besides painting, what are five or more disciplines that are considered part of the arts?

B Look at the photo. It shows a brush tipped with various paints. How does this photo suggest *art* rather than *house painting* or *furniture painting*?

C Read Camila's message. Why might her friend be unrealistic, and why might it not matter?

CAMILA RIVAS

@CamilaR

My friend thinks he'll become a famous artist. I hope so, but it could take decades to get there. In any case, I'm sure he'll enjoy trying.

LESSON 1 TALK ABOUT STREET ART

CAMILA RIVAS

@CamilaR

I finally moved to a new apartment. There's a lot of incredible art in the neighborhood. I need to learn more about these artists.

1 VOCABULARY Words related to street art

A Look at the photos in the infographic. Is street art an old or a new form of art? Where have you seen this type of art?

B ▶04-01 Read and listen. Do you know the words in bold?

The word ***graffiti*** originated from the ancient Greek word *graphein* meaning "to scratch, draw, write." Graffiti has been found in the Roman ruins at Pompeii and in prehistoric caves. There are many forms of graffiti.

Tagging began with a teenager in Philadelphia in 1967. The objective was not artistic **self-expression**. He only wanted to get the attention of a girl by writing his name anywhere she might see it.

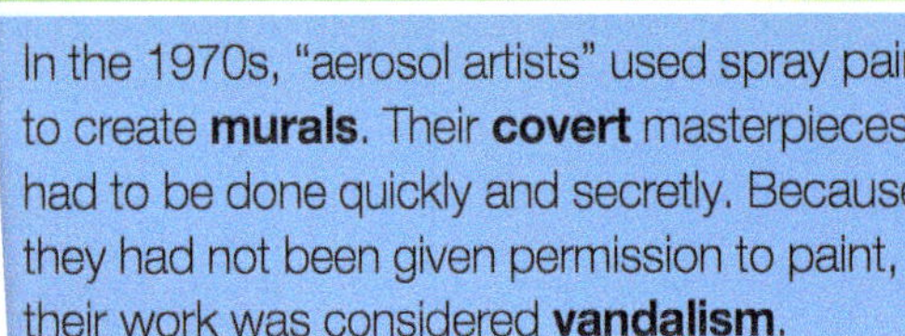

In the 1970s, "aerosol artists" used spray paint to create **murals**. Their **covert** masterpieces had to be done quickly and secretly. Because they had not been given permission to paint, their work was considered **vandalism**.

In the 1980s, graffiti was part of the **phenomenal** rise of hip-hop culture. The amazing popularity of hip-hop added an element of **commercial value** to street art.

In the late 1990s, murals by an artist known as Banksy began to **provoke** thought with their humor and social **commentary**. He is now so popular that his work has been **auctioned off** for millions of dollars.

>> FOR PRACTICE, PAGE 134 / DEFINITIONS, PAGE 158

2 LANGUAGE CHOICES Substitution with *so* and *not*

A Read the example sentences. Underline the phrases or clauses that have been replaced by *so* or *not*. Then circle the correct answers in the chart.

Example sentences

1. If we can increase the commercial value of this property, let's do so.
2. Are you going to the auction? If so, I'd like to go with you.
3. Do you like museums? If not, we can go somewhere else.
4. I may have shredded the receipt. I hope not, but I can't find it anywhere.
5. Did artists have permission to paint that mural? I don't believe so.
6. Is graffiti really art? I guess so.
7. Artists shouldn't paint on public buildings without permission. Doing so is vandalism.

Common words used with *so*: *assume, be afraid, believe, expect, guess, hope, imagine, presume, suppose, suspect, say, think*

Common words used with *not*: *assume, be afraid, guess, hope, suspect*

Substitution with *so* and *not*

- Use *do so* to avoid repeating a **subject / verb phrase**.
- Use *if so* to avoid repeating the clause in a **conditional / question**.
- *If not* means "if that situation is **true / not true**."
- Use *so* or *not* to avoid repeating a **verb / clause**.

>> FOR PRACTICE, PAGE 134

B Read the note about common words used with *so* and *not*. How can we make negative statements with these verbs?

3 CONVERSATION SKILL

A ▶04-04 Read the conversation skill. Listen. Notice the words the speakers use to ask for an opinion. Complete the sentences that you hear.

1. What ________________ on the city's decision to remove all the street art around here?
2. It's getting a lot of attention. ________________ it?
3. That's an interesting idea. ________________ it?

Ask for an opinion

Use questions like these to ask for an opinion in conversations, especially when discussing controversial topics:

What do you think / have to say about…?
What are your views / thoughts on…?
How do you feel about…?
What's your reaction to…?
How do you see the issue?
Which side are you on?

B PAIRS Discuss the issue of whether street artists should be arrested for vandalism and put in jail. Use an expression from the conversation skill box to ask for an opinion.

4 CONVERSATION

A ▶04-05 Listen. What do Edgar and Camila talk about?

B ▶04-05 Listen again. Answer the questions.

1. How does Camila feel about street art?
2. Why was the Banksy mural a problem for the garage owner?
3. Who shredded the Banksy picture after it was auctioned?
4. In your opinion, what might the buyer have been thinking when the Banksy picture was going through the shredder?

C ▶04-06 Listen. Complete the conversation.

Edgar: I would debate whether or not graffiti actually is art. What ________________ on that?

Camila: Personally, I don't like tagging, but I think Banksy's murals are art because they are a creative form of ____________. They provoke discussion on important social and political issues.

Edgar: OK. I guess ____________. But isn't street art meant to be temporary? And so, shouldn't it be available for everyone to see? In my opinion, it ________________ in a museum or in the home of a wealthy art collector.

5 TRY IT YOURSELF

A THINK What are some possible positive and negative effects of having street art like the Banksy mural in a neighborhood? Take notes in the chart.

Positive effects	Negative effects

B PAIRS Give your opinion about the most important effect from your charts.

☐ I CAN TALK ABOUT STREET ART.

LESSON 2 TALK ABOUT AI AND ART

CAMILA RIVAS

@CamilaR

As someone with a background in industrial design, I'm always interested in what machines can do. But can AI really create art?

1 BEFORE YOU LISTEN

A PAIRS THINK What do you know about artificial intelligence (AI)?

B ▶04-07 VOCABULARY Complete the chart. Then listen and check your answers.

	Verb	Noun	Adjective
1.	conceptualize	concept	
2.		endeavor	
3.	blur		
4.	compile		
5.		algorithm	
6.	utilize		
7.		depiction	
8.	emulate		
9.	evoke		

>> FOR PRACTICE, PAGE 135 / DEFINITIONS, PAGE 158

2 LANGUAGE CHOICES Phrasal verbs

Phrasal verbs consist of a verb + a particle. Some phrasal verbs are separable, and some are inseparable.

A Read the example sentences. Then read the rules in the chart. Are they true (*T*) or false (*F*)? Correct the false rules.

Use	Example sentences
Separable, with an object	1. How do you **tell apart** the two artists? It's impossible to **tell** them **apart**. They can't be **told apart**.
Inseparable, with an object	2. I don't know much about AI-generated art, but I'll **look into** it. It will be **looked into**.
No object	3. I missed part of the presentation because I **zoned out** a little. 4. We waited for 30 minutes, but the speaker never **showed up**.

Phrasal verbs

___ • When the object of a separable verb is a noun, it can separate the verb or follow the complete verb.

___ • When the object of a separable verb is a pronoun, it cannot separate the verb.

___ • In passive sentences, separable verbs are not separated.

___ • With inseparable verbs, the object always follows the complete verb in an active sentence.

___ • Phrasal verbs that do *not* take a direct object can be active or passive.

>> FOR PRACTICE, PAGE 135

B PAIRS Read the sentences. Which sentence contains a phrasal verb? What are some differences between phrasal verbs and verbs with prepositions?

Josh **lives down** the street. Josh thinks he'll never **live down** that mistake.

3 PRONUNCIATION

A ▶04-09 Listen. Read the pronunciation note.

B ▶04-10 Listen. Notice the stress in the underlined phrases. Then listen and repeat.

> **Stress in phrasal verbs**
>
> In two-word inseparable verbs, the main verb is usually stressed: ***agree** with*. In two-word separable verbs, the particle is usually stressed: *bring* **up**. In three-word phrasal verbs, the first particle is usually stressed: *look* **out** *for*, *put* **up** *with*.

A: I just found **out** that Rudy's going to rent **out** his art studio and **switch** to computer art.

B: Right. He had brought **up** that possibility. It's too bad. He's a talented painter.

A: I don't think he plans to give **up** painting entirely, but he needs to **catch** up on some bills.

B: Yeah, I can understand that. I hope this works **out** for him.

C ▶04-11 Listen. Mark the stressed words in the underlined phrases with a dot.

1. I ran into Samira at the museum today. She just started a new job there.
2. Do you think machines are going to take over the art world?
3. We just got back from the comedy show. It was hilarious.

4 LISTENING

> **LISTENING SKILL** Listen for signal phrases in conclusions
>
> Speakers sometimes use signal phrases in conclusions to summarize or restate important information. Listen for these phrases to both improve your understanding and review main ideas. For example: *Generally speaking,...; All things considered,...; Altogether,...; Ultimately,...; In short,...; As has been noted,...; We've seen that....*

A ▶04-12 Listen. What is the topic of the podcast?

B ▶04-12 Read the Listening Skill. Then listen for signal phrases in the conclusion. Write the signal phrases that you hear.

1. To show summary ______________
2. To show restatement ______________

C ▶04-12 Listen again. Answer the questions.

1. Why does *Portrait of Edmond Belamy* blur the lines between human and AI-generated art?
2. What are the two kinds of creativity that Professor Ramirez talks about?
3. What did the research at Rutgers University show?
4. Why can't human artists be replaced by artificial intelligence at the present time?

D PAIRS Why do you think an art collector paid $432,500 for *Portrait of Edmond Belamy*?

5 TRY IT YOURSELF

A THINK What is your opinion about artificial intelligence-generated paintings? Are the paintings art? Take notes in the chart.

Are AI-generated paintings art? Yes	No
Reason 1:	Reason 2:

B DISCUSS In small groups, discuss your answers from 5A.

C EVALUATE Find classmates who agree with your *Yes* or *No* response. Use information from the podcast and your own ideas to prepare for a debate with a group of classmates who have the opposing idea. Then have a debate.

☐ I CAN TALK ABOUT AI AND ART.

LESSON 3 DISCUSS THE BENEFITS OF IMPROVISATION

CAMILA RIVAS

@CamilaR

I'd love to try improvisation, but I just can't act! I don't think I have it in me. What about you?

1 BEFORE YOU LISTEN

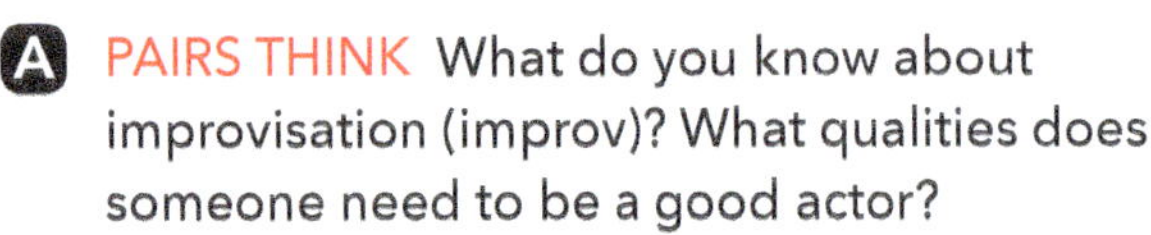

A PAIRS THINK What do you know about improvisation (improv)? What qualities does someone need to be a good actor?

B ▶04-13 VOCABULARY Read the words and listen to the sentences. Do you know these words?

on the spot	out of (your) comfort zone	empathy
checks all the boxes	face (your) fears	impartial
a daunting experience	a mindset	a conscious effort

>> FOR PRACTICE, PAGE 136 / DEFINITIONS, PAGE 159

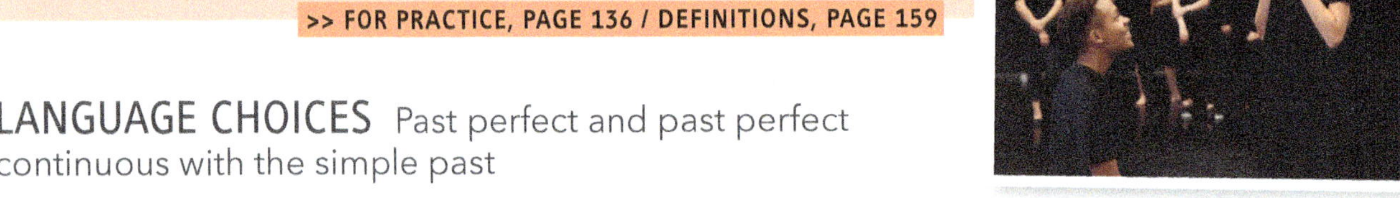

2 LANGUAGE CHOICES Past perfect and past perfect continuous with the simple past

A Read the example sentences. Then circle the correct answers in the chart.

Use	Example sentences
To describe an action that happened before another action in the past	1. The class **had** already **started** by the time I **arrived**. 2. I **hadn't understood** Lin's dilemma until I **put** myself in his shoes. 3. I**'d been considering** an improv class for years before I finally **tried** it.
To describe cause and effect	4. Masa **apologized** since he **had put** me on the spot. 5. We **were** finally able to begin once we **had checked** all the boxes. 6. His eyes **were** red because he**'d been crying**. 7. Yan **had been studying** for weeks, so she **did** really well on her exams.

Past perfect and past perfect continuous with the simple past

- Use the past perfect with the simple past to show the sequence of two actions. Use the past perfect or past perfect continuous for the **first / second** of the two actions.
- Use the past perfect continuous to show that the first action was **complete / in progress** when the second action began.
- Use the **simple past / past perfect** for an action that caused another action to happen.
- Use the **simple past / past perfect** for the resulting action.

>> FOR PRACTICE, PAGE 136

B The following sentence shows the sequence of two events. Why doesn't the speaker use the past perfect? Is it possible to replace one of the verbs with a past perfect or past perfect continuous verb?

Marta attended the improv class for six months before she felt comfortable.

3 VIDEO TALK

A ▶04-15 Listen or watch. What is the main idea of the talk?

B ▶04-15 Read the Note-taking Skill. Listen or watch again. Then complete the notes.

NOTE-TAKING SKILL Use an outline

The outline note-taking method is great way to organize information in a structured, logical manner. Write main points to the left. Indent supporting details and examples that follow.

Improvisation (aka improv): type of theater technique; not planned
Why do it?
- good for ______ (1), helps navigate life; ______ (2) can do improv

How does it work?
- typical improv class = teamwork, pairs, or groups; involves performance and role play; not competitive—collaborative

Benefits: everyday life
- builds ______ (3), teaches you to say ______ (4)
- prepares you for challenges, like ______ (5) issues, ______ (6) problems, etc.
- soft skills development; ______ (7), teamwork, problem solving, etc.
- helps you adjust ______ (8)
- helps develop ______ (9) listening—a very important ______ (10) skill; Say YES!

C The speaker persuades listeners to try improv classes. Which persuasive features did you notice?

D PAIRS REACT Did this talk make you want to try improv classes? Why or why not? If not, what could the speaker have said to persuade you?

4 DISCUSSION SKILL

Read the discussion skill. Do you use this strategy in your discussions now?

Say "yes" to keep a conversation going

When you're having a discussion, use the improv strategy of "saying yes" to put speakers at ease and keep the conversation going. If someone comes up with an idea, respond positively and add your own ideas. For example:

A: *You need to show teamwork if you're working on a group project at work.*

B: *Yes, and you might even need it on a small project with another person.*

5 TRY IT YOURSELF

A THINK Look at the list of skills mentioned in the video. Think of everyday scenarios where you might use these skills. Take notes.

- public speaking
- showing empathy
- teamwork
- problem solving
- adjusting to change
- active listening

B DISCUSS Share your ideas from 5A. Say "yes" and add your own ideas during your discussion.

C EVALUATE In groups, choose one of your scenarios from 5A. Improvise the scenario.

☐ I CAN DISCUSS THE BENEFITS OF IMPROVISATION.

LESSON 4 READ ABOUT A FAMOUS FESTIVAL

CAMILA RIVAS

@CamilaR

I love the principles of the Burning Man festival. Leaving no trace is so important—more festivals should do this.

1 BEFORE YOU READ

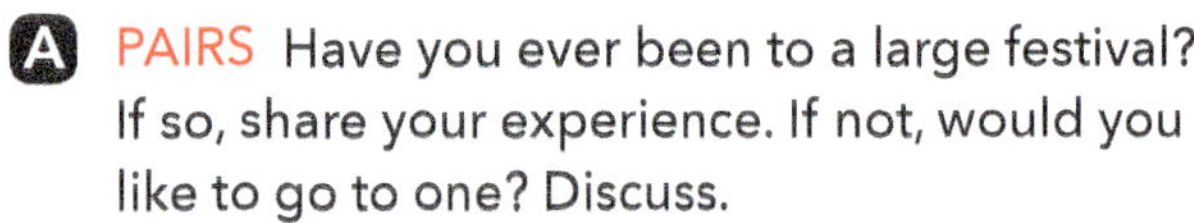

A PAIRS Have you ever been to a large festival? If so, share your experience. If not, would you like to go to one? Discuss.

B ▶04-16 VOCABULARY Read and listen. Do you know these words?

a gathering	a pop-up	communal	unconditional	an effigy	a bucket list
descend on (a place)	a vast array	radical	culminate	humble	

>> FOR DEFINITIONS, PAGE 159

2 READ

A PREVIEW Look at the title and layout. Where might you find a text like this?

B ▶04-17 Read and listen to the blog post. What does the writer think of Burning Man?

Blog | About | Destinations | Contact Logout

Burning Man Festival by Autumn Smith

Black Rock, Nevada

It started as a small bonfire gathering on a beach back in 1986. It's since evolved into one of the world's most famous celebrations of community, art, and self-expression. Every year, up to 70,000 people descend on Black Rock Desert in Nevada to attend Burning Man.

It's said that Burning Man is not a festival, it's an experience. In fact, organizers describe the event as a "culture of possibility." It's not a theory or an idea, it's a way of life. It's not political, it's moral. It's not sponsored, it's supported. It's unlike any other event on the planet—it truly is unique.

Burning Man is a nine-day event focusing primarily on arts and performance. It takes place in a pop-up city in the desert erected by the participants themselves. The Burning Man experience is built on active participation. The organizers don't book any entertainment—attendees provide entertainment for each other for free. You can find a vast array of activities at the event, including dances, theater performances, cooking sessions, parties, and art workshops. Some participants also offer services to their fellow attendees for free, including recycling, bike repairs, and even massages. The event is built around a communal effort and is open to everyone.

FOUNDING PRINCIPLES

as written by Burning Man founder Larry Harvey:

RADICAL INCLUSION: Burning Man is open to everyone.

GIFTING: The act of gifting is encouraged and is unconditional.

DECOMMODIFICATION: Burning Man is unmarketable. The event does not invite sponsorship from commercial organizations. In practice, this means that commerce is banned at the festival site.

RADICAL SELF-RELIANCE: Participants are encouraged to rely on their own resources. For example, they provide their own food and water for the duration of the event.

RADICAL SELF-EXPRESSION: Community members' self-expression, in whatever form, is a gift to others.

COMMUNAL EFFORT AND CIVIL RESPONSIBILITY: Cooperation, collaboration, and public welfare are emphasized.

LEAVING NO TRACE: The Burning Man community respects the environment, and cleanups are a communal responsibility.

PARTICIPATION AND IMMEDIACY: Direct, active involvement is encouraged. Participants create entertainment for each other and live the Burning Man experience in the here and now. >>

Given that entertainment is created by participants, you can't always predict the content of Burning Man. However, there are certain forms of art and expression that you can expect to see. Some participants arrive in mutant vehicles, which are creatively altered trucks and cars. Electronic dance music also features regularly at the event, as do large-scale interactive art installations. These are displayed across the desert, converting the vast landscape into an interactive gallery exhibition. Creative outfits are also likely to feature, as are bicycles, which are the preferred mode of transportation for attendees.

Burning Man has an annual theme to loosely guide the event's content. Past themes have included "Hope and Fear," "Metamorphoses," and "The Floating World." Although the theme changes each year, one thing remains the same: The event culminates in the ritual burning of a wooden effigy—the Burning Man itself. The effigy can be up to 30 meters tall, and attendees enjoy the hour-long bonfire spectacular, which includes an impressive fireworks display.

From humble beginnings, Burning Man has become an internationally renowned event. Despite its growth, it has stayed true to its founding principles throughout the years and is a vibrant and enriching experience that's well worth adding to your bucket list.

3 CHECK YOUR UNDERSTANDING

A **Answer the questions, according to the blog post.**

1. What changes at the Burning Man festival each year?
2. Why don't organizers book entertainment for Burning Man?
3. Why can't you buy merchandise at the event?
4. How is the principle of gifting demonstrated by participants?

B CLOSE READING **Reread lines 4-6 in the blog post. Then circle the correct answers.**

1. Why does the writer use the "It's not..., it's..." construction to compare ideas?
   a. She is suggesting that these are common misconceptions about Burning Man.
   b. She is suggesting that these are common features of other large events.
   c. She is paraphrasing the principles of Burning Man.
2. Which sentence best summarizes the lines?
   a. Burning Man is not what people might expect.
   b. It is difficult to define Burning Man.
   c. Burning Man is better than other festivals.

C **Read the Reading Skill. Then reread the blog post and follow the steps in the box. Summarize paragraphs 1-3 in about 10 words each.**

D PAIRS **Summarize the blog post in 3-5 sentences.**

READING SKILL **Summarize paragraphs**

Summarizing helps you identify the most important information in a text. To summarize a paragraph, follow these steps:

1. Identify the main idea of the paragraph. Identify any key words.
2. Paraphrase the main idea and key words, excluding any unnecessary information.

4 MAKE IT PERSONAL

Find out about the problems Burning Man organizers face.

A THINK **Reread the founding principles of Burning Man. Think of ways that participants and organizers could demonstrate each principle. Take notes.**

To promote more of an immediate experience, participants could be discouraged from videoing events to "live in the moment."

B GROUPS **Discuss your ideas from 4A. Give reasons to support your ideas.**

C EVALUATE **In the same groups, choose the best ways to demonstrate each principle. Make a flyer for festival attendees titled "Make the Most of Your Burning Man Experience." Remember, the Burning Man principles are guidance, not rules.**

One of the Burning Man principles is immediate experience—we encourage you to live life for the moment and not through a lens.

LESSON 5 WRITE A DESCRIPTIVE ESSAY

CAMILA RIVAS
@CamilaR
I visited this place recently. Amazing! Sometimes buildings can be art.

1 BEFORE YOU WRITE

A Read about descriptive essays.

A descriptive essay uses sensory details to describe a person, place, or object and to recreate an experience for the reader. Like a narrative essay, a descriptive essay is often organized with a flow of ideas from one paragraph to the next, rather than a strictly structured thesis with supporting points.

B Read the model. What adjectives does the writer use to describe how the building makes her feel?

A BUILDING A WORLD APART

Visiting the Galaxy SOHO building in Beijing is an experience unlike any other. The architect, Zaha Hadid, an Iraqi-British woman, is one of the most famous modern-day architects. I knew her name but had never before visited one of her buildings. I hadn't thought of architecture as an art form until I walked through the Galaxy SOHO.

To begin with, the building is vast. It is impossible to walk through without feeling awed and humbled. You enter and the walls rise around you like cliffs. They curve in a continuous flow, with no corners and no obvious transition from one room to the next. Indeed, the whole experience feels more like walking through a natural landscape, rather than something human-made. For me, this created the feeling of being part of something bigger than myself. It made me feel that people, and the art that people create, are simply another extension of our incredible natural world.

Hadid makes a conscious effort to change the way we think about space. The Galaxy SOHO has four large "pods," dome-like sections of building that reminded me of something out of a science fiction novel. The pods are connected with bridge-like sections, and on the ground level there is a courtyard. This enables a continuous flow between inside and outside space. Also, when you are inside, the huge windows further blur the distinction between inside and outside. You see patches of sky, sometimes through the window and sometimes through an open space. The Galaxy SOHO is appropriately named because it feels like a place of endless scope and variety, not just a building.

Before visiting Hadid's creation, I had always thought of buildings in more conventional ways—just something functional, with four walls and a roof. So, for me, walking through the Galaxy SOHO was a liberating experience. It gave me the feeling that people can move beyond the ordinary, think in unconventional ways, and share an experience that taps into what it means to be human. It is only through art that I experience moments like that—when it is as though, for a moment, someone has pulled back a curtain to reveal how everything interconnects. It had never occurred to me that a building could spark that feeling until I experienced the awe of walking through the Galaxy SOHO.

 PAIRS Discuss. What other objects or experiences does the writer compare the Galaxy SOHO to? Why does she choose these things for comparison?

5 SAY THAT AGAIN?

LEARNING GOALS

In this unit, you

- talk about diplomatic language
- talk about cultural differences
- discuss the origin of slang
- read about communicating with aliens
- write a rhetorical analysis

GET STARTED

A Read the unit title and learning goals. A common expression is, "It's not what you say but how you say it." What does this mean? How could a language choice impact your success in communicating?

B Look at the photo. It shows people holding speech bubbles. What do you think is the message behind this photo?

C Read Iris's message. Why do you think she believes that every part of a presentation needs to match?

IRIS LIN

@IrisL

When giving a presentation, it's critical to have a clear message. Everything should align, including how the materials look, how you dress, and how you speak.

LESSON 1 TALK ABOUT DIPLOMATIC LANGUAGE

IRIS LIN

@IrisL

Tip of the day: Never write an email when you're angry. It never ends well. 

1 VOCABULARY Words related to communication

A Look at the web page. Have you ever received an unprofessional email or letter?

B ▶05-01 Read and listen. Do you know the words in bold?

Be Professional When Writing

It is important to sound professional when you write a formal email, memo, or letter. Here are some basic tips to follow:

- Always be **diplomatic**; that is, be polite and clear, rather than **harsh** and accusatory. Be **tactful** so that the other person feels respected and does not lose face. Embarrassing someone is never a good thing, so be careful of how you **word** things.
- Avoid issuing **ultimatums**, such as, "If you do not do X, we will stop doing Y." The other person will feel backed into a corner and you might end up harming the relationship.
- Be politely direct in your requests and not **ambiguous**. If your **wording** is **vague**, at worst, you will sound **wishy-washy** and easy to push around. At best, you will confuse the other person.
- If you have bad news to deliver, be polite, but get to the point quickly. Do **not mince your words**.
- Avoid **jargon**. Use language that is easy to understand.

>> FOR PRACTICE, PAGE 137 / DEFINITIONS, PAGE 159

2 LANGUAGE CHOICES The subjunctive

A Read the example sentences. Then circle the correct answers in the chart.

Use	Example sentences
After the following verbs: *advise, ask, command, demand, insist, propose, recommend, request, suggest*	1. How do you propose this message **be worded**? 2. I recommend that you **be diplomatic**. 3. My co-worker suggested I **not send** the message.
After the following adjectives: *better / best, critical, crucial, essential, imperative, important, necessary, urgent*	4. It's best that you **not give** an ultimatum. 5. Is it essential we **schedule** a meeting this week? 6. It's imperative that we **be told** the truth.

The subjunctive

- The subjunctive expresses a **desired** / **completed** action.
- The subjunctive is formed with the **simple present** / **base form** of a verb.
- We **can** / **cannot** omit *that* before a subjunctive clause.
- Use *not* **before** / **after** the subjunctive verb to make it negative.
- The passive subjunctive is formed with *be* + **base form** / **past participle**.

>> FOR PRACTICE, PAGE 137

B Both of the following sentences have a negative meaning. What is the difference between them?

I don't recommend you use strong wording in your message.

I recommend you not use strong wording in your message.

3 CONVERSATION SKILL

A ▶05-04 Read the conversation skill. Listen. Notice the words the speakers use to communicate diplomatically. Complete the sentences that you hear.

> **Communicate diplomatically**
>
> When dealing with sensitive issues in formal communication, it's important to be clear and direct but also diplomatic in order to avoid offending the other party.
>
> To decline something:
> *I'm afraid that we cannot…*
> *I regret that I will be unable to…*
> *I'm sorry, but unfortunately we cannot…*
>
> To make a request:
> *We would appreciate…*
> *We strongly suggest that you…*
> *We request that you…*

1. I'm sorry, but ______________________ lower the price any further.
2. ______________________ it if you could have the professor schedule the exam a day earlier.

B PAIRS Imagine you are the people below. Make and decline requests. Use diplomatic language from the conversation skill box.

car salesperson / customer professor / student employer / employee

4 CONVERSATION

A ▶05-05 Listen. What does Artur need help with?

B ▶05-05 Listen again. Answer the questions.

1. What problem is Artur writing about?
2. What does Iris mean when she says, "You catch more flies with honey than with vinegar"?
3. What other advice does Iris give Artur?

C ▶05-06 Listen. Complete the conversation.

Iris: Well, it's OK to be direct, but this sentence might be a little too direct. "We ______________ that your director ______________ us immediately to set up a meeting." It sounds like an ______________ .

Artur: How about this: "We ______________ that your director contact us at his ______________________ to set up a meeting?"

Iris: Great! That wording is much more ______________ .

5 TRY IT YOURSELF

A THINK Read the email on page 167. Try to make it sound more professional and diplomatic. Take notes in the chart.

Wording that needs to be changed	Diplomatic wording

B ROLE PLAY Student A: You are an employee. Student B: You are a manager. Imagine that Student A is your employee and has shown you the email from 5A. Make suggestions on how to revise the email.

☐ I CAN TALK ABOUT DIPLOMATIC LANGUAGE.

TALK ABOUT CULTURAL DIFFERENCES

IRIS LIN

@IrisL

Communicating with someone from a different culture can be challenging sometimes, even when you both speak the same language.

1 BEFORE YOU LISTEN

A PAIRS THINK Have you ever heard the expression "Silence is golden"? What do you think it means?

B ▶05-07 VOCABULARY Read the words and listen to the sentences. Do you know these words?

neglected	reflective	a cultural gap	fill the silence
explicit	an utterance	unsettled	a counterpart

>> FOR PRACTICE, PAGE 138 / DEFINITIONS, PAGE 159

2 LANGUAGE CHOICES Embedded *yes/no* questions

A A *yes/no* question can be embedded as a noun clause in a sentence. Read the example sentences. Underline the embedded questions. Then read the rules in the chart. Are they true (*T*) or false (*F*)? Correct the false rules.

Example sentences

1. I can't say if / whether my attitude is reflective of my culture.
2. Should we ask someone if / whether that information is correct?
3. I have no idea if / whether I'll move back to Dubai or not.
4. The question is whether or not we should change our plans.
5. Whether or not this trend will continue is anyone's guess.
6. Whether it was a cultural gap or some other misunderstanding is not clear.

Embedded *yes/no* questions

___ • An embedded *yes/no* question uses question word order.

___ • *If* and *whether (or not)* have the same meaning when introducing embedded questions.

___ • *If* and *whether* can be omitted from embedded questions.

___ • An embedded question occurs only within statements.

___ • An embedded question can follow a noun or a verb.

___ • Use *whether* to introduce embedded questions that function as the subject of the sentence.

>> FOR PRACTICE, PAGE 138

B PAIRS Be careful not to confuse an embedded *yes/no* question with a conditional sentence. Look at the following sentences. Which is an embedded question? Which is a conditional? How can you tell?

I don't know if she needs help.

I'm always here if she needs help.

3 PRONUNCIATION

Contrastive stress

When two or more ideas are compared or contrasted, speakers often stress syllables in both words to draw attention to them. The stressed syllables are usually longer, louder, and higher-pitched: *Is it better to speak **formally** or **casually**?*

A ▶05-09 Listen. Read the pronunciation note.

B ▶05-10 Listen. Notice the stress on the contrasted words. Then listen and repeat.

1. Be **explicit** when you tell me your decision, not **indirect**.
2. Am I responsible for **all** of our South American markets or only **some**?

C ▶05-11 Listen. Underline the words that are compared or contrasted. Mark the stressed syllables with a dot.

1. Will I sound more natural if I speak slowly or quickly?
2. You heard me rehearsing my talk. Should I slow down or speed up?

4 LISTENING

LISTENING SKILL Listen for contrasts

Speakers use a variety of words and expressions to show a contrast. For example: *a comparison of, conversely, in contrast, instead, on the contrary, on the other hand, rather, unlike.*

A ▶05-12 Listen. What is the topic of the podcast?

B ▶05-12 Read the Listening Skill. Listen again for contrasting information. Complete the chart.

	Speaking cultures	Listening cultures
1. Speaking vs. listening cultures		value reflective silence, sign of respect
2. Countries	English-speaking countries + southern Europe / parts of South America	
3. Timing of utterances		Japanese: 8-second pause btw speakers
4. Feelings about silence		Silence is golden; offended if others jump in too quickly
5. Meaning of silence		silence = careful consideration, respect
	silence in response to question = don't know answer or disinterested	

C PAIRS REACT What surprised you most about this podcast?

5 TRY IT YOURSELF

A MAKE IT PERSONAL Look at rows 4-5 of your notes in 4A. Which culture do you relate to the most?

B DISCUSS In small groups, discuss your answers from 5A. Explain your answers.

C EVALUATE Based on what you learned in the podcast and your discussion, what issues do you think you would have living in a culture that communicates differently from yours? How would you approach these challenges?

I CAN TALK ABOUT CULTURAL DIFFERENCES.

LESSON 3 DISCUSS THE ORIGIN OF SLANG

IRIS LIN

@IrisL

I think it's OK to use slang most of the time, but I draw the line when it comes to legal documents! 🙁

1 BEFORE YOU LISTEN

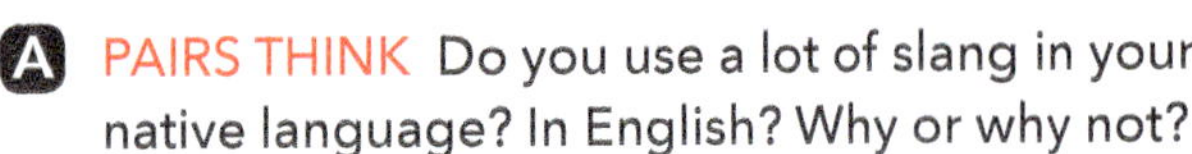

A PAIRS THINK Do you use a lot of slang in your native language? In English? Why or why not?

B ▶05-13 VOCABULARY Read the words and listen to the sentences. Do you know these words?

cringeworthy	an abbreviation	rebel	solidarity	concise	vulgar
a phenomenon	an emoji	the status quo	no hard and fast rules	a downside	hinder

>> FOR PRACTICE, PAGE 139 / DEFINITIONS, PAGE 160

2 LANGUAGE CHOICES Embedded *Wh-* questions

A Read the example sentences. Underline the embedded questions. Then complete the rules in the chart with words from the box.

Example sentences

1. I can't tell what this emoji means.
2. I'm not certain who is attending the meeting today.
3. a. I don't know where I should go.
   b. I don't know where to go.
4. a. Do you know how we can fix this?
   b. Do you know how to fix this?
5. a. How did you finish this report so quickly?
   b. I can't imagine how you finished it by yourself.
6. a. What does this abbreviation stand for?
   b. Can you remind me what it stands for?

Embedded *Wh-* questions

- An embedded question can begin with any ______________ word.
- When an embedded question contains *can* or *should*, we can replace it with a(n) ______________ .
- Embedded questions use ______________ word order.
- An embedded question with the subject *who* takes a(n) ______________ .
- Do not include the auxiliary verb ______________ in an embedded question.

singular verb
infinitive
Wh- question
do
statement

>> FOR PRACTICE, PAGE 139

B Change the two questions to embedded questions. Begin each sentence with *I don't know*. How does the word order change in each sentence?

Who called you? Who did you call?

3 VIDEO TALK

A ▶05-15 Listen or watch. What is the main idea of the talk?

B ▶05-15 Read the Note-taking Skill. Listen or watch again. Take notes in the chart.

NOTE-TAKING SKILL Know what to write

Knowing what and how much to write down is sometimes difficult. Follow these tips for what to include in your notes:

- definitions, word for word
- enumerations or lists of things that are discussed
- information that is repeated or spelled out
- examples

Unit 5: Stoked about Slang

Definition of slang / Why we use it	How slang is formed
• information, non-standard vocabulary • part of everyday conversation	• new words, e.g., ______________
Positive views on slang	**Negative views on slang**
• highly creative and fun	• inappropriate in certain situations

C Is the speaker for or against the use of slang?

D PAIRS REACT The speaker says, "Slang isn't appropriate in all situations. Critics say that it can make you sound vulgar, or less intelligent." Do you agree? Why or why not?

4 DISCUSSION SKILL

Read the discussion skill. Which of these phrases do you use in your discussions now?

Speculate

Speculating is when you form an idea about something without firm evidence. Use phrases like these for speculating:

It could be because…
Perhaps it's because…
It might have to do with…

These are usually followed by a noun phrase.

5 TRY IT YOURSELF

A THINK Make a list of slang terms you use. Analyze your own use of these terms. Think about…

- why you use them
- how they're formed
- their popularity
- others' attitudes towards them

B DISCUSS In small groups, share your thoughts from 5A. Use language to speculate.

C EVALUATE What causes a slang term to become widespread or even mainstream? With your group, list five possible reasons and then rank them based on likelihood. Share your list with another group.

☐ I CAN DISCUSS THE ORIGIN OF SLANG.

READ ABOUT COMMUNICATING WITH ALIENS

IRIS LIN

@IrisL

What's up with alien movies? Aliens always come to Earth speaking perfect English. Are there language schools on Mars?!

1 BEFORE YOU READ

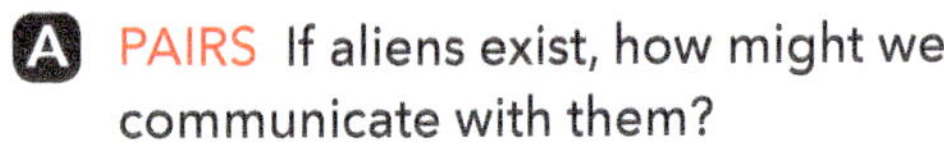

A PAIRS If aliens exist, how might we communicate with them?

B ▶05-16 VOCABULARY Read and listen. Do you know these words?

decipher	on the premise (that)	interstellar	a long way off
divided on	render (something) unnecessary	a cultural construct	a boundary

>> FOR DEFINITIONS, PAGE 160

2 READ

A PREVIEW Read the title and subtitles. Predict what you think each paragraph will include.

B ▶05-17 Read and listen to the article. What is the author's main argument?

COMMUNICATION WITH EXTRATERRESTRIALS—AN ALIEN CONCEPT?

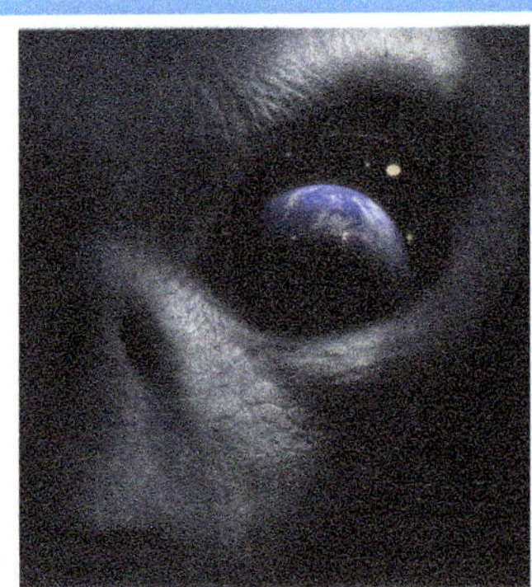

The 2016 blockbuster *Arrival*, which explores the theme of human interaction with extraterrestrials, suggests that communicating with visitors to Earth might be fairly easy. In the movie, a linguist deciphers symbols produced by the aliens and establishes a shared vocabulary to communicate. If aliens exist and we encounter them, how will we communicate? Experts are divided on this issue, but one thing seems clear—it will likely be much harder than it seems on the big screen.

Hello? Can you hear me?

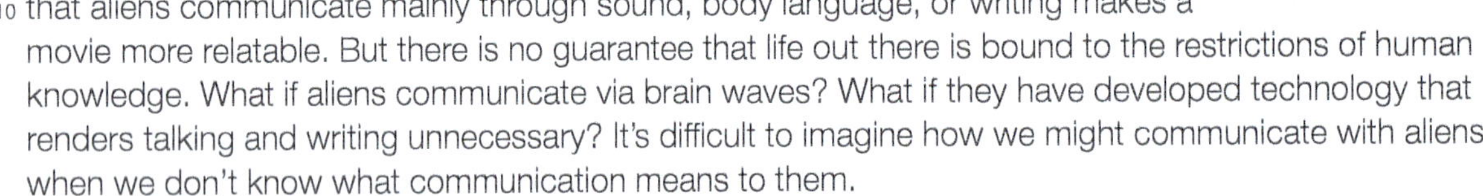

Arrival is a fascinating insight into how an alien encounter might play out. However, it works on the premise that humans and aliens have shared traits or skills. Assuming that aliens communicate mainly through sound, body language, or writing makes a movie more relatable. But there is no guarantee that life out there is bound to the restrictions of human knowledge. What if aliens communicate via brain waves? What if they have developed technology that renders talking and writing unnecessary? It's difficult to imagine how we might communicate with aliens when we don't know what communication means to them.

Just as aliens may not communicate in the same way that we do, they may not advance in the same way, or at the same speed. We are now better able to receive and interpret signals than we were 200 years ago due to advancements in technology. Where are alien civilizations in their development? And how fast have their communication systems advanced? We simply have no idea.

Huh? I don't get it.

Stephen Wolfram, an expert in computer languages, points out that alien communication could be all around us already. One example he gives is pulsars—an extraterrestrial source of radiation. Pulsars are widely accepted to be emissions from spinning neutron stars and were discovered back in 1967. Could these stars be beacons of communication that aliens have engineered for interstellar navigation? The blinking of a neutron star, caused by the pulsars emitted, could be the equivalent of a lighthouse on Earth.

Alternatively, the late philosopher and science fiction writer Stanislaw Lem suggested that aliens might use coded communication. They may not send a message directly, but instead send a code that someone (or something) would use to access a message. Only creatures with the right biological makeup and cognitive systems would be able to convert this code into a message.

>>

We should talk about this "in person."

However aliens communicate, deciphering that communication will prove difficult, perhaps impossible. Even interpreting a human message relies on some prior knowledge of cultural constructs and ideas. Put simply, you can't understand a mathematic formula, say $E = mc^2$, without understanding the concepts of energy, mass, and the speed of light. The same applies to alien communication, and we know nothing about extraterrestrial cultures or concepts. It is likely that this intelligence gap can only be overcome through face-to-face contact with extraterrestrial beings, yet no alien encounters have been confirmed to date. In order to learn how to communicate with something, first we need proof that it even exists!

It seems that communication with aliens is still a long way off. Science fiction can make fantastical concepts seem very real, but only within the boundaries of our own conceptual knowledge. It may be that the first step to understanding alien communication is not to limit ourselves to what we already know.

3 CHECK YOUR UNDERSTANDING

A Answer the questions, according to the article.

1. Why do science fiction movies feature aliens with familiar, human traits?
2. What is unknown about aliens and how they might communicate?
3. What examples does the writer give of possible types of alien communication?
4. What key information does the writer believe we need in order to understand alien communication, and how is it suggested we can attain that?

B CLOSE READING Reread lines 12-14 in the article. Then circle the correct answers.

1. What is the main purpose of the questions beginning with *What if…*?
   a. to introduce questions that the writer will answer later in the text
   b. to express the writer's opinions on the topic with hypothetical examples
   c. to support a statement with hypothetical examples
2. Which statements about these lines are true? There may be more than one correct answer.
   a. The writer uses personal pronouns to make us feel part of the discussion.
   b. The writer uses rhetorical techniques to draw the reader into the argument.
   c. The writer supports his argument with factual information.

C Read the Reading Skill. Scan the article in 2B. Circle the different ways the writer refers to *aliens*. Underline the different ways the writer refers to *communication*.

D PAIRS Summarize the article in 3-5 sentences.

READING SKILL Recognize word choices

Writers often vary the language they use to avoid repetition. For example, a writer may use the words *a concept* or *an idea* to explain *a theory*. Also, writers may give specific information about the same idea. For example, *scientists* might become *experts in biology*.

4 MAKE IT PERSONAL

Find out more about alien communication.

A THINK Imagine you are explaining one of these concepts to an alien: energy, anger, language, or peace. How might you do it? Would you use words, actions, demonstrations, or descriptions? Take notes.

B PAIRS Share your ideas. Are they similar? Which do you think would be the most effective?

C EVALUATE Work with another pair. Pair A: Explain one of the concepts in the way you think is most effective. Pair B: Guess which concept Pair A is explaining. Evaluate the strengths and weaknesses of the explanation.

☐ I CAN READ ABOUT COMMUNICATING WITH ALIENS.

LESSON 5 WRITE A RHETORICAL ANALYSIS

IRIS LIN

@IrisL

I'm fascinated by the messages ads send us. This ad is one of my faves!

1 BEFORE YOU WRITE

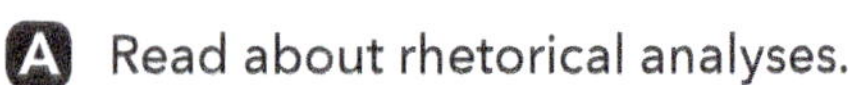

A Read about rhetorical analyses.

Rhetoric refers to the art of speaking or writing in order to persuade or influence people. Rhetoric is often used in politics and in marketing. A rhetorical analysis evaluates a piece of written or spoken language, such as an advertisement, and explains the strategies it uses to persuade people.

B Read the model. What is the main message of the advertisement being analyzed?

The Nike™ ad campaign "Find Your Greatness," which aired during the London Olympics, explored the idea that ordinary people could be great. The series of advertisements featured everyday people attempting to do difficult or scary things. One ad showed a young boy standing at the top of a high dive, looking down, obviously anxious, for example. And then, he jumped. The narration for the ad said, "Greatness is scary. Until it isn't." The words "Find your greatness," then appeared on the screen.

The tagline "Find your greatness" works in a number of rhetorical ways. First, it uses one of the most common modern advertising strategies: It takes the form of a command. This makes the audience feel compelled to follow the advice being given. Second, it's very personal. By using the pronoun "your" (instead of omitting the pronoun and saying simply, "Find greatness"), the ad suggests that everyone, *including you*, can be great. It speaks directly to the viewer, who, is likely to be an ordinary person. The ad suggests, then, that greatness is not about whether you are special; it is about what you're willing to push yourself to do, even as an ordinary person.

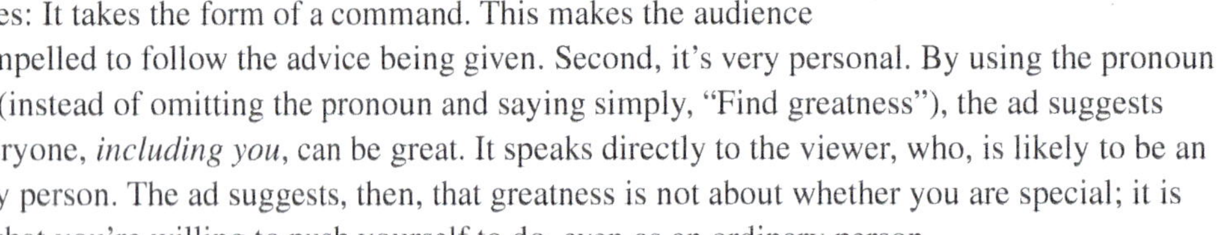

And, more subtly but perhaps most importantly, the ad successfully connects the idea of greatness with athletics. On the one hand, we understand "Find your greatness" to mean that we can be great at anything, if we only try. On the other hand, by viewing images of athletics, we are connecting the concept of greatness with sports—specifically with the product being advertised. So if we wear Nike shoes, we will be brave enough and persistent enough to become great.

In the complete ad, we can see further examples of how Nike makes this case. "Somehow we've come to believe that greatness is a gift reserved for a chosen few…and the rest of us can only stand by watching," the ad says. By using the pronouns *we* and *us*, the sentence aligns the brand Nike with the ordinary people who are watching the commercial. Then the ad goes on to state, "You can forget that. Greatness is not some rare DNA strand…We're all capable of it. All of us." The wording appeals to our desire to be better than we are. It inspires us to get out and do something. The repetition of the word *all* in the final sentence reiterates the feeling that the viewer is being personally included.

As a brand, Nike is a master of creating concise, motivational phrases, such as their famous "Just do it" slogan. The campaign "Find Your Greatness" further aligns Nike with the everyday person who wants to be more.

C PAIRS According to the writer, what is the importance of each word in the advertising slogan "Find your greatness"? Discuss.

D PAIRS Read the model again. Complete the chart.

Word	Type of phrase	Impact
find	______	creates feeling of something you have to do
your	______	speaks directly to ______
greatness	______	the concept being advertised; connects to ______ and to ______
we've...the rest of *us*	personal pronouns	aligns the brand with ______
We're all capable of it.	sentence	appeals to ______
All of us.	phrase / repetition from previous sentence	reiterates the feeling of being ______

2 FOCUS ON WRITING

Read the Writing Skill. Then reread the model. Underline the transitions. Label their placement in the sentence: beginning (*b*), middle (*m*), or end (*e*).

WRITING SKILL Vary placement of transitions

English grammar allows for the placement of transition words or phrases at several different points in a sentence. We can start a sentence with a transition, or we can place it in the middle or at the end. Varying this placement makes your writing more interesting and fluent.

3 PLAN YOUR WRITING

A Choose an advertisement with interesting rhetoric. You will analyze the rhetorical strategies used in this advertisement. Write down the script and underline the words and phrases that you can analyze. Then create a chart like the one in 1D to organize your ideas.

B PAIRS Discuss your ideas.

There's an ad for that guy who's running for governor. He says, "A vote for me is a vote for security."

Writing tip

Get a second opinion. When writing an analysis, you might be making statements about something subjective, so another person might have a different reaction. Run your ideas by a friend to see if your friend agrees or has any other thoughts to add.

4 WRITE

Write a first draft of a rhetorical analysis of the advertisement you described in 3A. Remember to vary the placement of transitions. Use the essay in 1B as a model.

5 AFTER YOUR FIRST DRAFT

A PEER REVIEW Read your partner's rhetorical analysis.

- Does the opening paragraph state what the product is and give a description of the ad?
- Does the analysis break down the script into words and phrases, explaining the importance of each one?
- Is the placement of transitions varied, making the analysis more interesting and fluent?
- Do you have an overall sense of what the message is and how it is being conveyed?

B REVISE Write another draft, based on the feedback you got from your partner.

C PROOFREAD Check the spelling, grammar, and punctuation in your analysis. Then read it again for overall sense.

☐ I CAN WRITE A RHETORICAL ANALYSIS.

PUT IT TOGETHER

1 PROBLEM SOLVING

A CONSIDER THE PROBLEM New words are created every day. Slang is an example of this. How do experts decide which new slang terms should be added to the dictionary? Review the flowchart and circle the correct answers.

1. A dictionary team identifies a new word or meaning.

2. The dictionary team asks:
- Has a famous person used it?
- Is it important / useful?
- Is it consistently used?
- Is there a standard definition?
- Is it used across fields?

3. Key question: Is it likely to remain popular?
- yes — Include it in the dictionary.
- no — Ignore it.

1. If a famous person has used a new word, it probably means the word is ______ .
   a. used infrequently   b. intelligent   c. popular
2. Technology has likely ______ the amount of slang that dictionary teams are able to identify.
   a. increased   b. decreased   c. had no impact on
3. New words are likely to remain popular if they have ______ .
   a. limited usefulness   b. a wide audience   c. various forms

B THINK CRITICALLY Why do people use slang? In what contexts is it helpful? When might it be harmful? Discuss with a partner.

C FIND A SOLUTION Consider the data, the problem, and possible solutions in small groups.

Step 1 **Brainstorm** Slang often defines a group and its ideas. Do you think a slang term's group of origin affects its inclusion in the dictionary? Why or why not?

Step 2 **Evaluate** Review your answer. Consider the type of slang and where you might use it.

Step 3 **Present** Explain your ideas to the class.

2 REFLECT AND PLAN

A Look back through the unit. Check (✓) the things you learned. Highlight the things you need to learn.

Speaking Objectives
- ☐ Talk about diplomatic language
- ☐ Talk about cultural differences
- ☐ Discuss the origin of slang

Vocabulary
- ☐ Words related to communication

Conversation
- ☐ Communicate diplomatically

Pronunciation
- ☐ Contrastive stress

Listening
- ☐ Listen for contrasts

Note-taking
- ☐ Know what to write

Language Choices
- ☐ The subjunctive
- ☐ Embedded *yes/no* questions
- ☐ Embedded *Wh-* questions

Discussion
- ☐ Speculate

Reading
- ☐ Recognize word choices

Writing
- ☐ Vary placement of transitions

B What will you do to learn the things you highlighted?

Notes   Done

In the app, do the Lesson 2 Listening activities: Talk about cultural differences.

______

______

______

6 WHAT ARE THEY HIDING?

LEARNING GOALS

In this unit, you

- talk about financial crime
- talk about a system of government
- discuss power in society
- read about a public crisis
- write a letter of advice

GET STARTED

A Read the unit title and learning goals. *Corruption* is defined as dishonest, immoral, or illegal behavior. What are three examples of corruption you have heard about?

B Look at the photo. It shows an envelope being passed under a table. What kind of information might someone illegally pay for?

C Read Ariya's message. What do you think she may have learned at the training session?

ARIYA SUKSUAY

@AriyaS

Just finished a training session about how to avoid corrupt business practices. I learned a lot!

LESSON 1 TALK ABOUT FINANCIAL CRIME

ARIYA SUKSUAY

@AriyaS

Is it possible to find an honest politician? I want to believe it is, but...

1 VOCABULARY Words related to financial crime

A Look at the newspaper article. Who has been arrested and why?

B ▶06-01 Read and listen. Do you know the words in bold?

STATE REP ARRESTED IN FINANCIAL SCANDAL

State representative Jamie Small was arrested this morning at his home. He has been **charged** with **bribing** a public official, **fraud**, **embezzlement**, and **misappropriation of funds**. The far-reaching **scandal** involves a number of unnamed public officials. According to a source, Small bribed top officials with $100,000 for their silence and got half of the money by misappropriating funds that were intended for his campaign. The source **tipped off** the FBI, and an **internal audit** was conducted, uncovering the embezzlement. The money was **traced** back to Small's personal accounts. Small has been the subject of numerous **accusations** of corruption and fraud. He has denied involvement in the scandal, blaming the media for their "**inexcusable** attacks" on his character.

>> FOR PRACTICE, PAGE 140 / DEFINITIONS, PAGE 160

2 LANGUAGE CHOICES Restrictive and non-restrictive relative clauses

A Read the example sentences. Then complete the chart with *restrictive* or *non-restrictive*.

Use	Example sentences
Restrictive relative clauses	1. My sister is a detective **who / that specializes in fraud cases**. 2. She is someone **who(m) / that people trust**. 3. What were the results of the audit **that / which we conducted last spring**? 4. The director was involved in a scandal **that / which lasted for years**.
Non-restrictive relative clauses	5. My sister, **who is a detective**, specializes in fraud cases. 6. Dan Wong, **whom everyone suspected of bribery**, was found not guilty. 7. Embezzlement, **which is a misappropriation of funds**, is a serious crime.

Restrictive and non-restrictive relative clauses

- ______________ relative clauses express necessary information that distinguishes the person or thing we are talking about.
- ______________ relative clauses can modify pronouns such as *anyone, someone, everyone*, or *the one*.
- ______________ relative clauses provide extra information that is not necessary for understanding the sentence.
- In ______________ relative clauses, we can replace *who(m)* or *which* with *that*.
- ______________ relative clauses are separated from the rest of the sentence by commas.

>> FOR PRACTICE, PAGE 140

B Compare the following sentences. The relative pronoun has been omitted in the first two sentences but not in the third sentence. Why not?

She is a leader people trust. What were the results of the audit we conducted last spring?

Dan Wong, whom everyone suspected of bribery, was found not guilty.

3 CONVERSATION SKILL

A ▶06-04 Read the conversation skill. Listen. Notice the words the speakers use to show that they are interested and engaged. Complete the sentences that you hear.

1. A: Twenty students are accused of breaking into the computer system and changing their grades.
   B: ______________ ! That's ______________ !
2. A: I'm so tired of all the corruption in politics.
   B: ______________________________ !

Show interest with interjections

When you're listening to a story or are involved in a conversation, it's important to show that you are interested in what the other person is saying. Use interjections to show that you're interested or surprised:

Interest:	Surprise:
Uh-huh.	*Really!*
Awesome!	*You're kidding!*
Great!	*No way!*
I know. Wow!	*That's crazy!*
Interesting.	*That's unbelievable!*
You can say that again!	

B PAIRS Student A: Talk about something interesting or surprising that happened to you. Student B: Use interjections to show that you are interested and engaged.

4 CONVERSATION

A ▶06-05 Listen. What do Ariya and Iris talk about?

B ▶06-05 Listen again. Answer the questions.

1. What did the More Corporation do?
2. What crimes has the mayor been accused of?
3. Why was it a bad idea for the mayor to hire his wife?

C ▶06-06 Listen. Complete the conversation.

Ariya: They discovered the ______________ when they did an ______________ . And you'll never believe this.

Iris: There's more?

Ariya: He hired his wife, ______________ is an interior decorator, to do the work!

Iris: ______________ ! That's crazy! He's not only ______________ , but he's also stupid.

Ariya: I ______________ . What a stupid way to spend the money. Just think of all the trips ______________ he could have taken!

5 TRY IT YOURSELF

A THINK Think of a recent financial scandal or other example of corruption, or make one up. Take notes in the chart.

Who did it?	What did he or she do?	What evidence is there?

B PAIRS Student A: Tell your story. Student B: Use interjections from the conversation skill box.

☐ I CAN TALK ABOUT FINANCIAL CRIME.

LESSON 2 TALK ABOUT A SYSTEM OF GOVERNMENT

ARIYA SUKSUAY
@AriyaS

It's election day, and I'm heading out to vote. Have you voted yet? If not, there's still time!

1 BEFORE YOU LISTEN

A PAIRS THINK Do you think voting is important? Why or why not?

B ▶06-07 VOCABULARY Read the words and listen to the sentences. Do you know these words?

random	have a say	a campaign	naïve	on hold	diversity
eligible	restore	a lobbyist	susceptible	employable	

>> FOR PRACTICE, PAGE 141 / DEFINITIONS, PAGE 161

2 LANGUAGE CHOICES Relative clauses after prepositions and quantity expressions

A Read the example sentences. Then read the rules in the chart. Are they true (*T*) or false (*F*)? Correct the false rules.

Example sentences

1. a. He launched a campaign **in which local residents were actively involved**.
   b. He launched a campaign **(which / that) local residents were actively involved in**.
2. a. She had the support of the legislators **with whom she had developed strong relationships**.
   b. She had the support of the legislators **(who[m] / that) she had developed strong relationships with**.
3. We're working with lobbyists, **many of whom are lawyers**, to address our clients' issues.
4. We started some major projects, **most of which were put on hold** as negotiations were underway.
5. That politician used to be an actor, **several of whose films were very popular**.
6. The candidate ran several ad campaigns, **the most common of which were on social media**.

Relative clauses after prepositions and quantity expressions

____ • A preposition can go at the beginning or end of a relative clause.
____ • A preposition in a relative clause can go immediately before *who, whom, that*, or *which*.
____ • A quantifier + *of* can go immediately before *whom, which*, or *whose*.
____ • Relative clauses with quantity expressions are *not* separated from the rest of the sentence by a comma.
____ • Relative clauses with a noun + *of which* can refer to people or things.

>> FOR PRACTICE, PAGE 141

B Relative clauses with prepositions at the beginning of the clause are very formal; it is much more common to place the preposition at the end of the clause. What are three ways the following sentence can be rewritten with the preposition at the end of the clause?

Is he the politician to whom you were referring?

3 PRONUNCIATION

A ▶06-09 Listen. Read the pronunciation note.

B ▶06-10 Listen. Notice the dropped vowels. Then listen and repeat.

1. average
2. family
3. general
4. business
5. favorite
6. different

Dropped vowels

In some words, unstressed vowels are usually dropped. For example, the word *every*, which looks like a three-syllable word, is often pronounced as a two-syllable word because the second vowel is dropped: *every* /ˈɛvri/. The word *comfortable* is often pronounced as a three-syllable word: *comfortable* /ˈkʌmftərbəl/.

C ▶06-11 Listen. Draw a line through the dropped vowels in the underlined words.

A: I think voting is a privilege. I wonder why so many eligible voters don't vote.
B: Probably for many reasons. I agree that we need to do something to boost participation.
A: Let's go to the Youth Center this evening. There's a campaign to register first-time voters.

4 LISTENING

A ▶06-12 Listen. What is sortition?

B ▶06-12 Read the Listening Skill. Listen again and complete the sentences.

LISTENING SKILL Recognize arguments

Speakers use a variety of words and expressions to present an argument. For example: *You are correct about X. However…; On the contrary…; X is not true. In fact…; Far from doing X, Y does Z.; You can't be serious.; I disagree.*

1. A: Taking away this right threatens our democracy.
   B: ______________ . ______________ , sortition would help to restore democracy.
2. A: It's completely impractical!
   B: ______________ . We could make laws to protect selected representatives from losing their jobs.

C ▶06-12 Listen again. Identify who made each argument. Then take notes for both sides.

Argument	Speaker	Notes
1. Sortition is anti-democratic.		
2. The current system is corrupt		
3. A randomly-selected representative would be easy to bribe.		
4. Citizens cannot put their lives on hold for years.		
5. Citizens would gain valuable experience after serving.		

D PAIRS REACT In your opinion, who won the debate?

5 TRY IT YOURSELF

A THINK Look at the list of arguments in 4C. Which are the strongest? Why?

B DISCUSS Compare lists with a partner. Add to your notes any arguments that you missed.

C EVALUATE Would sortition work in your country? Why or why not? Explain to the class.

☐ I CAN TALK ABOUT A SYSTEM OF GOVERNMENT.

LESSON 3 DISCUSS POWER IN SOCIETY

ARIYA SUKSUAY

@AriyaS

Remember this quote from *Spider-Man*? "With great power comes great responsibility." I think world leaders today should consider that!

1 BEFORE YOU LISTEN

A PAIRS THINK How would you define power? Explain your idea with examples.

B ▶06-13 VOCABULARY Read the words and listen to the sentences. Do you know these words?

ubiquitous	aspire to (something)	condemnation	diminish
a dynamic	ambivalent	liberating	a barrier
idolize (someone)	adulation	coercion	conformity

>> FOR PRACTICE, PAGE 142 / DEFINITIONS, PAGE 161

2 LANGUAGE CHOICES Reducing relative clauses to phrases

A Relative clauses can be reduced or changed to adjective phrases. Read the example sentences. Then circle the correct answers to complete the chart.

Example sentences		
	Relative clauses	**Adjective phrases**
1.	I have a brother **who is aspiring to run for office**.	I have a brother **aspiring to run for office**.
2.	There are some politicians **who are known for abusing their powers**.	There are some politicians **known for abusing their powers**.
3.	We often idolize **people who are famous**.	We often idolize **famous people**.
4.	He published a study **that explained power dynamics**.	He published a study **explaining power dynamics**.
5.	People **who lack empathy** are less likely to rise to a position of power.	People **lacking empathy** are less likely to rise to a position of power.

Reducing relative clauses to phrases

- An adjective phrase **has** / **doesn't have** a subject and verb.
- In a relative clause with a single adjective, the adjective is usually moved to **before** / **after** the noun in the adjective phrase.
- If a relative clause contains the verb *be*, **change** / **omit** the subject pronoun and *be* to reduce the clause to a phrase.
- If a relative clause does *not* contain the verb *be*, omit the subject pronoun and change the verb to an ***-ing*** / ***-ed*** form to reduce it to a phrase.

>> FOR PRACTICE, PAGE 142

B A relative clause that modifies an entire sentence can also be reduced to a phrase. This type of phrase is always separated by commas. Change the relative clauses in the following sentences to adjective phrases. Pay attention to the punctuation.

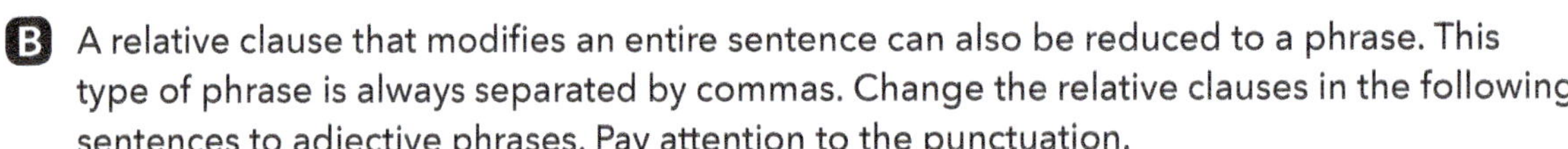

Ava Peng, who is a psychologist and professor, conducted a study on power dynamics.
Min-ki has a new corner office, which probably means he got a promotion.

3 VIDEO TALK

A ▶06-15 Listen or watch. Does the speaker think that power corrupts?

B ▶06-15 Read the Note-taking Skill. Listen or watch again. Then complete the notes.

NOTE-TAKING SKILL Note the main points

At the beginning of lectures, speakers often outline the main points they plan to discuss. Write down these points first. Use your notes to add details later.

What is power?

- Definition: Power is the ability to ______ (1) people.

How do we feel about it?

- Joe Magee – Power is ______ (2).

How do we get it?

- Dacher Keltner – We gain power by ______ (3) with others.

What happens when we get it? Does power corrupt?

- Dacher Keltner – Once we gain power, our ability to empathize ______ (4).
- Pamela Smith – Self-centered people become more ______ (5) as they gain power.

  ______ (6) people become more concerned with others when they gain power.

C What is the purpose of the talk? How do you know?

D PAIRS REACT Do you agree with Keltner that all people in power become less empathetic or with Smith that only some do?

4 DISCUSSION SKILL

Read the discussion skill. Which of these phrases do you use in your discussions now?

Explore alternative viewpoints

Some speakers play "devil's advocate" during discussions. They introduce alternative viewpoints because they feel it will help test the strength of their own or others' ideas. For example:

OK, that might be the case, but what if…?
I'm just putting this out there, but what if…?
I'm playing devil's advocate here, but…?
What if it's actually…?

5 TRY IT YOURSELF

A THINK Think about a power dynamic you have observed in society. Who were the participants? What was the type of power in the relationship (e.g., reputational, coercive, social)? How might that power have affected the relationship between participants?

B DISCUSS Share your thoughts from 5A with a partner. Have you observed similar situations?

C EVALUATE In groups, read the list below. Discuss the following: Which role holds the most power in each pair? How might the trait of emotional intelligence relate to each role?

- politicians and voters
- a company and its employees
- a teacher and a student
- a social media company and its users

☐ I CAN DISCUSS POWER IN SOCIETY.

LESSON 4 READ ABOUT A PUBLIC CRISIS

ARIYA SUKSUAY

@AriyaS

It's clear that the authorities were at fault for this crisis. Cutting corners to save money is never the right option.

1 BEFORE YOU READ

A PAIRS Whose responsibility is it to provide safe water for a city? Why?

B ▶06-16 VOCABULARY Read and listen. Do you know these words?

stunted	armed with (something)	dispel	the tipping point
an isolated occurrence	cognitive impairment	unearth (something)	an accolade
overexposure	fall on deaf ears	afflict	

>> FOR DEFINITIONS, PAGE 161

2 READ

A PREVIEW Read the headline and look at the photo. Predict the content of the article.

B ▶06-17 Read and listen to the article. What was the main impact of Walters's and Edwards's work?

THE WHISTLEBLOWERS WHO EXPOSED A WATER CRISIS

In December 2014, LeeAnne Walters, a stay-at-home mother from Flint, Michigan, noticed something strange about her tap water. It had turned brown. Within a few months, her husband and children developed serious health problems, and her 3-year-old son's growth had become stunted.

Tests by the local water department confirmed that the water supply was contaminated, but the department insisted that the issue was an isolated occurrence. However, at one point, tests showed Walters's tap water included 800 times the legal limit of lead particles. Overexposure to lead can damage the kidneys and nervous system in children and adults and cause cognitive impairment in children.

Armed with these test results, Walters filed a complaint with the local authorities, as did many other Flint residents. Their complaints fell on deaf ears. Over the next few months, authorities refused to fully investigate and continually denied that there were serious issues with the city's water supply. The mayor of Flint, Dayne Walling, even drank Flint water on local television to dispel residents' fears.

Walters began researching the water system in Flint herself. What she found was striking. In an attempt to cut costs, the city government had recently switched its water supply from a nearby lake to the Flint River. The Flint River had been a dumping ground for industrial waste for nearly two centuries, yet the government's desire to clear debts led officials to ignore this fact.

Walters contacted Marc Edwards, a scientist who had experience uncovering water-supply scandals. Ten years earlier, Edwards had investigated claims from the public that the water supply in Washington, D.C., had become contaminated. He discovered rising lead levels in the water systems and unearthed a monumental government cover-up that had resulted in thousands of children being left with lifelong health problems.

Edwards sensed that a similar cover-up might be afflicting Flint. He collaborated with Walters to arm Flint residents with hundreds of water-testing kits. Analysis of samples taken from around the city showed dangerous levels of lead, confirming Edwards's suspicions that this was not a localized, isolated occurrence. >>

Supporting evidence from local health agencies proved to be the tipping point. A pediatrician based in Flint named Mona Hanna-Attisha released data showing elevated levels of lead in blood samples taken from children in the area. Hanna-Attisha's data clearly correlated with that of Walters and Edwards.

The findings were conclusive, and authorities had no choice but to accept blame for the water-supply crisis. Many government employees were forced out of their jobs after being found complicit in a state-wide cover-up. To date, the state of Michigan has spent $240 million to address the crisis, funding a range of public health programs, and has stopped using the Flint River as a source for drinking water.

LeeAnne Walters and Marc Edwards have received numerous awards and accolades for their efforts, and their work has inspired other communities worldwide to fight for clean water.

3 CHECK YOUR UNDERSTANDING

A Answer the questions, according to the article.

1. How did local authorities respond to Walters's initial complaints?
2. Why / How did these problems occur in the first place?
3. How did Walters, Edwards, and Hanna-Attisha work together to address this issue?

B CLOSE READING Reread lines 29-30. Then circle the correct answers.

1. Which sentence is the best paraphrase of these lines?
   a. Authorities made excuses, but the evidence proved they were at fault.
   b. Authorities were not given the chance to defend their actions, as the evidence against them was too strong.
   c. The authorities' only real option was to admit fault for the water supply crisis.
2. What is meant by employees being "found complicit"?
   a. Employees directly took part in activities that were illegal and were therefore guilty.
   b. Employees didn't know about the cover-up. However, they should have known.
   c. Employees were aware of illegal activities taking place but may not have been directly involved.

C Read the Reading Skill. Then reread the article and follow the steps in the box.

D PAIRS Summarize the article in 3-5 sentences.

Find out more about the work of Marc Edwards.

READING SKILL Process information

Pause while you're reading to think about ideas in the text. This can help you to better process the information. Follow these steps:

1. Read the first paragraph. Clarify any information that you have trouble understanding.
2. State the main idea of the paragraph.
3. Summarize the supporting ideas.
4. Predict the content of the next paragraph.

Repeat this process with each paragraph of the text.

4 MAKE IT PERSONAL

A THINK Do you think that governments around the world are doing enough to tackle problems affecting local communities? If so, give specific examples. If not, what more could they do? You may think about your own ideas or consider the following problems.

- air pollution
- deforestation
- overfishing
- intensive farming
- water pollution
- endangered species

B PAIRS Share your ideas. Do you agree?

C EVALUATE In groups, choose one problem from 4A that you feel should be addressed urgently. What do you think would be the most effective ways to address it? Consider the role of citizens, industries, organizations, or authorities in your response.

☐ I CAN READ ABOUT A PUBLIC CRISIS.

LESSON 5 WRITE A LETTER OF ADVICE

ARIYA SUKSUAY

@AriyaS

My company deals with ethical problems, big and small, every day. That's why I love this advice column.

1 BEFORE YOU WRITE

A Read about letters of advice.

Many news sites publish columns offering advice on moral or ethical issues, and sometimes you may need to write an email (or a letter) of advice to a friend or family member. First, analyze the situation and ask questions (or use *if*-statements) if there are aspects you do not fully understand. Then offer solutions or steps that the person could take to resolve the issue. Make sure the language you use throughout is sympathetic and helpful rather than judgmental.

B Read the model. What is the ethical problem?

Home | Discussion Board | Logout 

I have a friend who sometimes struggles with the work required for a class we take together. Recently, I learned that he cheated on an essay that was part of our final grade. He found an essay online and copied it, changing only a few sentences. Should I report this to the professor? I feel bad because my friend works so hard, but the class is really difficult, and he just can't keep up. What should I do?—Honest

Dear Honest,

The first question you should ask yourself is, how certain are you about exactly what happened? Plagiarism is a serious accusation, as it seems you are aware. It's understandable that you may not wish to report your friend, as this would get him into a lot of trouble, not to mention possibly ending your friendship. So if you have any doubt about whether he copied or not, then you should not report it without speaking to him first. I suggest that you start by having a conversation with him. Ask him what happened and why.

If your friend did copy the essay, he needs to understand the possible consequences. Plagiarism is a form of stealing, and it is unfair to the other students who have actually put in time to write original essays. Most colleges have strict plagiarism policies, which usually involve failing the class in which the cheating occurred. Also, be aware that colleges usually have a policy requiring students to report plagiarism when they know it has happened. So if your friend did plagiarize and you don't report it, you could be putting yourself at risk, too. You should make sure that your friend understands this.

If your friend made a mistake and simply didn't realize he was cheating, then he needs your help, not your condemnation. There may be a way to deal with the issue discreetly. Speak to your professor about your concerns. Professors are people, too, and it's likely that he or she will want to find a way to help your friend before raising it to the next level of an official report. Perhaps she could give your friend some extra time to submit a new essay. Or perhaps the professor could suggest a makeup project for your friend to complete. Many schools provide services in the form of tutoring or support classes for students who need some extra help. Your professor could point your friend in the right direction.

The bottom line is that cheating and plagiarism often happen because of an emphasis that society places on grades rather than on learning. Sometimes, we learn more by failing than by succeeding. Ultimately, your friend will do better in school—and in life—if he puts his efforts into learning how to do the work by himself, without relying on copying someone else's efforts.

C PAIRS Discuss. Why is "Honest" asking for advice? What do you think you would do in this situation?

D PAIRS Read the model again. Complete the chart.

The problem:
A friend may have ______________ .

Analysis of the problem:
- Is "Honest" sure that ______________ ?
- Plagiarism is serious because ______________ .
- If "Honest" reports his friend, ______________ ______________ .
- If he does *not* report his friend, ______________ ______________ .

Solution / Step 1:
Talk to the friend. Find out ______________ . Make sure he understands ______________ .

Solution / Step 2:
Talk to ______________ . Can that person offer solutions like ______________ ?

Concluding comment:
______________ is more valuable than getting ______________ .

2 FOCUS ON WRITING

Read the Writing Skill. Then reread the model. Underline the pronoun *you* and all contractions. Circle the imperative sentences.

WRITING SKILL Speak directly to the reader

A letter of advice is more personal and casual than other writing. You can use the personal pronoun *you*, the imperative form, abbreviations, and other casual constructions.

3 PLAN YOUR WRITING

A Think of an ethical problem. You can use one of the situations below or come up with your own. You will write a letter of advice to someone dealing with this situation. Create a chart like the one in 1D to organize your ideas.

- The advice seeker's co-worker regularly steals small office supplies.
- The advice seeker's friend lied to her partner about an important issue.

B PAIRS Discuss your ideas.

I think I'll write advice to someone whose friend lied to her partner.

4 WRITE

Write a first draft of a letter of advice on the topic you chose in 3A. Remember to speak directly to the reader. Use the letter in 1B as a model.

Writing tip

Strike the right tone. Read your letter out loud after you write a first draft. Does it sound friendly and kind yet instructive? If it sounds too authoritative, change some of your imperatives to suggestions. If it sounds too uncertain, add more confident-sounding imperatives.

5 AFTER YOUR FIRST DRAFT

A PEER REVIEW Read your partner's letter.

- Does the letter analyze the situation and ask questions or use *if* statements to clarify unknown information?
- Does the letter offer at least two possible solutions or steps to take to resolve the issue?
- Is the advice clear and helpful?
- Does the writer use sympathetic language and avoid judgmental language?
- Is the letter written in a casual way, using the pronoun *you* and imperatives?

B REVISE Write another draft, based on the feedback you got from your partner.

C PROOFREAD Check the spelling, grammar, and punctuation in your letter. Then read it again for overall sense.

☐ I CAN WRITE A LETTER OF ADVICE.

PUT IT TOGETHER

1 PROBLEM SOLVING

Corruption and Education

Average global test score = 100

120 110 100 90 80 70 60 50 40 30 20 10 0

High corruption | Medium corruption | Low corruption

A CONSIDER THE PROBLEM Corruption usually affects the operations of businesses and governments directly. But the impact of corruption could be felt in other areas. Review the data and circle the correct answers.

1. Corruption has ____ effect on test scores.
   a. an adverse
   b. a positive
   c. no
2. One factor that might affect test scores in high-corruption countries is ____ .
   a. more funding reaching schools
   b. corrupt students
   c. less funding reaching schools
3. Countries that have medium levels of corruption are closest in scores to countries with ____ .
   a. high corruption
   b. no corruption
   c. low corruption

B THINK CRITICALLY How does corruption affect other parts of society? Discuss in pairs.

C FIND A SOLUTION Consider the data, the problem, and possible solutions in small groups.

Step 1 **Brainstorm** Think of specific instances of corruption you are aware of. Brainstorm 3-5 ways individuals and governments might fight this corruption.

Step 2 **Evaluate** Choose the best solution. Which solution is most likely to be both affordable and effective?

Step 3 **Present** Explain the best solution to the class.

2 REFLECT AND PLAN

A Look back through the unit. Check (✓) the things you learned. Highlight the things you need to learn.

Speaking Objectives
- ☐ Talk about financial crime
- ☐ Talk about a system of government
- ☐ Discuss power in society

Vocabulary
- ☐ Words related to financial crime

Conversation
- ☐ Show interest with interjections

Pronunciation
- ☐ Dropped vowels

Listening
- ☐ Recognize arguments

Note-taking
- ☐ Note the main points

Discussion
- ☐ Explore alternative viewpoints

Reading
- ☐ Process information

Language Choices
- ☐ Restrictive and non-restrictive relative clauses
- ☐ Relative clauses after prepositions and quantity expressions
- ☐ Reducing relative clauses to phrases

Writing
- ☐ Speak directly to the reader

B What will you do to learn the things you highlighted?

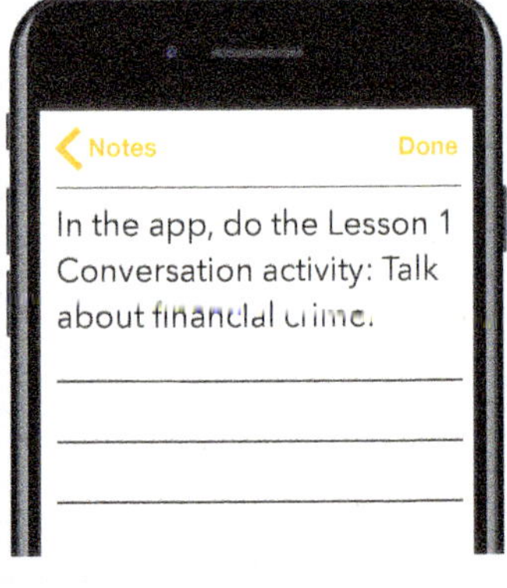

7 SO YOU THINK WE SHOULD BREAK UP?

LEARNING GOALS

In this unit, you

- talk about the art of persuasion
- talk about a breakup
- discuss monopolies
- read about the global plastic crisis
- write an argumentative essay

GET STARTED

A Read the unit title and learning goals. Breakups are common not only in personal relationships, but also in business. What do both kinds of breakups have in common?

B Look at the photo. It shows a broken heart. Part of falling in love is the risk of a broken heart. Why do some relationships end with broken hearts and others succeed?

C Read Artur's message. Why do you think he feels this way?

ARTUR TAVARES

@ArturT

Thinking of ending a relationship in my life. I'm dreading it, but I think it's better to just rip off the bandage and do it.

LESSON 1 TALK ABOUT THE ART OF PERSUASION

ARTUR TAVARES
@ArturT
Important meeting with a client today. Wish me luck!

1 VOCABULARY Words related to persuasion

A Look at the article. What is win-win negotiating?

B ▶07-01 Read and listen. Do you know the words in bold?

THE ART OF PERSUASION: WIN-WIN NEGOTIATING

How good are you at **talking someone into** doing something? How about **dissuading** someone from doing something? A good negotiation is about making both sides feel like winners. Here are some tips about how to engage in *win-win negotiating*.

1. Identify the issues and evaluate how **far apart** you are. If the gap is too wide, you might need to **reconsider** and walk away. If the situation is **out of your counterpart's hands**, you might need to talk to someone with more authority. Don't waste your time trying to **coax** someone to do something that he or she can't.
2. If you do have some **wiggle room**, it's time to plan. **Top-notch** negotiators identify a wide range of options. It makes no sense to **twist someone's arm**. It will only make the person resentful.
3. Keep an open mind. **Assure** your negotiating partner that you are indeed partners. Do not **make up your mind** on every issue before you start the negotiation.
4. Be ready to **sweeten the pot**. Prepare to give something up or give something extra to your partner.

>> FOR PRACTICE, PAGE 143 / DEFINITIONS, PAGE 162

2 LANGUAGE CHOICES Negative gerunds and infinitives

A Read the example sentences. Then circle the correct answers in the chart.

Example sentences

1. The sales team complained about **not having** more wiggle room in the negotiations.
2. **Not accepting** this offer would be a mistake.
3. Because the price is nonnegotiable, there will be **no coaxing** the seller.
4. The company lost a major client when it chose **not to sweeten** the pot a little.
5. **Not to dissuade** you from accepting the offer, but I think you should read the fine print first.

Negative gerunds and infinitives

- Use *not* / *no* + a gerund to give the gerund a negative meaning.
- Use *not* / *no* + a gerund to mean *not any*.
- A negative gerund **can** / **can't** be used as either a subject or an object.
- Use *not* / *no* + an infinitive to give the infinitive a negative meaning.
- Use *not* + **a gerund** / **an infinitive** at the beginning of a sentence to mean *I don't want to*.

A gerund is a verb + *-ing*. An infinitive is *to* + the base form of a verb.

>> FOR PRACTICE, PAGE 143

B Read the first pair of sentences. How does the meaning of the sentence change when the main verb is negative versus when the infinitive is negative? Read the next sentence. What happens to the meaning when both the main verb and the infinitive are negative?

I **wasn't** happy to be there. / I was happy **not to be** there.

Our manager **didn't tell** us **not to negotiate**.

3 CONVERSATION SKILL

A ▶07-04 **Read the conversation skill. Listen. Notice the words the speakers use to negotiate. Complete the conversation.**

A: I'm ________________ that we can reach an agreement today.

B: I am, too.

A: ________________ we start with the pricing? Do you have any wiggle room?

B: What do you have in mind?

A: Well, ________________ to meet me halfway? Say 5% less?

B: ________________ 4%?

A: OK. That ________________ !

Negotiate

When we try to persuade someone, we often use the language of negotiation. These are some common expressions for negotiating:

Make suggestions:

Don't you think that…

Why don't…

I'm hoping that…

I'm wondering if…

How about if…

Make concessions:

Is there anything I can do to change your mind?

I could…

If I X, would you be willing to Y?

Would you be willing to meet me halfway?

Express agreement:

I think you'll agree that…

I couldn't agree more.

Great! So, we agree that…

That works for me!

B ROLE PLAY **Student A: You want to go bowling. Student B: You want to go to the movies. Negotiate a solution. Use language from the conversation skill box.**

4 CONVERSATION

A ▶07-05 **Listen. Who is Amy?**

B ▶07-05 **Listen again. Answer the questions.**

1. What does Amy like about working with TSW Media?
2. Why is Amy switching to a new design company?
3. What tactics does Artur use to try and persuade Amy?

C ▶07-06 **Listen. Complete the conversation.**

Artur: I know you said that you'd made up ____________ about going with another design company, but I'm ____________ there is some way I can persuade you to ____________ .

Amy: I ____________ I could say yes, but I'm ____________ this is out of my ____________ . You know I've always enjoyed working with you.

Artur: That's why I was so surprised by your decision. I'm ____________ if there is anything we can do to ________________________ .

5 TRY IT YOURSELF

A THINK **Look at the situations. Think about how you will persuade your partner. Take notes.**

Situation 1: Persuade your professor to give you more time to complete an assignment.

Situation 2: Persuade your boss to give you time off from work.

B ROLE PLAY **Student A: Try to persuade your partner. Student B: Agree or refuse to do what your partner wants. Use language from the conversation skill box.**

■ I CAN TALK ABOUT THE ART OF PERSUASION.

LESSON 2 TALK ABOUT A BREAKUP

ARTUR TAVARES
@ArturT
Feeling a little blue today. Broke up with my girlfriend last night. It was a mutual decision, but it still hurts.

1 BEFORE YOU LISTEN

A PAIRS THINK What is the worst breakup story you've ever heard?

B ▶07-07 VOCABULARY Read the words and listen to the sentences. Do you know these words?

let (someone) down easy	go for it	get back at (someone)	hang out with
tons	shoot (someone) a text	hideous	romantic
figure	the perils of	smash	dump

>> FOR PRACTICE, PAGE 144 / DEFINITIONS, PAGE 162

2 LANGUAGE CHOICES Perfect gerunds and infinitives

A Read the example sentences. Underline the perfect gerunds and infinitives. Then read the rules in the chart. Write the number of the example sentence that demonstrates each rule.

Example sentences
1. They are believed to have been dating for the past several months.
2. Tyler regrets having smashed his alarm clock when it went off at 5:00 this morning.
3. It was kind of her to have let him down easy.
4. She was upset about having been told what to do.
5. That package was supposed to have been sent weeks ago.

Perfect gerunds and infinitives use *have* to emphasize that the action occurred or began in the past.

Perfect gerunds and infinitives

____ • A perfect gerund (*having* + past participle) emphasizes the gerund occurred in the past.

____ • A perfect infinitive (*to have* + past participle) emphasizes the infinitive occurred in the past.

____ • A perfect continuous infinitive (*to have been* + verb + *-ing*) shows an action began before the time expressed in the main verb.

____ • A perfect infinitive in the passive (*to have been* + past participle) expresses an action was done to the subject.

____ • A perfect gerund in the passive (*having been* + past participle) expresses an action was done to the subject.

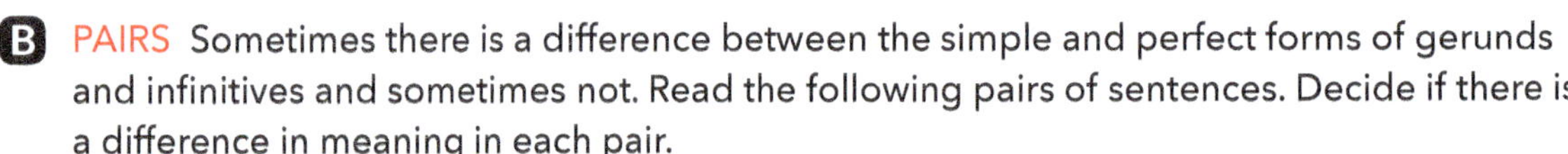

>> FOR PRACTICE, PAGE 144

B PAIRS Sometimes there is a difference between the simple and perfect forms of gerunds and infinitives and sometimes not. Read the following pairs of sentences. Decide if there is a difference in meaning in each pair.

It was a mistake to post that photo online. / It was a mistake to have posted that photo online.
She regrets marrying him too soon. / She regrets having married him too soon.
He's happy to spend time with his friends. / He's happy to have spent time with his friends.
She denied being in a relationship with her colleague. / She denied having been in a relationship with her colleague.

3 PRONUNCIATION

A ▶07-09 Listen. Read the pronunciation note.

B ▶07-10 Listen. Notice how the bold words are pronounced. Then listen and repeat.

A: How **did** you break up with Ahmed?
B: I called Mona and asked **her** to tell him.
A: His sister Mona? You asked **his** sister to tell him **you** wanted to break up?
B: I know. I **shouldn't** have! I'm feeling pretty miserable about it.

Stress in pronouns and auxiliary verbs

Pronouns and auxiliary verbs, which are normally unstressed, can be emphasized when they are used as key words or are used to contrast or correct information. Emphasize the pronoun or auxiliary verb by using heavy stress, different pitch, and more length.

This time, I ***am*** *going to break up with him.*
She *broke up with* ***me****, not the other way around.*

C ▶07-11 Listen. Mark the stressed words with a dot.

A: Have you told Rob the bad news yet? He does deserve to know.
B: I did tell him. I sent him a text.
A: Hmm. You should have talked to him in person, let him down more easily.
B: You're right. I thought I was letting him down easily, but I guess he didn't agree.

4 LISTENING

LISTENING SKILL Recognize stress on key words

Speakers place more emphasis, or stress, on key words in a story. Key words are often content words, such as nouns, verbs, and adjectives. New information or contrasting information is also stressed, and those words might include non-content words, such as pronouns. Stressed words have a higher or lower pitch, and the vowel in the stressed syllable is lengthened.

A ▶07-12 Listen. Circle the best title for the episode.

a. Angry Breakups
b. Breaking Up Is Hard to Do
c. The Problem with Relationships

B ▶07-12 Listen again. Circle the person who initiated the breakup. Then take notes.

	Notes
1. **Lena / Lucas**	
2. **Max / Sara**	
3. **Trudy / Dan**	

C ▶07-13 Read the Listening Skill. Listen. Mark the stressed words with a dot.

Lena: Almost immediately, Lucas shot me an angry text, asking me how I could possibly know what was best for him!
Host: So, what did you do?
Lena: I wrote him back saying, "I'm sorry that I wasn't clear. In fact, I am sure that you are not the right person for me."

D PAIRS REACT Which of the three stories did you find the most surprising? Why?

5 TRY IT YOURSELF

A MAKE IT PERSONAL Think of a breakup that you or a friend has experienced. Think of who was involved, where and when it happened, and why it happened. Take notes.

B DISCUSS Student A: Tell your story. Stress the key words. Student B: Take notes.

C EVALUATE Retell your partner's story. Then discuss how your partner might have handled the situation differently.

☐ I CAN TALK ABOUT A BREAKUP.

LESSON 3 DISCUSS MONOPOLIES

ARTUR TAVARES
@ArturT
I don't think large tech firms can be trusted with our data. There have been some big scandals in recent years.

1 BEFORE YOU LISTEN

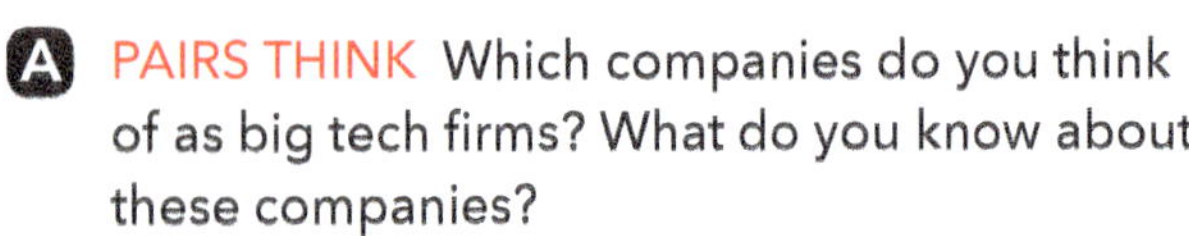

A PAIRS THINK Which companies do you think of as big tech firms? What do you know about these companies?

B ▶07-14 VOCABULARY Read the words and listen to the sentences. Do you know these words?

an innovation	monopolize	a start-up	clout	exert	harvest
distribute	stifle	deter	a patent	manipulative	breach

>> FOR PRACTICE, PAGE 145 / DEFINITIONS, PAGE 162

2 LANGUAGE CHOICES Reported speech

A Read the example sentences. Underline the changes from direct speech to reported speech. Then circle the correct answers to complete the chart.

Example sentences		
	Direct speech	Reported speech
1.	"Large companies have too much power."	He complained (that) large companies had too much power.
2.	"Some tech companies are breaching your privacy."	He told us (that) some tech companies were breaching our privacy.
3.	"Why does competition matter?"	She asked why competition mattered.
4.	"I'll file a patent tomorrow."	She said (that) she would file a patent the next day.
5.	"You should have attended the meeting yesterday."	She said (that) I should have attended the meeting the day before / the previous day.
6.	"I can't be here this week."	He told me (that) he couldn't be there that week.
7.	"I listened to a podcast about monopolies."	He said (that) he had listened to a podcast about monopolies.

Reported speech

When changing a direct quote to reported speech:

- present verbs often change to the **simple past** / **present perfect**.
- the simple past often becomes the **present perfect** / **past perfect**.
- *you* becomes ***she*** / ***I***.
- the word order changes when the direct speech is a **statement** / **question**.
- *this* becomes ***these*** / ***that***, and *here* becomes ***there*** / ***then***.
- *tomorrow* becomes ***today*** / ***the next day***, and *yesterday* becomes **that day** / **the previous day**.

>> FOR PRACTICE, PAGE 145

B PAIRS In some cases, we don't change the verbs or pronouns in reported speech. Read the sentences. Discuss why the speaker chose *not* to change the verb tense or *this* to *that*.

Allen just called to tell me that he **is running** a little late **this** afternoon.

Mr. Wang told us that **this** building **is** over 100 years old.

3 VIDEO TALK

A ▶07-16 Listen or watch. What is the speaker's main idea?

B ▶07-16 Read the Note-taking Skill. Listen or watch again. Take notes on the impact of big tech firms in the chart.

NOTE-TAKING SKILL Take notes in different colors

Colors can be used to show main ideas, important or emphasized material, or movement from one topic to another. Also, when reviewing notes, you can use several colors of highlighters.

Topic	Notes
Monopolies are powerful enough to stifle competition.	
Big tech companies don't play by the rules.	
The behavior of big tech companies is unethical and affects us all.	

C What is the aim of the talk? What language does the speaker use that makes this clear?

D PAIRS REACT Do you agree with the speaker's views? What is her strongest argument?

4 DISCUSSION SKILL

Read the discussion skill. Which of these phrases do you use in your discussions now?

Signpost

Signposting helps a discussion stay on track. Use language like this to signpost more formal discussions:

Begin a discussion: *OK, let's start by discussing…*

Continue to the next topic: *OK, moving on…; OK, next up we have…*

Summarize a point: *Let's just recap.*

Bring a point to a close: *Are we (all) agreed then?*

Keep to the point: *I think we're getting sidetracked.*

5 TRY IT YOURSELF

A THINK Look at the following issues. How can big tech firms be held accountable for their actions? What are some possible solutions? Take notes.

- The dominance of tech giants deters innovators from creating start-up companies.
- Large companies allow third parties to access our personal data.

B DISCUSS Share your ideas with a partner. Offer feedback on your partner's ideas.

C EVALUATE In small groups, discuss your ideas from 5A. Decide on the best solution for each issue listed. Share your ideas with the class.

☐ I CAN DISCUSS MONOPOLIES.

READ ABOUT THE GLOBAL PLASTIC CRISIS

ARTUR TAVARES

@ArturT

I can't believe the scale of the plastic pollution crisis. People around the world should commit to addressing this issue.

1 BEFORE YOU READ

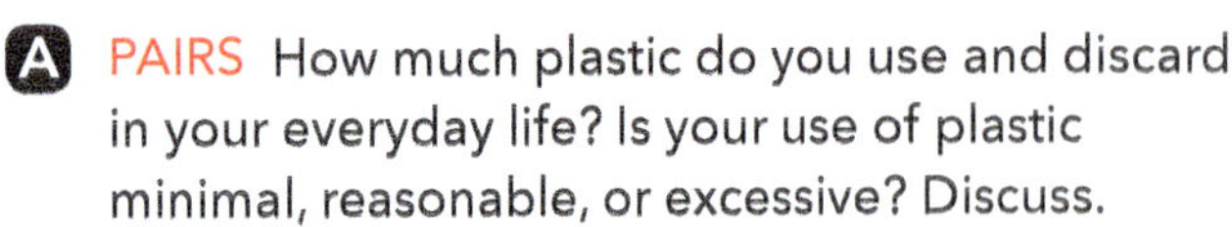

A PAIRS How much plastic do you use and discard in your everyday life? Is your use of plastic minimal, reasonable, or excessive? Discuss.

B ▶07-17 VOCABULARY Read and listen. Do you know these words?

outweigh	profound	mitigate	a raw material
debris	viable	derive	dispose of

>> FOR DEFINITIONS, PAGE 163

2 READ

A PREVIEW Read the title and look at the photo. What information do you expect this text to include?

B ▶07-18 Read and listen to the article. Was your prediction correct?

PLASTIC POLLUTION EMERGENCY

The global plastic waste crisis is much worse than you think. Imagine 700 plastic bags being produced every year for every single person on the planet. Imagine the amount of plastic outweighing the number of fish in the ocean by the year 2050. It's almost unimaginable, but it's happening.

Around 9 million tons of plastic finds its way into the ocean every year. Nearly 700 species of plants and animals have been affected by this, including some endangered species. The Great Pacific Garbage patch, a spiral of floating marine debris full of plastic waste and trash, is currently estimated to cover over 1,550,000 square kilometers of ocean. That is three times the size of Thailand. The damage is profound. This is not a problem that will go away on its own. But we do have some viable options to combat this threat to our oceans.

Collecting plastics is one option, and cleanups are happening daily. However, this doesn't prevent plastic from entering the world's oceans in the first place. Another complication is that collecting plastics can increase the need for landfills. Experts highlight that the environmental impact of landfills, such as air pollution, makes them unsuitable in the long term.

Recycling plastics is another option. Institutions, governments, and organizations are already working together to introduce initiatives that promote public recycling. These range from small-scale changes like creating green office spaces to creating policies that ensure companies mitigate any environmental harm they cause due to plastic waste.

But perhaps a better approach to dealing with the crisis involves rethinking our attitude towards plastic overall. If people opt to use biodegradable and reusable plastics, then the global plastic crisis may become manageable, with only minimal changes to our own lifestyles.

Various companies have produced plant-based plastics, or bioplastics, for use around the world. Avani Eco, a company based in Bali, has received publicity for its production of plant-based bioplastic bags, which are fully biodegradable. Minima, Asia's leading provider of bioplastics, produces a whole range of goods, such as cups, bowls, and straws, using only naturally derived polymers. The Thai-owned company NatureWorks™ uses greenhouse gases as the raw material for plastic production.

When it comes to dealing with the plastic crisis, any action is better than none. However, it may be that the long-term solution lies in the production of bioplastics as an alternative to single-use plastics that cannot be disposed of easily.

3 CHECK YOUR UNDERSTANDING

A Answer the questions, according to the article.

1. What is one of the major causes of the global plastic crisis?
2. Why aren't landfill sites a good solution to the crisis?
3. What are some examples of uses for bioplastics that have been produced?
4. What are some changes you could make in your own life?

B CLOSE READING **Reread lines 17-19 and 25-26. Then circle the correct answers.**

1. To summarize lines 17-19, changing how we view plastics ____ .
   a. won't solve the crisis, because plastic isn't always harmful
   b. will help solve the crisis, but it will require major changes to our lifestyles
   c. may help the crisis, and it may be easier than we think
2. In lines 25-26, the author encourages consumers to shun single-use plastics because ____ .
   a. any action is better than no action
   b. we cannot get rid of these plastics easily
   c. bioplastics are easy to produce

C Read the Reading Skill. Then follow the steps in the box to complete the chart.

Figure	Information
700	*number of plastic bags produced for every person on the planet*
2050	
9	
700	
1,550,000	
3	

READING SKILL Scan for data

Scientific articles or articles about global issues often include numerical data to support their findings. To scan an article for data, follow these steps:

1. Move your eyes quickly over the article, looking only for figures. Remember that these figures may be in written or numerical form.
2. Find the unit that the figure is referring to. Note if it's a percentage, currency, or amount.

D PAIRS **Summarize the article in 3-5 sentences.**

4 MAKE IT PERSONAL

Find out more about the Pacific Garbage Patch.

A THINK **Imagine that you work for a bioplastics company. What do you think would be an effective way to promote bioplastics? Think about the following ideas.**

- What kinds of products might you sell (e.g., cups, plates, bags)?
- Where and how might you promote them (e.g., social media, newspapers, TV, ads)?
- Who might your target audience be and why?
- What might help your promotion have maximum impact?

B PAIRS **Share your ideas. Were they similar?**

C EVALUATE **Work in small groups. Prepare an advertising campaign for your bioplastics company to promote your products. Choose the format and medium that you feel is most appropriate. Share your campaign with another group. Justify the choices you made.**

☐ I CAN READ ABOUT THE GLOBAL PLASTIC CRISIS.

LESSON 5 WRITE AN ARGUMENTATIVE ESSAY

ARTUR TAVARES

@ArturT

My ex-girlfriend told me that I never apologized for anything. She was right. And it looks like I'm not the only one.

1 BEFORE YOU WRITE

A Read about argumentative essays.

Argumentative essays seek to persuade the reader about a particular point of view. The introductory paragraph states the writer's point of view on the topic. Body paragraphs one and two present arguments to support this point of view. In the third body paragraph, opposing arguments are presented, refuted, and dismissed. The concluding paragraph re-affirms the writer's point of view.

B Read the model. What benefits of apologizing does the writer point out for both of the people involved in an argument?

Why should I apologize?

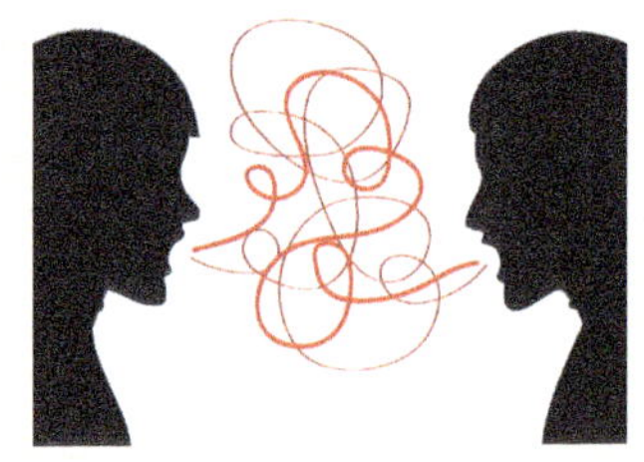

Are you one of those people who never apologizes? Is it difficult for you to admit to ever being wrong? Perhaps this describes not only the arguments you have about big issues but also the small ones—like being late to meet someone, for example. If this sounds like you, then you should consider changing your ways. Rather than weakening us, apologizing actually offers many benefits to everyone involved.

It is, of course, easy to see how apologizing benefits the person receiving the apology. That person is likely to be holding on to a lot of anger and hurt. When an apology is offered, the receiver can move past the anger and experience emotional healing. Moreover, he or she can once again see the wrongdoer as an empathetic person; this allows for reciprocal feelings of empathy. In cases of a two-sided argument, the hurt person may even realize that he or she also needs to apologize.

However, it is not only the receiver of an apology who benefits. When you have hurt another person (intentionally or not), feelings of guilt can eat away at you. By apologizing, you can relieve yourself of these harmful feelings. Furthermore, you can repair and even strengthen your relationship with the other person. This is true even if you do not feel that you we were in the wrong. Psychological studies show that by acknowledging that you have hurt another person, you communicate that the person is more important to you than any one particular issue. Needless to say, this prioritizing of the relationship allows the other person to feel valued, and then that person is likely to value you more highly, too.

Many people believe that offering an apology makes them look weak. However, this is simply not true. In fact, it is the opposite: We see people who are able to humble themselves and take responsibility as strong and confident. Consider public apologies. When a political leader makes a mistake and says something offensive, we are more likely to view him or her as a strong person and a good leader if the person offers an apology for his or her behavior. By not apologizing, the person risks being seen as stubborn, small-minded, and insecure. This is also true in everyday work situations. Although some people might think that apologizing makes them lose authority, it actually helps co-workers trust and respect them more.

When you consider all of the benefits of apologizing, it becomes clear that accepting responsibility for wrongdoing should be the norm. If it is hard for you to admit that you were wrong, you can perhaps start by acknowledging that the other person is hurting. Opening yourself up to empathy is the first step in setting things right and repairing the relationships in your life.

C PAIRS Do you apologize often, sometimes, or never? Do you think your friends would agree with your answer? Can you think of situations where an apology shouldn't be given?

D PAIRS Read the model again. Complete the chart.

Benefits of apologizing	Possible drawbacks of apologizing
The receiver of the apology can move past ______ and feel ______ for the wrongdoer.	Some people think it makes them look ______ .
The receiver may realize that he / she also ______ .	Some people think apologizing might make them ______ .
The person apologizing can let go of ______ and ______ the relationship.	

2 FOCUS ON WRITING

Read the Writing Skill. Then reread the model. Underline the conjunctions and conjunctive adverbs. Are they being used to support the writer's point of view or to refute opposing arguments?

WRITING SKILL Use conjunctions and conjunctive adverbs strategically

In an argumentative essay, you can use subordinating conjunctions and conjunctive adverbs strategically to support your own point of view and to refute opposing arguments. Subordinating conjunctions like *however, in fact,* and *although* can be used to refute an argument. Conjunctive adverbs like *moreover* and *furthermore* add weight to your argument. Phrases like *needless to say* make your statements sound unarguable.

3 PLAN YOUR WRITING

A Choose one of the topics below. You will write an argumentative essay explaining and supporting your point of view on the topic. Create a chart like the one in 1D to organize your ideas.

- Which is preferable: being an empathetic leader who listens to employees' ideas, or being an authoritative leader who sets clear goals and guidelines for workers?
- Which is preferable: breaking up with someone while the person is going through a difficult time, or waiting until things are better for that person?

B PAIRS Discuss your ideas. I prefer leaders who are authoritative.

4 WRITE

Write a first draft of an argumentative essay on the topic you described in 3A. Remember to use conjunctions and conjunctive adverbs strategically. Use the essay in 1B as a model.

Writing tip

Find the right balance between supporting ideas and arguments to refute. If you have far more supporting ideas than arguments to refute, then you may not have much of an argument to make. If the balance is too equal, you might have a difficult time persuading others of your point of view.

5 AFTER YOUR FIRST DRAFT

A PEER REVIEW Read your partner's essay.

- Does the introductory paragraph clearly state the topic and the writer's point of view?
- Do the first two body paragraphs provide sufficient supporting ideas?
- Does the third body paragraph successfully explain and refute opposing arguments?
- Are conjunctions and conjunctive adverbs used strategically throughout?
- Is there an appropriate balance of supporting ideas and opposing arguments?
- Does the concluding paragraph reaffirm the writer's point of view?

B REVISE Write another draft, based on the feedback you got from your partner.

C PROOFREAD Check the spelling, grammar, and punctuation in your essay. Then read it again for overall sense.

☐ I CAN WRITE AN ARGUMENTATIVE ESSAY.

PUT IT TOGETHER

1 PROBLEM SOLVING

A CONSIDER THE PROBLEM Couples break up for many different reasons. Review the data and answer the questions.

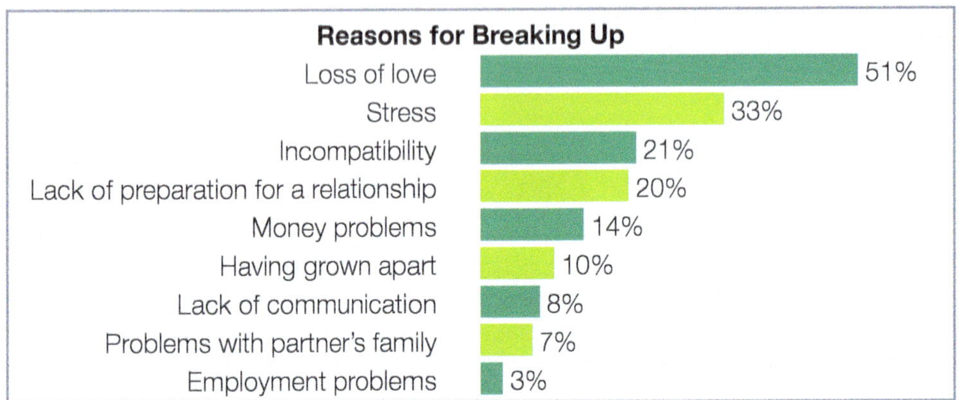

1. Which reason for breaking up means that the couple is not well matched? ____________
2. How many reasons for breaking up deal with finances? ____________
3. Which reason for breaking up is similar in meaning to "loss of love"? ____________

B THINK CRITICALLY Should couples attend training sessions for marriage? Consider arguments for and against marriage training. Talk about them with a partner.

C FIND A SOLUTION Consider the data, the problem, and possible solutions in small groups.

Step 1 **Brainstorm** Think of a list of questions that would help couples decide if they are suited to marry each other.

Step 2 **Evaluate** Choose the best 3–5 questions. Consider questions that help identify each partner's most important issues and concerns.

Step 3 **Present** Explain your list of questions to the class.

2 REFLECT AND PLAN

A Look back through the unit. Check (✓) the things you learned. Highlight the things you need to learn.

Speaking Objectives
- ☐ Talk about the art of persuasion
- ☐ Talk about a breakup
- ☐ Discuss monopolies

Vocabulary
- ☐ Words related to persuasion

Conversation
- ☐ Negotiate

Pronunciation
- ☐ Stress in pronouns and auxiliary verbs

Listening
- ☐ Recognize stress on key words

Note-taking
- ☐ Take notes in different colors

Discussion
- ☐ Signpost

Reading
- ☐ Scan for data

Language Choices
- ☐ Negative gerunds and infinitives
- ☐ Perfect gerunds and infinitives
- ☐ Reported speech

Writing
- ☐ Use conjunctions and conjunctive adverbs strategically

B What will you do to learn the things you highlighted?

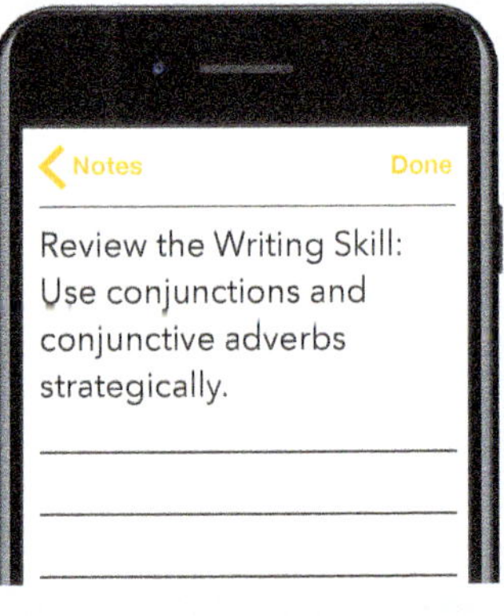

8 GET IT?

LEARNING GOALS

In this unit, you

- talk about humor
- talk about laughter
- discuss the art of joke telling
- read about the funniest jokes
- write an opinion essay

GET STARTED

A Read the unit title and learning goals. Almost everyone enjoys humor. What kind of humor do you enjoy most? Why?

B Look at the photo. It is an example of *anthropomorphizing*, which means giving human qualities to a nonhuman thing. Why does this make the photo humorous?

C Read Edgar's message. Do you think this joke is funny? What type of audience might find this funny?

EDGAR VELA

@EdgarV

Did you hear about the new restaurant on the moon? Great food but no atmosphere.

LESSON 1 TALK ABOUT HUMOR

EDGAR VELA
@EdgarV
Looking forward to my presentation today!

1 VOCABULARY Words related to humor

A Look at the blog. What types of humor are mentioned?

B ▶08-01 Read and listen. Do you know the words in bold?

THE LAUGHING BLOGGER Using Humor to **Break the Ice**

When giving a presentation, humor can be a great way to get even the most difficult audience member to relax and **crack a smile**. But humor doesn't always translate very well; jokes can **fall flat** if they contain **sarcastic** remarks that your audience may not understand. So if you don't want to **bomb**, try one of these easy-to-use joke types.

One-liners A one-liner is a short, humorous remark, usually not more than one sentence. One-liners are easier to understand than jokes since they don't have a story and a **punchline**. If you can **pull off** the perfect one-liner, your audience will **crack up**. Then the rest of what you say will go much more smoothly.

Slapstick Slapstick humor is generally well-understood by people from many cultures, so if you can pull it off, it's a fairly safe form of humor to use with multicultural groups. For example, falling down or tripping over something at the right moment can be **hilarious**. If you're a good clown, you will have the whole audience **in hysterics**.

>> FOR PRACTICE, PAGE 146 / DEFINITIONS, PAGE 163

2 LANGUAGE CHOICES Reduced adverb time clauses

A Read the example sentences. Underline the adverb phrases in the second column. Then read the rules in the chart. Are they true (*T*) or false (*F*)? Correct the false rules.

Example sentences		
	Adverb clauses	Adverb phrases
1.	Before you use humor in a presentation, make sure you know your audience.	Before using humor in a presentation, make sure you know your audience.
2.	We worked until we were exhausted.	We worked until exhausted.
3.	I got a lot of ideas as I listened to a podcast.	I got a lot of ideas while listening to a podcast.
4.	She feels embarrassed when she is chosen to participate.	She feels embarrassed when chosen to participate.
5.	When they heard the joke, they cracked up.	Upon / On hearing the joke, they cracked up.

Reduced adverb time clauses

____ • Adverb phrases can go only at the beginning of the sentence.
____ • To reduce a clause to a phrase, omit the subject and change the verb to the *-ed* form.
____ • If the clause contains the verb *be*, omit the subject and *be*. Don't change anything else.
____ • Change *as* to *while* in an adverb phrase.
____ • Change *when* to *upon* or *on* if the phrase happened in the past. If the phrase is in the present, do not change *when*.

>> FOR PRACTICE, PAGE 146

B Read the sentence. Why is it not possible to reduce the adverb clause to a phrase?
Some speakers have a hard time recovering when a joke falls flat.

3 CONVERSATION SKILL

Express concern

Use these expressions to express concern for someone who is having a bad day:

I'm sorry to hear that.
What a shame!
Don't beat yourself up.
Take it easy.
I wouldn't worry about it too much.
Don't be so hard on yourself.

A ▶08-04 **Read the conversation skill. Listen. Notice the words the speakers use to express concern. Compete the sentences that you hear.**

1. A: It's going to cost $1,000 to get my car fixed.
   B: Ouch. ________________ . That's expensive.
2. A: I'm really upset. I only got a B on the exam.
   B: ________________ . That's still a pretty good grade.
3. A: I just found out I didn't get that job I applied for.
   B: ________________ ! But I wouldn't ________________ . You'll find something soon.

B ROLE PLAY **Read the following situations and act them out. Use language from the conversation skill box to express concern.**

1. Your friend is upset because he lost his wallet.
2. Your co-worker didn't get the raise that she was expecting.

4 CONVERSATION

A ▶08-05 **Listen. What is Edgar upset about?**

B ▶08-05 **Listen again. Answer the questions.**

1. Why is Artur surprised?
2. Why didn't the audience laugh at Edgar's humor?
3. How many types of humor did Edgar use during his presentation? What were they?
4. What is Edgar likely to change during his next presentation?

C ▶08-06 **Listen. Complete the conversation.**

Artur: Well, don't beat yourself up. Even now, after ____________ with people from different cultures all these years, I'll sometimes hear a joke and think I'm understanding everything. Then they get to the ____________ and everyone else is ____________ , but I just don't get it.

Edgar: Yeah, that's happened to me, too. I usually just pretend I get it and laugh along, ____________ that no one asks me a question about it. But today no one was pretending. They just stared at me. And to make matters worse, I tried again a little bit later with a ____________ and they stared at me again.

5 TRY IT YOURSELF

A THINK **Think of an embarrassing or difficult situation that you found yourself in because of a misunderstanding involving humor. Where were you, who was there, and what happened? Take notes.**

B PAIRS **Student A: Tell your partner about the situation from 5A. Student B: Express concern. Use expressions from the conversation skill box.**

☐ I CAN TALK ABOUT HUMOR.

LESSON 2 TALK ABOUT LAUGHTER

EDGAR VELA

@EdgarV

I was playing with my dog this morning and had the strangest feeling that he was laughing at me! Am I nuts? Do pets laugh?

1 BEFORE YOU LISTEN

A PAIRS THINK Do you think laughter is important? Why?

B ▶08-07 VOCABULARY Read the words and listen to the sentences. Do you know these words?

evolutionary	bonding	exclude	dominate	a mammal
a species	a territory	alleviate	tickle	

>> FOR PRACTICE, PAGE 147 / DEFINITIONS, PAGE 163

2 LANGUAGE CHOICES Cause and effect in participial phrases

A Read the example sentences. Underline the participial phrases. Then circle the correct answers in the chart.

Example sentences		
	Adverb clauses	**Participial phrases**
1.	Because Frida tends to dominate the conversation, she should present last.	Given that Frida tends to dominate the conversation, she should present last.
2.	Because we didn't want to exclude Mario, we invited him to lunch.	Not wanting to exclude Mario, we invited him to lunch.
3.	Because laughter alleviates stress and tension, it makes us feel better.	Alleviating stress and tension, laughter makes us feel better.
4.	Since we were finished with our work, we went home.	Finished with our work, we went home.
5.	Because we were unable to keep up with our workload, we hired an assistant.	(Being) unable to keep up with our workload, we hired an assistant.
6.	Because I had heard that joke a million times, I didn't laugh.	Having heard that joke a million times, I didn't laugh.

Cause and effect in participial phrases

- *Because* or *since* **is / is not** included in the participial phrase.
- For active clauses, change the verb to ***-ed*** / ***-ing*** in the participial phrase.
- For passive clauses, omit ***be*** / ***-ing*** and keep the past participle verb.
- ***Being*** / ***Given that*** means "because we understand this."
- To make a participial phrase negative, add ***no*** / ***not*** before the verb.
- To emphasize past time, use ***being*** / ***having*** + past participle.

>> FOR PRACTICE, PAGE 147

B Participial phrases expressing cause usually go at the beginning of a sentence, but sometimes it's possible to reverse the order. Look at example sentences 1 and 2 in 2A. Then read the sentences below. What do you notice about the sentences below?

Frida should present last, given that she tends to dominate the conversation.

We invited Mario to lunch, not wanting to exclude him.

3 PRONUNCIATION

Pausing with participial phrases

Speakers do not usually pause between a noun and a restrictive participial phrase: *My dog is the one rolling on the grass.* Speakers do use pauses to separate a non-restrictive participial phrase from a noun: *Having regularly gone to the comedy club, I know who the best comedians are.*

A ▶08-09 **Listen. Read the pronunciation note.**

B ▶08-10 **Listen. Notice whether the speaker pauses around the underlined phrases. Then listen and repeat.**

1. Given that laughter is relaxing, it's not surprising that psychologists study it.
2. Scientists studying laughter conclude that it's socially and emotionally beneficial.

C ▶08-11 **Listen. Add commas where you hear pauses.**

A: I just participated in a laughter study that was sponsored by the psychology department.

B: That's interesting. What was it about?

A: Computer-generated laughter. Because laughter can be contagious spreading from one person to the next television producers often add recorded laughter to soundtracks.

4 LISTENING

A ▶08-12 **Listen. Which of the questions is *not* answered in the podcast?**

a. Which animals laugh? b. Why do humans laugh? c. Why do only mammals laugh?

B ▶08-12 **Listen again. Answer the questions.**

1. Why do we laugh? 2. When do we laugh? 3. Do animals laugh? How do we know?

C ▶08-13 **Read the Listening Skill. Listen. Draw a / where you hear long pauses.**

LISTENING SKILL Recognize pauses

Speakers often pause before introducing a new topic or important information. They will often also use signal words such as *first*, *next*, *now*, or *another* to introduce important information or a change in topic, but this is not always the case.

So, let's get started with the most basic question: Why do we laugh? Evolutionary biologists are always interested in why certain behaviors evolve. How did it benefit the survival of our species? After much study, scientists believe that laughter serves several important purposes. First, it leads to social bonding. Given that our species is highly social and we rely on each other for survival, it seems that laughter gives us an evolutionary advantage by bringing us together. Laughter can also be used to mark group territory–to create an in-group and exclude those who do not belong in the group.

D PAIRS REACT **What part of the podcast did you find most interesting? The most surprising?**

5 TRY IT YOURSELF

A MAKE IT PERSONAL **Keep a record for a day of the things that make you laugh. Note the number of times each type of thing made you laugh. For example, you may laugh when you: hear a joke, read a cartoon, watch a video, feel nervous, listen to a story, or do something stupid.**

B DISCUSS **Compare notes. What made you laugh? Did you and your partner laugh at the same things?**

C EVALUATE **How does your experience support or refute what you heard in the podcast? Discuss in groups. Then explain your experience to the class.**

☐ I CAN TALK ABOUT LAUGHTER.

LESSON 3 DISCUSS THE ART OF JOKE TELLING

EDGAR VELA
@EdgarV
Sometimes I get halfway through telling a joke and then realize I've forgotten the punchline!

1 BEFORE YOU LISTEN

A PAIRS THINK What makes a good joke? Brainstorm ideas. Think about the audience, content, and delivery.

B ▶08-14 VOCABULARY Read the words and listen to the sentences. Do you know these words?

wish the ground would swallow (you) up	antiquated	a hook
a fit	current affairs	an anecdote
vice-versa	personalize	signpost
tailor		

>> FOR PRACTICE, PAGE 148 / DEFINITIONS, PAGE 164

2 LANGUAGE CHOICES Participial adjectives and nouns as adjectives

A Read the example sentences. Underline the modified noun and circle the adjective that modifies it. Then circle the correct answers in the chart.

Use	Example sentences
Participial adjectives	1. a. Yu-jin is experienced at speaking. b. She's an experienced speaker. 2. a. The audience was not impressed. b. It's intimidating to deliver a presentation to an unimpressed audience. 3. a. The story was extremely entertaining. b. It was an extremely entertaining story. It was extremely entertaining.
Nouns as adjectives	4. Telling jokes is an art form. 5. We appreciated all the audience participation. 6. The comedian told a lot of politician jokes.

Participial adjectives and nouns as adjectives

- Nouns as adjectives **usually** / **never** take a plural -s ending.
- Nouns as adjectives go **before** / **after** the noun that they are modifying.
- We can modify **participial adjectives** / **nouns as adjectives** with intensifiers such as *very*, *extremely*, *more*, and *less*.
- When the noun performs an action or causes a feeling, use a **present (-*ing*)** / **past (-*ed*)** participial adjective.
- When the noun receives the action or feeling, use a **present (-*ing*)** / **past (-*ed*)** participial adjective.
- A participial adjective can go before a noun or after the verb ***have*** / ***be***.

>> FOR PRACTICE, PAGE 148

B PAIRS Some participial adjectives are composed of a noun + a participle. Examples include *storytelling (skills)*, *time-consuming (project)*, and *decision-making (power)*. These adjectives are usually separated with a hyphen (-). Make a list of other examples.

3 VIDEO TALK

A ▶08-16 Listen or watch. Did the speaker mention any of your ideas from 1A?

B ▶08-16 Read the Note-taking Skill. Listen or watch again. Complete the chart.

NOTE-TAKING SKILL Make lists

As you listen, try to identify categories of information. Then make lists under the appropriate headings. Arrange the lists vertically so they are easy to read when you review your notes.

Tip 1: Know your audience.	Tip 2: Get the material right.	Tip 3: It's all in the delivery.
______(1)______ your joke to your audience.	Joke about ______(4)______, celebrities or everyday situations.	Joke telling requires ______(9)______.
Stick to broader, ______(2)______ contexts.	Use your ______(5)______ as inspiration.	______(10)______ words in a punchline, or pause before the punchline.
Avoid jokes that play on ______(3)______.	______(6)______ a joke to hook your audience.	Liven up a joke with ______(11)______.
	Use ______(7)______ elements, such as characters, setting, plot, conflict, and an element of ______(8)______.	Be confident. But don't ______(12)______ at your own jokes!

C What is the speaker's goal?

D PAIRS REACT Share two sentences about the video for each of the prompts.

I heard… I thought… I wonder…

4 DISCUSSION SKILL

Read the discussion skill. Which of these phrases do you use in your discussions now?

Take feedback well

When someone offers feedback, the person usually has a positive intention. Focus on the message the person is sharing, not your feelings about it. Consider how you could apply the comments and make useful changes. Remember to thank the person for his or her contribution. For example: *That's useful feedback.*; *Those points are worth considering.*; *Thank you. I appreciate your feedback.*

5 TRY IT YOURSELF

A THINK Read each joke. Then think of a joke you know. Decide which one is the funniest and why. Imagine how a speaker might deliver that joke. Which words might they stress, or when might they pause? Take notes.

- I've decided to go on a seafood diet. So I see food, and I eat it.
- I don't really know if I enjoy riding elevators. I mean, they have their ups and downs.

B DISCUSS Tell a partner your favorite joke from 5A. Take feedback from your partner.

C EVALUATE In small groups, choose the best joke from 5A. Choose one person to deliver the joke to the class. As a class, vote on which joke has the best content and delivery.

☐ I CAN DISCUSS THE ART OF JOKE TELLING.

LESSON 4 READ ABOUT THE FUNNIEST JOKES

EDGAR VELA

@EdgarV

I think I have a pretty good sense of humor but I found none of the jokes in this article funny. Does anyone else agree?

1 BEFORE YOU READ

A Read the Reading Skill. Then create a chart with three columns labeled *K*, *W*, and *L*.

B PAIRS The article is about what makes a joke funny. Write at least three things you know about this topic in column *K* in your chart.

C ▶08-17 VOCABULARY Read and listen. Do you know these words?

set out (to do something)	glazed (over)	a respondent	yield
cast a vote	incongruity	offbeat	dying to know

>> FOR DEFINITIONS, PAGE 164

READING SKILL Use a KWL chart

A KWL chart is a graphic organizer with three columns labeled *K* (what I *know*), *W* (what I *want to know*), and *L* (what I *learned*). It can help you prepare to read a text, engage with it, and organize what you learned.

2 READ

A PREVIEW What do you want to know about this topic? Write three questions in column *W* in your chart.

B ▶08-18 Read and listen to the article. Did the article answer your questions from 2A?

WHAT KINDS OF JOKES MAKE PEOPLE LAUGH? THE ANSWER IS QUACKERS!

Is it possible to identify the funniest joke in the world? A few decades ago, a research project called the LaughLab project set out to do just that. The findings were, as you'd expect, very amusing!

Participants from around the world were invited to submit their favorite jokes online. They were also asked to rate other peoples' jokes on a 5-point scale of funniness. The 40,000 English jokes submitted were rated by around 350,000 participants from seventy different countries. The data collected allowed researchers to explore which types of jokes had universal appeal, which humor was popular in certain countries, and crucially, what was the world's greatest gag.

After all votes were cast, this joke submitted by UK psychiatrist Gurpal Gosall topped the ratings:

Two hunters are out in the woods when one of them collapses. He doesn't seem to be breathing and his eyes are glazed. The other guy whips out his phone and calls emergency services. He gasps, "My friend is dead! What can I do?" The operator says "Calm down. I can help. First, let's make sure he's dead." There is silence, then a shot is heard. Back on the phone, the guy says "OK, now what?"

The project also shed some light on why this joke is considered so hilarious. Dr. Robert Wiseman, the LaughLab project leader, noted that jokes with universal appeal often include certain similar elements. He explained, "Sometimes [they] make us feel superior to others, reduce the emotional impact of anxiety-provoking situations, or surprise us because of some kind of incongruity. The hunters joke contained all three elements."

Further findings revealed that people from different countries have different senses of humor. For example, respondents from France and Denmark preferred more offbeat,

>>

surreal humor, such as the cow joke (see below, left). British and Australian respondents showed a preference for word play, such as the fly joke (see below, right). Americans and Canadians tended to prefer jokes that made others look foolish, like the hunter joke. Germans, on the other hand, tended to find every type of humor funny.

Two cows are in a field. One says "moo." The other says, "I was going to say that!"

Q: What do you call a fly with no wings?
A: A walk.

The project yielded plenty more curious findings. Results revealed that the funniest animal jokes usually include a duck and jokes including around 100 words were rated funnier than others. Furthermore, researchers learned that the least funny joke in the world was actually one of the most frequently submitted! The childhood classic, "What's brown and sticky? A stick," was submitted over 300 times, yet it failed to receive any positive ratings.

The LaughLab project taught us a lot about what's considered funny and by whom. Its findings can't be taken as scientific fact, but the project did offer a fun insight into humor around the globe. Most importantly, it revealed something we've all been dying to know. For the best chance of having a successful stand-up comedy show, you should pack your material with duck jokes, because they quack people up!

3 CHECK YOUR UNDERSTANDING

A PAIRS **Read the article again. In column *L* of your chart, write three things you learned. Then share and discuss your charts.**

B **Answer the questions, according to the article.**

1. What were the goals of the LaughLab project and how were they achieved?
2. Why was the winning joke considered so funny?
3. What were the key findings of the LaughLab project?
4. What, if any, was the overall impact of the LaughLab project?

C CLOSE READING **Reread lines 5-7. Then circle the correct answers.**

1. Which area of research does the writer consider the most important?
   a. which types of jokes had universal appeal
   b. which humor was popular in certain countries
   c. what was the world's greatest gag
2. What does it mean for a joke to have "universal appeal"?
   a. It includes all the elements of a perfect joke.
   b. Most people will be able to relate to and understand it.
   c. It is funny in general, but not to people from specific countries.

D PAIRS **Summarize the article in 3-5 sentences.**

4 MAKE IT PERSONAL

A THINK **Write down some jokes you like, either in English or in your native language. Think about what makes the jokes funny. Use these questions to help you:**

- Do the jokes relate to the criteria of universal appeal outlined by Dr. Robert Wiseman?
- Are the jokes similar to any sample jokes in the reading? If so, how?

B PAIRS **Discuss your jokes. Explain what you like about them and see if your partner agrees.**

C EVALUATE **Share your jokes in small groups. Then decide together which joke is the funniest and why. Share your ideas with the class.**

☐ I CAN READ ABOUT THE FUNNIEST JOKES.

LESSON 5 WRITE AN OPINION ESSAY

EDGAR VELA

@EdgarV

I've learned the hard way that there's a time and place for humor. Knowing your audience is key!

1 BEFORE YOU WRITE

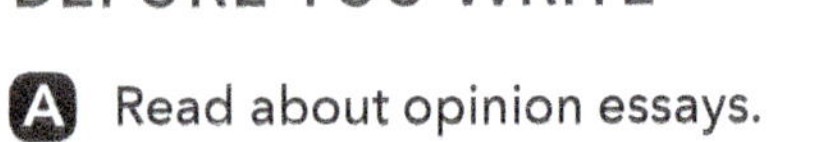

A Read about opinion essays.

An opinion essay is a five-paragraph essay that states your opinion on a topic and gives reasons to support that opinion. These essays are often written in response to a question prompt–in the essay section of a standardized test, for example. An opinion essay usually has a standard organization, starting with an introduction, continuing with three supporting body paragraphs, and ending with a conclusion that restates the thesis.

B Read the model. In one or two sentences, summarize the writer's opinion about the question prompt.

Question prompt:

Humor is often a way to connect with other people, but it can also sometimes push people away. Do you believe that teasing or using humor is a good way to connect with people or something best avoided unless you know a person very well?

Humor can be a wonderful way to connect with other people. Joking and lighthearted teasing with a friend can communicate that you have a strong friendship and that you accept the other person as they are. However, in the absence of a close relationship, humor is best avoided because it can be confusing or even hurtful, it can give people a bad first impression of you, and it can have serious cross-cultural implications.

Consider the following scenario: Two people meet at a conference. Person A, noticing that Person B is very assertive, teases her about it, saying, "You sure are the boss around here." How might Person B respond? Because she doesn't know Person A well, she might be confused about what Person A means. Does the joke mask a more serious criticism? Maybe Person A really thinks she is being too bossy. She can't know for sure, and it would be awkward to ask. So either Person B keeps her feelings to herself and feels bad, or she voices her feelings and risks making Person A feel bad, too. Neither outcome is desirable.

Furthermore, in the above scenario, Person A has run the risk of making a very bad first impression. He has been neither forthright nor sincere. Person B probably finds Person A rude, at best. It is possible that she considers him not only unflattering, but also presumptuous to make such a joke upon first meeting her. Any bond of trust, so crucial to business relationships, will be lacking between them at the outset.

The problem is magnified if the two people involved are from different cultures. In this case, the risk of offending each other is even greater. A joke that is perfectly acceptable in one culture may be rude in another culture. Making jokes when you don't know someone from another culture well both risks making that person feel bad, and also communicates an insensitivity on the part of one's own culture. This makes the cultural divide even wider, and in a business situation, it can have serious negative consequences for any discussion that is to take place.

Used wisely, humor can bring people closer together. People who know each other well can use humor to connect and have a good time. But people who do not know each other well would do better to avoid using humor, as it can be not only confusing or even hurtful, but it can also create a bad first impression of one's self or one's culture.

C PAIRS Discuss. Do you agree with the writer's opinion? Why or why not?

D PAIRS Read the opinion essay again. Complete the chart.

Reasons to use humor	Reasons not to use humor
It can help you to ____________ to other people. If you know someone well, teasing communicates ____________ ____________.	If you don't know someone well, teasing might ____________. The person who is teased might think that the joke masks ____________. It can create a bad ____________. The person might think you are being ____________ ____________. There will be a lack of ____________. ____________ divide: A joke that is acceptable in one culture may be rude in another. This conveys ____________ and can have ____________.
Conclusion / Thesis: Humor is ____________ when first meeting someone.	

2 FOCUS ON WRITING

Read the Writing Skill. Then reread the model. Underline the sentences with paired conjunctions.

WRITING SKILL Use parallel structure with paired conjunctions

Parallel structure makes writing clearer and more fluent. It also adds emphasis to your argument and makes your points sound stronger. One way of creating parallel structure is to use paired conjunctions:

Either…or…	*Not only…but also…*
Neither…nor…	*Both…and…*

3 PLAN YOUR WRITING

A Choose one of the following prompts. You will write an opinion essay with your answer to the question prompt. Create a chart like the one in 1D to organize your ideas.

- **Prompt 1:** There is an expression that says, "Laughter is the world's best medicine." Do you think that laughter can cure most of a person's problems? Why or why not?
- **Prompt 2:** Sometimes laughter can defuse a tense situation, but sometimes it can make the situation worse. Do you think humor is a good strategy to use to get out of a tense situation?

B PAIRS Discuss your ideas. *I'm choosing prompt 2. Sometimes when I do something really embarrassing, like forgetting someone's name, if I laugh at myself, it's really helpful.*

4 WRITE

Write a first draft of an opinion essay with your notes from 3A. Remember to use parallel structure with paired conjunctions. Use the essay in 1B as a model.

Writing tip

If you're working on a timed writing task for an exam, structure your time rigorously. Take a few minutes to plan what you want to say. Then move on quickly to writing the essay. It doesn't matter if you agree with what you're saying; what matters is your ability to effectively argue one side of a topic. Leave yourself ten minutes at the end to read over what you have written and to make changes.

5 AFTER YOUR FIRST DRAFT

A PEER REVIEW Read your partner's essay.

- Does the introduction have a clear thesis statement that answers the prompt?
- Do the body paragraphs provide clear supporting arguments?
- Are there examples of parallel construction with paired conjunctions?
- Does the conclusion restate the thesis in a new way?

B REVISE Write another draft, based on the feedback you got from your partner.

C PROOFREAD Check the spelling, grammar, and punctuation in your essay. Then read it again for overall sense.

☐ I CAN WRITE AN OPINION ESSAY.

PUT IT TOGETHER

1 PROBLEM SOLVING

A CONSIDER THE PROBLEM **Humor is a very persuasive sales method and is prevalent in advertising today. Review the data and circle the correct answers.**

1. One reason people might feel better about buying a product based on a humorous advertisement is that they ______ .
   a. don't worry about its quality
   b. associate it with happiness
   c. find such products cheaper
2. People's purchase of trusted brands is based on ______ .
   a. having confidence in the quality
   b. not caring about the quality
   c. being part of a group
3. Celebrities may have a minor impact on people's buying decisions because their endorsements are usually ______ .
   a. based on expertise
   b. about money
   c. only good for personal products

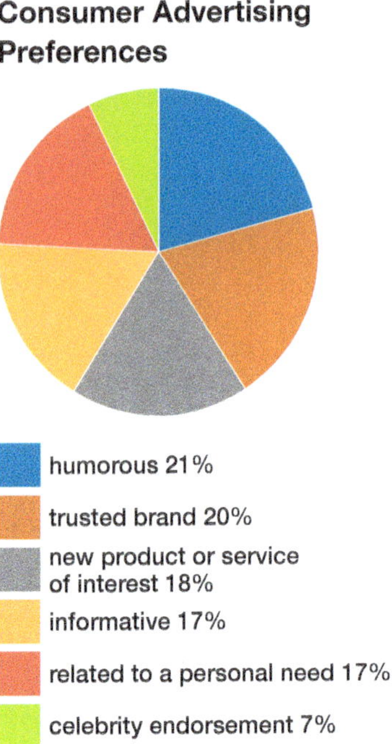

B THINK CRITICALLY **What are the pros and cons of using humor to sell a product? Discuss with a partner.**

C FIND A SOLUTION **Consider the data, the problem, and possible solutions in small groups.**

Step 1 **Brainstorm** Think of 3-5 ways consumers could be encouraged to think more critically about the advertising they encounter.

Step 2 **Evaluate** Choose the best idea. Think of an ad you're familiar with and discuss how your idea might help consumers better evaluate the product being sold.

Step 3 **Present** Explain your idea to the class. Use the ad you chose to provide an example of how your idea could work.

2 REFLECT AND PLAN

A **Look back through the unit. Check (✓) the things you learned. Highlight the things you need to learn.**

Speaking Objectives
- ☐ Talk about humor
- ☐ Talk about laughter
- ☐ Discuss the art of joke telling

Vocabulary
- ☐ Words related to humor

Conversation
- ☐ Express concern

Pronunciation
- ☐ Pausing with participial phrases

Listening
- ☐ Recognize pauses

Note-taking
- ☐ Make lists

Discussion
- ☐ Take feedback well

Reading
- ☐ Use a KWL chart

Language Choices
- ☐ Reduced adverb time clauses
- ☐ Cause and effect in participial phrases
- ☐ Participial adjectives and nouns as adjectives

Writing
- ☐ Use parallel structure with paired conjunctions

B **What will you do to learn the things you highlighted?**

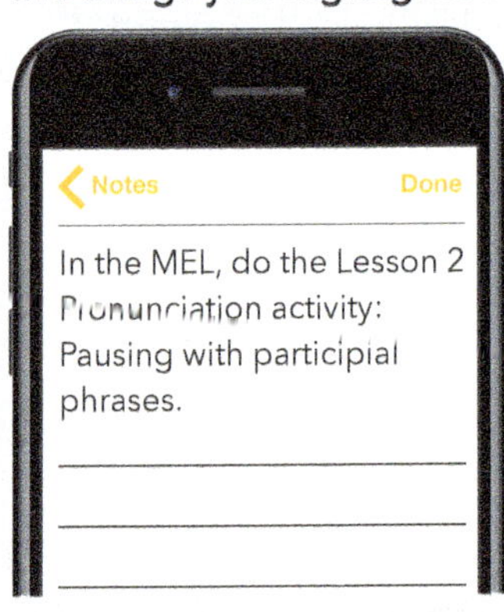

9 CAN WE TALK ABOUT THIS?

LEARNING GOALS

In this unit, you

- talk about conflict
- talk about how to deal with conflict
- discuss conflict in narratives
- read about action movies
- write a process essay

GET STARTED

A Read the unit title and learning goals. Conflict is everywhere in our lives. What is at the root of most conflicts? Explain.

B Look at the photo. It shows two contradictory signs. You are given no good choice. How is this typical of some conflicts? Explain with an example.

C Read Camila's message. What does her message suggest about her clients?

CAMILA RIVAS

@CamilaR

The hardest part of my job is making clients understand that they need to choose two of three things: cost, speed, or quality. They can't have all three.

LESSON 1 TALK ABOUT CONFLICT

CAMILA RIVAS

@CamilaR

I don't like conflict, but I've found that if I talk to the other person honestly and openly, things usually work out.

1 VOCABULARY Words related to conflict

A How do you usually deal with conflict? Do you confront the person or try to ignore it?

B ▶09-01 Complete the phrases with the words from the box. Then listen and check your answers.

with	wrong	bygones	at	out	on
into	a disservice	up	odds	amends	

1. come down ____________
2. single someone ____________
3. lay ____________
4. be at ____________
5. be short ____________
6. point the finger ____________
7. be in the ____________
8. patch ____________
9. make ____________
10. do someone ____________
11. let bygones be ____________

>> FOR PRACTICE, PAGE 149 / DEFINITIONS, PAGE 164

2 LANGUAGE CHOICES Implied conditionals

In a conditional sentence, the condition may be implied or introduced by *if*. The result clause expresses what would happen if the condition were true.

A Read the example sentences. Then check (✓) the rules in the chart that apply to implied conditionals.

Example sentences

1. I wouldn't have said anything, but you kept bringing it up.
2. He was very rude. Otherwise, there wouldn't have been a problem.
3. Why didn't you tell me you needed help? I would have been there for you.
4. We couldn't have figured out the problem without your insight.
5. She probably said something rude, or else he wouldn't have been so upset.
6. I wish they'd patched things up. He would be a lot happier now.

Implied conditionals

- ☐ The result clause is implied, not stated.
- ☐ The result clause uses conditional verbs (*would / could* + *have* + verb, or *would / could* + *have* + past participle).
- ☐ The condition is always in the past perfect.
- ☐ The condition can be introduced in a variety of ways, such as with *otherwise, but, or else, I wish,* or a question.
- ☐ *If* is always used in the condition.

>> FOR PRACTICE, PAGE 149

B Reread the example sentences in 2A. Identify the implied conditions by stating the full *if*-clause.

1. I wouldn't have said anything if you hadn't kept bringing it up.

3 CONVERSATION SKILL

A ▶09-04 **Read the conversation skill. Listen. Notice the words the speakers use to repair breakdowns in communication. Complete the conversations that you hear.**

1. A: Can we just let bygones be bygones?
   B: I'm not sure ________________.
   A: I'm sorry. ________________. I know I was short with you, and I apologize. Can you forgive me?
   B: Oh, of course! It was no big deal.
2. A: Hiro and I are really at odds over this deal.
   B: I'm sorry. ________________. What deal?
   A: Oh, I thought you knew about it. ____________. Hiro wants to sign a new lease, but I don't.

Repair communication breakdowns

Sometimes misunderstandings occur during a conversation. These are called *breakdowns in communication*. Use these expressions to fix these breakdowns:

Expressing confusion:

I'm afraid I'm not following.

I'm not sure what you're getting at.

I'm not with you.

Clarifying:

I'm sorry. Let me try again.

Let me put it another way.

Let me clarify.

I'm sorry. I wasn't being clear. What I meant was…

B ROLE PLAY **Student A: You're the boss. Give your employee negative feedback on a project he or she was involved in. Student B: You're the employee. You don't understand your boss's feedback very well. Ask for clarification. Resolve the conflict.**

4 CONVERSATION

A ▶09-05 **Listen. What is the conflict?**

B ▶09-05 **Listen again. Write *C* for Camila, *I* for Iris, or *B* for both.**

___ 1. At first, she was confused.

___ 2. She thinks the meeting was a success.

___ 3. She was blamed for not meeting the deadline.

___ 4. She came down on someone during the meeting.

___ 5. It was not completely her fault.

___ 6. She apologized.

___ 7. She accepted the apology.

C ▶09-06 **Listen. Complete the conversation.**

Iris: I'm not sure what you're ____________. Whose fault was it?

Camila: The art department was late with their designs, and that slowed us all down. I ________________ something, but I didn't want to point ____________ anyone.

Iris: Oh, I see. I'm sorry if I was ____________ you. I didn't mean to ____________, but I guess I can see how you might have felt that way.

5 TRY IT YOURSELF

A THINK **Think of a misunderstanding you had with someone, or invent one. What was it about? What were both of your perspectives? How was it resolved? Take notes.**

B ROLE PLAY **Explain the misunderstanding to a partner. Then role-play the situation together. Use language from the conversation skill box.**

☐ I CAN TALK ABOUT CONFLICT.

LESSON 2 TALK ABOUT HOW TO DEAL WITH CONFLICT

CAMILA RIVAS

@CamilaR

I'm getting better at dealing with conflicts at work, but I find it harder to do in my personal life. Any tips?

1 BEFORE YOU LISTEN

A PAIRS THINK When was the last time you got into a conflict with someone? What happened?

B ▶09-07 VOCABULARY Read the words and listen to the sentences. Do you know these words?

an intervention	cool off	trivial
down-to-earth	at hand	self-talk
de-escalate	minimize	food for thought
absorb		

>> FOR PRACTICE, PAGE 150 / DEFINITIONS, PAGE 165

2 LANGUAGE CHOICES Inverted conditionals

A Read the example sentences. Underline the inverted conditionals. Then circle the correct answers in the chart.

Use	Example sentences
Real conditionals	1. Should you need help next week, just call or text me. 2. Consider taking a walk to cool off, should you find you're unable to calm down.
Unreal conditionals in the present or future	3. Were I you, I would try to de-escalate the situation. 4. We wouldn't be having these problems were he not on our team.
Unreal conditionals in the past	5. Had we not intervened, they'd still be arguing. 6. I could've made a better decision, had I been given time to absorb the information.

The usual order of words in a sentence is subject + verb. In an inverted structure, the word order is verb + subject.

Inverted conditionals

- To invert a real conditional, replace *if* with ***were*** / ***should***.
- Use *were* for all subjects to indicate the conditional is in the **past** / **present**.
- Inverted conditionals in the past begin with ***had*** / ***were***.
- The inverted conditional can occur in **only the first** / **the first or second** clause.
- To form a negative inverted conditional, place *not* **before** / **after** the subject.

>> FOR PRACTICE, PAGE 150

B Rewrite the example sentences from 2A. Change the inverted clauses to *if*-clauses.

1. If you need help next week, just call or text me.

3 PRONUNCIATION

A ▶09-09 **Listen. Read the pronunciation note.**

B ▶09-10 **Listen. Notice the intonation in the parenthetical expressions. Then listen and repeat.**

1. First, I want to thank Carla Rojas, the head of the department, for inviting me here.
2. I used to work here, as some of you may know, and it's a pleasure to be back.

C ▶09-11 **Listen. Complete the sentences. Then practice the conversation.**

A: ______________, this confrontation with my boss has done some damage, ______________.
B: ______________, I think you should talk to him about what happened and apologize.
A: You're right, ______________. But I feel he needs to apologize, too, ______________.

Intonation in parenthetical expressions

Parentheticals are expressions that are set apart from the main sentence. Examples include comments (*I think*), direct address (*Mr. Chen*), reporting expressions (*he said*), and signal words (*finally*). Parentheticals are pronounced as a thought group and can occur at the beginning, middle, or end of a sentence. In beginning parentheticals, intonation usually starts high on the stressed word and then falls. Middle and final parentheticals are usually pronounced with lower pitch and volume.

4 LISTENING

A ▶09-12 **Listen. Circle the best title for the podcast.**

a. How to Avoid Conflict
b. How to Communicate More Effectively
c. How to De-escalate Difficult Situations

LISTENING SKILL Listen for signal words

Speakers often use signal words to help listeners follow their main points. For example: *First, Second, Another…, And…, At the same time, One of the most…, Next, Finally.*

B ▶09-12 **Read the Listening Skill. Listen again. Pay attention to the signal words and put the main points in order. Write *1* next to the first main point.**

___ Don't respond to challenges.
___ Don't judge.
___ Give the other person space.
___ Don't fill the silence.
___ Don't overreact.
___ Pay attention to the entire person.
___ Keep your nonverbal communication neutral.

C ▶09-12 **Listen again. Check (✓) the statements that Dr. Phipps would probably agree with.**

- [ ] It is best to avoid conflict.
- [ ] Conflict is a normal part of everyday life.
- [ ] It is extremely difficult to learn how to deal with conflict.
- [ ] We communicate a lot of information through our body language.
- [ ] Words do not matter very much in a conflict situation.
- [ ] Challenging another person's ideas can escalate a conflict.

D PAIRS REACT **Which of the pieces of advice in the podcast seemed the most useful to you? Why?**

5 TRY IT YOURSELF

A THINK **Look at the techniques in 4B. Do you use these techniques when you're in a conflict? If so, how effective are they? If not, which would be the most difficult to apply? Take notes.**

B DISCUSS **Discuss your answers to 5A. Which new techniques would you like to try?**

C EVALUATE **Over the next week, use at least one of the techniques when you are in a conflict, even a minor one. Share your experience with the class. Was the technique helpful?**

- [ ] I CAN TALK ABOUT HOW TO DEAL WITH CONFLICT.

LESSON 3 DISCUSS CONFLICT IN NARRATIVES

CAMILA RIVAS

@CamilaR

I wonder if it's possible to write a book or movie that doesn't involve conflict. I'm sure these books and films exist, right?

1 BEFORE YOU LISTEN

A PAIRS Think about the plot of your favorite book or movie. What is it about?

B ▶09-13 VOCABULARY Read the words and listen to the sentences. Do you know these words?

captivate	a confrontation	escapism
a resolution	a premise	woes
fundamental	a triumph	insurmountable
a circumstance	literary heritage	

>> FOR PRACTICE, PAGE 151 / DEFINITIONS, PAGE 165

2 LANGUAGE CHOICES *Hope* and *wish*

A Read the example sentences. Then circle the correct answers in the chart.

Example sentences		
	Hope	***Wish***
1.	I **hope** the plot of this film isn't too predictable. Do you think it will be?	I **wish** Hollywood movies weren't so predictable.
2.	I **hope** we can watch a movie this weekend. Do you have time?	I **wish** I could watch a movie, but I'm too busy.
3.	I **hope** you haven't read that book yet. I don't recommend it.	I **wish** I hadn't wasted my time on that book. It was awful!
4.	I **hope** Tim won't be confrontational during our meeting tomorrow.	I **wish** he wouldn't be so confrontational. I wonder why he's like that?
5.	It's been raining all day. I **hope** it stops soon.	I want to take a walk. I **wish** it would stop raining.

Hope* and *wish

- *Hope* indicates a situation is **possible / not possible**.
- *Wish* indicates a situation is **true / not true**.
- In a clause with *wish*, use the **present perfect / past**.
- Use ***can / could*** after *hope*. Use ***can / could*** after *wish*.
- In a clause with *wish*, change ***will* to *would* / *would* to *will***.
- Use *wish + would stop* to express the desire for a current situation to **continue / change**.

>> FOR PRACTICE, PAGE 151

B *Wish* is often expressed with *if only*. Rewrite the example sentences from 2A. Replace *wish* with *if only*.

1. If only Hollywood movies weren't so predictable.

3 VIDEO TALK

A ▶09-15 Listen or watch. What is the main idea of the talk?

B ▶09-15 Read the Note-taking Skill. Listen or watch again. Take notes in the chart.

NOTE-TAKING SKILL Prioritize important information

Prioritize important information by using asterisks, circles, or boxes around the things you want to review later. You can also indent or underline important items. If you are unsure of something, mark the information with a circled question mark.

What conflict is:	How conflict is structured:
Types of conflict:	Why we like conflict:

C What is the purpose of the talk?

D PAIRS REACT Which reason for "why we like conflict" can you relate to the most?

4 DISCUSSION SKILL

Read the discussion skill. Which of these phrases do you use in your discussions now?

Invite others to participate

During a discussion, it's important to invite others to participate. Use expressions like these:

What do you think about...?

Do you have any thoughts on this?

Do you want to add anything?

What is your opinion?

5 TRY IT YOURSELF

A THINK Think about the book or movie you discussed in 1A. What type of conflict does it feature? What do you enjoy most about this part of the storyline? Take notes.

Book or movie	Type of conflict	What I enjoy most

B DISCUSS Share your thoughts with a partner. Were your answers similar?

C EVALUATE In small groups, evaluate which type of conflict is the most common and discuss why you think it's the most common. Share your ideas with the class.

☐ I CAN DISCUSS CONFLICT IN NARRATIVES.

READ ABOUT ACTION MOVIES

CAMILA RIVAS
@CamilaR
I knew there had to be a reason why I don't like action movies. They're all the same!

1 BEFORE YOU READ

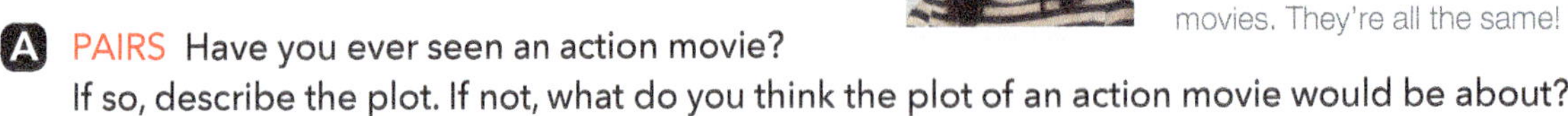

A PAIRS Have you ever seen an action movie? If so, describe the plot. If not, what do you think the plot of an action movie would be about?

B ▶09-16 VOCABULARY Read and listen. Do you know these words?

a genre	a hijacking	cheesy	retaliation	a conspiracy	emotive
a guise	a franchise	hard-hitting	substance	vast	oppression

>> FOR DEFINITIONS, PAGE 165

2 READ

A PREVIEW Look at the headings. Are any of them like the plots you described in 1A?

B ▶09-17 Read and listen to the article. Who do you think is the intended audience of this article?

Top 5 themes used in action movies

Do action movies all seem the same? That's because there are five basic plot devices all action movies recycle. It doesn't matter which subgenre you're watching; they all feature a variation on one of these five themes.

1. Kidnapping

The kidnapping plot device appears in many different guises, such as hostage situations, like *Speed* (1994), and hijackings, like *Captain Phillips* (2013). Standout movies featuring kidnapping or abduction include *Ransom* (1996), *Montage* (2013), and *Prisoners* (2013). The movie *Taken* (2008), which focused on a former government officer's attempts to find his abducted daughter, was a huge commercial success.

2. Revenge

There are thousands of action movies where characters seek revenge against those who have wronged them. The *Kill Bill* movies are perhaps the best examples, although the long-running *Death Wish* franchise managed to single-handedly do this plot line to, well, death. The cheesy *Desperado* (1995), the hard-hitting *Sleepers* (1996), the intense *The Fury of a Patient Man* (2016), and one of the best-ever martial arts movies, *Enter the Dragon* (1973) are some other highlights. Revenge can be about personal retaliation, but this theme also includes getting justice for others (insert cop movie here).

3. Assassination

Action movies based on politics or war often feature an assassination attempt. Some of these films are based on factual events, such as *JFK* (1991) and *Hero* (2002), while others are fictional—*Apocalypse Now* (1979) and *13 Assassins* (2011) being two of the most famous. As with any plot line, there are some movies that add substance to the theme, like the complex conspiracy *The Bourne Identity* (2002) and others that realize the theme is a winner and repeat it at every opportunity—see the *James Bond* franchise.

>>

4. Escape

The list of places and things that actors have tried to escape from is pretty vast. It includes *Planet of the Apes* (1968), *Escape from Alcatraz* (1979), *Train to Busan* (2016), and "repetitive movies." OK, that one's a lie. A struggle for freedom is emotive, and eventual success is heartwarming, hence Hollywood revisits this theme so often. *The Great Escape* (1963), which tells the story of soldiers tunneling out of a POW camp during World War II, is genre defining. Interestingly, one of the most popular escape-themed movies of all time is the animated action-adventure *Chicken Run* (2000). This just shows how this theme really does reach every subgenre you can imagine.

5. Oppression

This common plot device in action movies calls for a change in tone. Most oppression-themed movies deal with serious or important topics. Films like *I, Robot* (2004) and *Django Unchained* (2012) address slavery. *Mississippi Burning* (1988) and *American History X* (1998) address racism. *The Frontier* (1991) addresses military oppression, *V for Vendetta* (2005) addresses political oppression, *Seven Samurai* (1954) addresses social oppression, and so on. Power struggles between oppressors and the oppressed are certainly a common theme in action movies.

3 CHECK YOUR UNDERSTANDING

A Answer the questions, according to the article.

1. What specific examples does the writer give of kidnapping being used as a plot device?
2. Which of the revenge movies listed does the writer like? How do you know?
3. Is the writer critical of any movies featuring assassination? If so, how?
4. How are the examples of escape and oppression connected?

B CLOSE READING **Reread lines 19-20 and 22-23. Then circle the correct answers.**

1. In line 20, the word *well* is used to ___ .
   a. highlight that the word that follows is obvious, because the phrase *done to death* is common
   b. show that the word that follows is meant to be humorous in some way
   c. show that he is thinking while he is writing
2. In line 23, the writer uses the phrase in parentheses to ___ .
   a. say that he can't think of a good example of a cop movie
   b. encourage readers to think of their own cop movie
   c. suggest that all cop movies are the same

C Read the Reading Skill. Reread the article and underline the informal language.

D PAIRS **Summarize the article in 3-5 sentences.**

READING SKILL Use informal tones

Writers use a variety of tones to express informality, such as the following:

a personal tone: addresses the reader directly (*you*)

a chatty tone: includes features of spoken language (*Um…; You know…; Well…*)

a humorous tone: includes jokes or sarcastic asides

an exaggerated tone: includes hyperbole or grand statements

4 MAKE IT PERSONAL

A THINK **Think of another genre, such as romantic comedy or science fiction. List five common plot themes that appear in this genre, such as war, coming of age, or good versus evil. Add examples of movies or books that fit with each theme.**

B PAIRS **Share your ideas. Offer advice and suggestions on your partner's ideas.**

C EVALUATE **Work with a group who chose the same genre as you. Make a list of the five most common plot themes that appear in that genre. Rank your ideas in order of importance and present your ideas to the class.**

☐ I CAN READ ABOUT ACTION MOVIES.

CAMILA RIVAS

@CamilaR

Just read this piece by a colleague of mine. Sometimes the hardest conflicts to resolve are our own internal ones!

1 BEFORE YOU WRITE

A Read about process essays.

Process essays describe the process of doing something, with the goal of having readers understand and be able to follow the process on their own. They are structured in a step-by-step way, with each paragraph describing and explaining one step in the overall process. Some process essays are educational in nature, such as "How to Apply for a Job"; others are written about more personal topics, for example, "The Secrets to Looking Fashionable with Limited Money."

B Read the model. What are the three main steps in the process that the writer describes?

Blog | About | Destinations | Contact   Logout

How to Make Important Decisions

About

RSS Feed

Social

Email

Posts

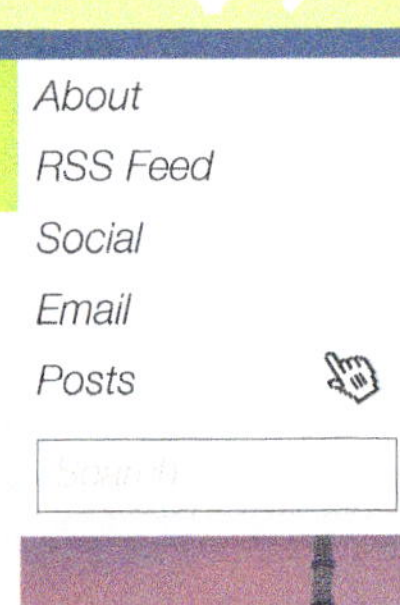

When I was 24 years old, I had to choose between a job and a boyfriend. My boyfriend had been offered a job in Tokyo and wanted me to move there, too, but I had just been promoted to a bigger production role in the media company where I worked. I was torn. To make a decision, I came up with a process that I have been using ever since. I recommend this process to anyone who has a difficult decision to make.

The first step was to talk to my "listeners" about the decision. By "listeners" I mean people who listen well and help me to better understand my own perspective. I can talk to my brother, for example, but not to my mother, who has her own ideas about what she wants for me. Good listeners support you but are also unafraid of contradicting you if you have overlooked something. For example, when I told my brother how great my job was, he said, "True, but there may also be good job opportunities for you in Tokyo." Talking to your listeners is a crucial first step to help you get all the information in front of you.

The second step was to make a pro / con list. I wrote down all of the points I had discussed with my listeners. Then I applied a version of a technique from Benjamin Franklin, applying a numerical value to each item. For example, I gave a value of 1 to the item "Tokyo would be a fun adventure," whereas I gave a value of 3 to the item "My salary will increase if I stay here," because it was something of more practical and lasting consequence. After assigning a value to each item, I added up the total numbers on each side to see whether the pros outweighed the cons. It is critical to apply such a technique; otherwise, you might overvalue intuition and undervalue important practical consequences.

Intuition does, however, play a critical role in the final step of the process, especially if your pro / con list ends up balanced. During the final stage, I ruminated alone. I took long walks and wrote in a journal. I tried to imagine myself in five years' time. Could I picture myself in Tokyo? Was I working? Was I happy? In the end, despite the thrilling idea of moving to Tokyo, I realized that I was not ready to give up the opportunities at my current job. The time I spent thinking alone allowed me to realize this.

Sometimes I wonder what my life would be like had I decided to go to Tokyo. But I never regret the decision I made because I trust the process I used. So I recommend following these steps whenever you have a difficult decision of your own to make. Good luck!

C PAIRS Discuss. Do you think the writer's process is a useful one? Can you think of other techniques that she could have used in coming to her decision?

D PAIRS Read the model again. Complete the chart.

PROCESS: HOW TO MAKE A DECISION

Decision: whether to ______________________________

Step 1: Talk to people who ____________ and ________________________. Good listeners ____________ but can also ________________________.	→	Step 2: Make a(n) ____________ and apply a technique of assigning ________________________.	→	Step 3: Think by yourself; take ____________, write ____________, imagine ________________________.

2 FOCUS ON WRITING

Read the Writing Skill. Then read the following sentences, taken from different process essays. Circle the sentences written for an informal audience.

1. The first thing you need to do is gather the ingredients.
2. The correct area to administer the injection is 1–2 inches below the acromion process.
3. When my friend told me, "There's a better way to do it," I was very curious.
4. If you have flipped the sandwich too soon, don't worry! You can flip it back over.

WRITING SKILL Determine your audience

Process essays are written for a variety of audiences, depending on the topic and on where the essay is published. The model essay is intended for an informal audience, so it's based on a personal anecdote and includes common vocabulary, direct quotations, and frequent use of the word *I*. If you're writing a process essay for a formal audience, you should write in a formal style.

3 PLAN YOUR WRITING

A Think of a time when you had to go through a process, for example, how you chose a university. What were the steps? Create a chart like the one in 1D to organize your ideas.

B PAIRS Discuss your ideas.

I'm going to write about choosing a degree in school.

4 WRITE

Write a first draft of a process essay about the process you chose in 3A. Remember to use language appropriate for an informal audience. Use the essay in 1B as a model.

Writing tip

Keep your goal in mind. A process essay seeks to outline a clear, easy-to-follow process, and uses personal anecdotes in pursuit of that goal. Notice that the final sentence of each paragraph generalizes the step being discussed and emphasizes the importance of the process for the reader.

5 AFTER YOUR FIRST DRAFT

A PEER REVIEW Read your partner's essay.

- Does the introduction explain what process will be described? Is the personal example introduced?
- Do the body paragraphs follow a step-by-step order in the process?
- Is the essay written for an informal audience? Are personal anecdotes used?
- Does the final sentence of each paragraph generalize the step being described?
- Does the conclusion reemphasize how the process can benefit the reader?
- After reading the essay, would you be able to follow this process?

B REVISE Write another draft, based on the feedback you got from your partner.

C PROOFREAD Check the spelling, grammar, and punctuation in your essay. Then read it again for overall sense.

☐ I CAN WRITE A PROCESS ESSAY.

1 PROBLEM SOLVING

How to resolve conflicts

ASSERTIVE (High ↑ / Low)	Low COOPERATIVE →	High
High	Competing	Collaborating
	Compromising	
Low	Avoiding	Accommodating

A CONSIDER THE PROBLEM **We all experience conflicts in many aspects of our lives, including among loved ones, at school, and in the workplace. There are many ways of resolving large and small conflicts. Look at the graphic and circle the correct answers.**

1. Being assertive means being confident or forceful. Avoiding conflict is a low-assertive strategy. It's also a low-cooperative strategy because there's no search for ____ .
   a. an argument b. an issue c. a solution
2. Compromising is one way of settling a conflict but it may lead to ____ .
   a. both sides being happy b. neither side being happy c. both a and b
3. When you collaborate, you work to understand and meet others' needs. When you ____ , each person's needs are only partially fulfilled.
   a. compromise b. avoid c. compete

B THINK CRITICALLY **Are all compromises fair? Discuss with a partner.**

C FIND A SOLUTION **Consider the data, the problem, and possible solutions in small groups.**

Step 1 **Brainstorm** Create a conflict scenario. Think of 3–4 responses to the situation that illustrate some of the strategies in the graphic.

Step 2 **Evaluate** Choose the best solution to the conflict. Ensure that it is something that both sides will consider fair.

Step 3 **Present** Explain the best solution to the class. Refer to the graphic to support your ideas.

2 REFLECT AND PLAN

A **Look back through the unit. Check (✓) the things you learned. Highlight the things you need to learn.**

Speaking Objectives
☐ Talk about conflict
☐ Talk about how to deal with conflict
☐ Discuss conflict in narratives

Vocabulary
☐ Words related to conflict

Conversation
☐ Repair communication breakdowns

Pronunciation
☐ Intonation in parenthetical expressions

Listening
☐ Listen for signal words

Note-taking
☐ Prioritize important information

Language Choices
☐ Implied conditionals
☐ Inverted conditionals
☐ *Hope* and *wish*

Discussion
☐ Invite others to participate

Reading
☐ Use informal tones

Writing
☐ Determine your audience

B **What will you do to learn the things you highlighted?**

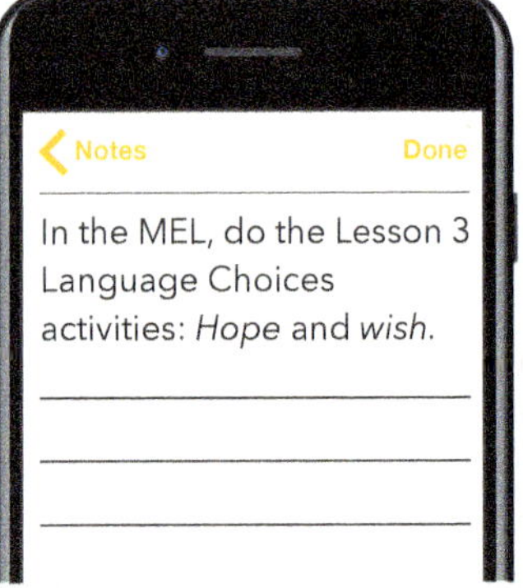

10 HOW DO YOU FEEL?

LEARNING GOALS

In this unit, you
- talk about emotions
- talk about sadness
- discuss happiness
- read about the pursuit of happiness
- write an analytical essay

GET STARTED

A Read the unit title and learning goals. Psychologists have identified dozens of emotions. What emotions do you think children experience the most? Teens? Adults?

B Look at the photo. It shows a woman sitting with her head in a cloud. What emotion is this meant to reflect?

C Read Sam's message. What kinds of "little things" have you experienced that have made you happy?

SAM BENNETT
@SamB
A perfect stranger bought me a coffee this morning. It made my day! Sometimes it's the little things that make the biggest difference.

LESSON 1 TALK ABOUT EMOTIONS

SAM BENNETT
@SamB
Missing my grandma, but I treasure the memories I have of her.

1 VOCABULARY Words related to emotions

A Look at the pamphlet. Do you know of any ways to deal with grief?

B ▶10-01 Read and listen. Do you know the words in bold?

Dealing with grief

If you've recently suffered a loss, it's perfectly normal to feel **heartbroken**—even **devastated**. But know that you are not alone. There are many people and organizations ready to offer their **compassion** and **condolences**. Here are some things to remember.

1. Try not to isolate yourself. It's OK to spend time alone, but being around people who can **console** you is very important. Even if you don't talk at first, knowing that someone else cares can be **uplifting** during this dark time.
2. Sharing memories of your loved one can be deeply **gratifying**, particularly if you share them with someone who is also grieving. **Savoring** your good memories can be very healing.
3. While you cannot expect to get over your loss quickly, if you **are** still **down in the dumps** after a few months, it might be a good idea to seek professional help. Contact our office for information on local grief counselors.

>> FOR PRACTICE, PAGE 152 / DEFINITIONS, PAGE 165

2 LANGUAGE CHOICES Articles

A Read the example sentences. Underline all the nouns and noun phrases. Circle the articles. Then complete the chart with *indefinite article, definite article,* or *no article.*

Example sentences

1. Miriam had a nice trip, but she's been down in the dumps ever since she returned from Toronto.
2. Caleb has an upbeat attitude and really seems to savor the small things in life.
3. Offering condolences is hard. Just remember the goal of expressing sympathy is to show compassion for the bereaved.
4. I'm reading the book you recommended. It's an uplifting story.

Indefinite articles = *a, an*
Definite article = *the*

Articles

- singular count nouns that are *not* specific ______________
- most proper nouns, such as the names of countries or people ______________
- previously mentioned nouns ______________
- specific nouns known to the listener or reader ______________
- noncount nouns and plural nouns that are *not* specific ______________

>> FOR PRACTICE, PAGE 152

B Articles are difficult because there are exceptions to the rules. The sentence below has exceptions to the rule that proper nouns do *not* take articles. Write two rules for these exceptions.

The Taylors lived in **the Dominican Republic** before they moved to **the Netherlands**.

3 CONVERSATION SKILL

A ▶10-04 **Read the conversation skill. Listen. Notice the words the speakers use to show empathy. Complete the sentences that you hear.**

1. A: I got the job!
   B: Good for you! ________________________.
2. A: Both of my kids caught the flu and my husband is out of town.
   B: That must be hard. Please let me know ________________________.

B ROLE PLAY **Choose four expressions from the conversation skill box. Make short conversations, using one expression in each conversation.**

Show empathy

Use these expressions to show empathy when someone shares emotional news:

Reacting to sadness:

That's terrible. I'm so sorry you're going through this.

That must be hard.

I can imagine (how you must be feeling).

I'm here for you.

Please let me know if there's anything I can do.

Reacting to happiness:

That's great! Congratulations!

Good for you! You must be so happy.

You've worked hard. You deserve it.

Good job! I'm really proud of you.

4 CONVERSATION

A ▶10-05 **Listen. Circle the statement that Sam's grandmother would agree with.**

a. Don't waste time on the small things in life.
b. Human beings are often cruel.
c. Spend your life traveling.
d. Focus on the good things in your life.

B ▶10-05 **Listen again. Answer the questions.**

1. What was unusual about Sam's grandmother's attitude toward life?
2. What did his grandmother never lose?
3. What advice from his grandmother is Sam likely to use in the future?

C ▶10-06 **Listen. Complete the conversation.**

Sam: She had such a great attitude ______________. Even when she knew she was dying, she never felt sorry for herself. She was grateful for ______________ she had led and was always encouraging me to follow my dreams.

Ariya: This must be so hard. She sounds like a really special person.

Sam: She was. She always said that the secret to ______________ was living each day as if it were your last. And she really ______________ that philosophy. Even at the end when she was in pain, she ______________ a positive attitude.

5 TRY IT YOURSELF

A THINK **Choose two of the situations below: one happy and one sad. Take notes about how you will share the news with your partner.**

- Your best friend is moving away.
- Your partner just broke up with you.
- You got into your first-choice university.
- You just got engaged to be married.

B ROLE PLAY **Student A: Explain what has happened to you. Student B: Respond empathically to your partner. Use the language from the conversation skill box.**

LESSON 2 TALK ABOUT SADNESS

SAM BENNETT
@SamB
Still missing my grandma a lot. I've been down in the dumps for a couple of weeks. Any suggestions for cheering me up?

1 BEFORE YOU LISTEN

A PAIRS THINK Do you like sad movies? Why or why not?

B ▶10-07 VOCABULARY Read the words and listen to the sentences. Do you know these words?

intriguing	a documentary	subjective	a boost	preliminary
dull	suppress	fellow	enhance	illuminating

>> FOR PRACTICE, PAGE 153 / DEFINITIONS, PAGE 166

2 LANGUAGE CHOICES *Too and enough*

A Read the example sentences. Then complete the chart with *too* and *enough*.

Example sentences

1. I can't watch this documentary. It's **too** depressing.
2. Mike just broke up with his girlfriend. It's **too** soon for him to date someone new.
3. There are **too** many people in here. There's **too** much noise to concentrate.
4. I decided to apologize. The guilt was **too** overwhelming.
5. There haven't been **enough** good movies this year.
6. If you suppress your feelings long **enough**, you could develop health problems.
7. I hate going to the dentist. My appointment can't end quickly **enough**!
8. The review was vague and subjective **enough** to avoid a lawsuit.
9. I don't have **enough** time to listen to him complain all day.
10. We don't have to talk about this right now. There'll be time **enough** to talk when we get together next week.

Too and enough

- ______________ means *sufficient*.
- ______________ means *very* or *a lot*. It usually has a negative meaning, as in *more than what is wanted or needed*.
- Use ______________ + a noun.
- Use ______________ + *much* / *many* + a noun.
- Use ______________ + an adjective or an adverb.
- Use an adjective or an adverb + ______________ .
- In some cases, we can use a noun + ______________ .

>> FOR PRACTICE, PAGE 153

B Read the sentences. What does each sentence suggest about the listener?

Was the movie sad enough for you?
Was the movie too sad for you?

3 PRONUNCIATION

Intensifiers and emphatic stress

Intensifiers like *really, too, so,* and *definitely* add emphasis to other words. Intensifiers are often pronounced with emphatic stress. The stressed vowel of the intensifier is longer, louder, and usually higher-pitched: *I'm* ***definitely*** *intrigued.*

A ▶10-09 Listen. Read the pronunciation note.

B ▶10-10 Listen. Notice the stress on the words in bold. Then listen again and repeat.

1. I don't want to watch a sad movie at **all**. I've had **enough** sadness lately.
2. My mother felt **so** heartbroken when her father died. She was **really** close to him.
3. I woke up feeling **incredibly** good this morning.

C ▶10-11 Listen. Complete the sentences. Listen again and mark the stressed syllables in the intensifiers with a dot.

A: That documentary on climate change was ______________ dull. It was ______________ a disappointment.

B: Oh, no. I ______________ disagree. I thought it was ______________ intriguing.

A: But there was ______________ that wasn't ______________ familiar.

B: Yeah, but the narrator's passion ______________ made the familiar information powerful.

4 LISTENING

A ▶10-12 Listen. Which of the questions is answered in the podcast?

a. Why do different people have different reactions to pain?

b. Why is *Titanic* one of the saddest movies ever made?

c. What is the connection between sadness and social bonding?

LISTENING SKILL Listen for questions

During a talk such as a podcast or lecture, speakers often use questions to highlight main ideas or important points. Writing down these questions will help you remember the answers, even if you're not able to catch every word.

B ▶10-12 Read the Listening Skill. Listen again. Complete the questions that you hear.

1. **Host:** So, Dr. Davis, one question I've had for a long time is ______________________________ .
2. **Host:** That's interesting, but ______________________ tolerance in the first place? ______________________ ______________ the reasons we enjoy sad movies?
3. **Host:** Wait a minute—if participants reported a negative mood after watching the sad movie, ______________________________ ?
4. **Host:** Could this be related in some way ______________________________ ?

C ▶10-12 Listen again. Answer the questions in 4B.

D PAIRS REACT What was most surprising to you in the podcast?

5 TRY IT YOURSELF

A THINK Summarize the main points of the podcast. Use your answers from 4C to help you.

B DISCUSS Talk about a time in your life when you were sad. Was the experience valuable in the way that the speaker in the podcast describes?

C EVALUATE After listening to the podcast, have you changed your ideas about sadness? Do you agree that sadness can sometimes be a positive thing?

☐ I CAN TALK ABOUT SADNESS.

LESSON 3 DISCUSS HAPPINESS

SAM BENNETT

@SamB

I hate memes with quotes about happiness. Happiness isn't something you can easily define—it means different things to different people.

1 BEFORE YOU LISTEN

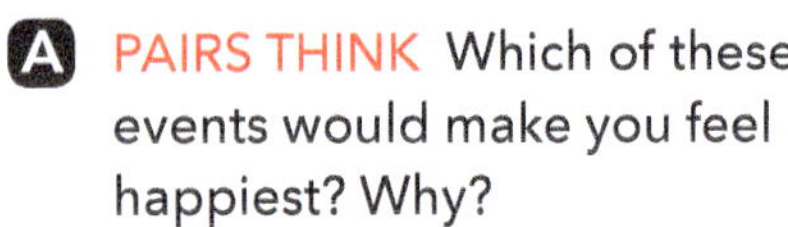

A PAIRS THINK Which of these events would make you feel happiest? Why?

- winning the lottery
- hearing your child's first words
- finishing your PhD
- surviving a plane crash
- meeting the love of your life
- beating an illness

B ▶10-13 VOCABULARY Read the words and listen to the sentences. Do you know these words?

a trauma	synthetic	a coping mechanism	overestimate	relative	be confined to
an obstacle	an immune system	miscalculate	a paraplegic	tedious	a contribution

>> FOR PRACTICE, PAGE 154 / DEFINITIONS, PAGE 166

2 LANGUAGE CHOICES Adverbs

A Read the example sentences. Look at the adverbs in bold. What do they modify? Then circle the correct answers in the chart.

Use	Example sentences
Sentence adverbs	1. a. **Fundamentally,** we all need coping strategies. b. We all need coping strategies, **fundamentally**. c. We all **fundamentally** need coping strategies.
Focus adverbs	2. We were so happy, we couldn't **even** speak. 3. **Even** Adrian was excited, and he's normally very serious. 4. **Only** Maya was in a bad mood. Everyone else was happy. 5. Runa **only** attended the meeting. She didn't participate.
Negative adverbs	6. **Never** have I made such a terrible miscalculation. 7. **Rarely** does the immune system fully eliminate a virus.

Adverbs

- If a sentence adverb comes **first or last in / in the middle of** a sentence, it is usually separated with a comma.
- **Sentence / Focus** adverbs express a viewpoint about the whole idea or sentence.
- **Sentence / Focus** adverbs draw attention to a specific word or phrase.
- **Focus / Negative** adverbs are often used at the beginning of a sentence with an inverted subject and verb.

>> FOR PRACTICE, PAGE 154

B PAIRS You can place adverbs in various places in a sentence. Discuss how shifting the adverb changes the focus or meaning of the following sentences.

Remarkably, Isabel seems to have recovered from the trauma.
Isabel seems to have remarkably recovered from the trauma.
Isabel seems to have recovered from the trauma remarkably.

3 VIDEO TALK

A ▶10-15 Listen or watch. What have we learned from Daniel Gilbert's research?

B ▶10-15 Read the Note-taking Skill. Listen or watch again. Take notes in the chart.

NOTE-TAKING SKILL Use charts for organization

The charting note-taking method uses columns to organize information. Label each column by category. Then add details below. This method is useful for organization and helps you group your ideas in a way that makes them easy to review.

Natural happiness	Synthetic happiness

C What is the purpose of the talk?

D PAIRS REACT Gilbert explains that we have a psychological immune system that can manufacture happiness in response to negative experiences. Do you think there are any downsides to having this system? If so, what?

4 DISCUSSION SKILL

Read the discussion skill. Which of these phrases do you use in your discussions now?

Tell an anecdote

An anecdote is a brief story that illustrates a point. You can begin an anecdote with phrases like these:

Back in the day, I… *I'll never forget the time I…*
Listen to this story. *Here's a good one.*

5 TRY IT YOURSELF

A THINK Think about different times in your life when you felt happy. What was happening in your life, and why did you feel happy? Do you think it was natural happiness or synthetic happiness? Take notes.

B DISCUSS Share your experiences with a group. What was similar? What was different?

C EVALUATE In the same groups, create a final list of things that define happiness based on the similarities from 5B. Prepare to justify your views to the class.

☐ I CAN DISCUSS HAPPINESS.

LESSON 4 READ ABOUT THE PURSUIT OF HAPPINESS

SAM BENNETT
@SamB
I really admire Elizabeth Gilbert. She had the courage to drop everything and pursue her dreams.

1 BEFORE YOU READ

A PAIRS What kinds of things do you think make people happy?

B ▶10-16 VOCABULARY Read and listen. Do you know these words?

tremendous	sheer	a turning point	spirituality	relentlessly
death-defying	a memoir	throw caution to the wind	strive	rags-to-riches

>> FOR DEFINITIONS, PAGE 166

2 READ

A PREVIEW You are going to read some personal stories about finding happiness. Read each heading and look at the photos. What do you think each person's story is about?

B ▶10-17 Read and listen to the article. Were your predictions in 2A correct?

THE PURSUIT OF HAPPINESS

What does happiness mean to you? Is it having new experiences, finding true love, being successful, or something different? Here are three stories about how people found happiness.

Reaching for happiness

In 2017, Alex Honnold achieved the greatest feat ever accomplished in free-soloing, a kind of climbing. He completed the first ever rope-free ascent of the famous El Capitan rock in Yosemite National Park. El Capitan is over 2,300 meters tall from its base and has sections that require almost vertical climbing. Honnold reached the peak in just under four hours without safety gear, using only his bare hands and tremendous willpower.

Most of us would panic at the thought of being stuck 450 meters up on a rockface, knowing that one slip could prove deadly. But not Honnold, who seeks out death-defying challenges like El Capitan for sheer happiness. Why? Honnold says that climbing gives him the most joy out of anything in life. These days, he's pretty famous for it, too, after the story of his climb was made into an Oscar-winning documentary.

Traveling for happiness

Elizabeth Gilbert's story of searching for happiness is also well-known. She is the author of the best-selling memoir *Eat, Pray, Love*, which documents a year of her life spent traveling the world in search of fulfilment. Prior to setting off on her travels, Gilbert had a home, a husband, and a successful writing career. However, she was unhappy in her marriage and decided to get a divorce. Facing a turning point in her life, she threw caution to the wind and headed out to see the world. She spent time eating delicious food in Italy, exploring spirituality in India, and eventually finding love again while in Bali, Indonesia.

Reflecting on her travels and search for happiness, Gilbert says finding joy isn't about luck but it is a result of personal effort. "You fight for it, strive for it, insist upon it, and sometimes even travel around the world looking for it. You have to participate relentlessly."

Working for happiness

A different type of journey to happiness involves one of the most famous businesses in the world. It is the rags-to-riches story of Soichiro Honda. Honda was born in the small village of Kyomo, Japan. He spent his early childhood helping his father with his bicycle repair business. At an early age, Honda developed a strong interest in cars.

Honda left home at age 15 and headed to Tokyo. He found work at a garage, where he was a mechanic for six years, before returning home. His first attempt at the personal motor business came in the mid-1940s when he invented a small bicycle engine. Encouraged by his success, he organized the Honda Motor Company™ in 1948. The company has since grown into one of the world's largest automobile businesses.

Honda once stated, "My biggest thrill is when I plan something and it fails. My mind is then filled with ideas on how I can improve it." He believed that "real happiness lies in the completion of work using your own brains and skills." Honda died in 1991, having seen the Honda Motor Company grow into a multi-billion-dollar business.

3 CHECK YOUR UNDERSTANDING

A Answer the questions, according to the article.

1. Why was Honnold's feat so impressive, and how has it become so well-known?
2. How does Gilbert believe we can find happiness?
3. How did inventing the bicycle engine help Honda start his company?

B CLOSE READING Reread lines 9-11 and 35-37. Then circle the correct answers.

1. Which option is the best paraphrase of lines 9-11?
   a. Free-soloing would be very frightening for most people, but Honnold isn't scared because he doesn't fear death.
   b. Free-soloing is too scary for most people, but Honnold does it for pleasure.
   c. Free-soloing is dangerous, so most people don't do it. However, Honnold loves danger.
2. What can we infer from Honda's views in lines 35-37? More than one answer may be correct.
   a. We must take risks if we want to be happy.
   b. Happiness comes from hard work.
   c. Failure is a part of success.

C Read the Reading Skill. Choose one of the stories from the article. Divide a page of your notebook into three boxes. Storyboard the story in three frames.

D PAIRS Summarize the article in 3-5 sentences.

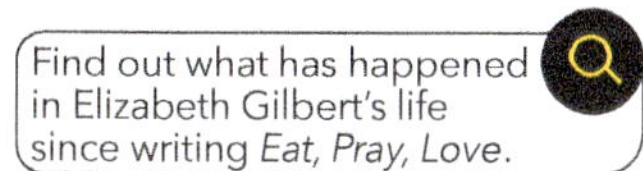

READING SKILL Visualize a story

Visualizing a story helps you to understand both the storyline and the emotions of the characters.

Storyboarding is a good technique for visualization. To practice this technique, draw pictures of each scene in a story, like it is a movie. You can use thought bubbles or speech bubbles to help explain the emotions of each character.

4 MAKE IT PERSONAL

A THINK What kinds of things make you happy? How do you feel when you're doing these things? Take notes.

B PAIRS Share your thoughts with a partner. Ask questions about his or her activities.

C EVALUATE Share your thoughts in a group. What do you have in common? Which activities would you like to try? Organize these activities into three categories: *I really want to try…*, *I might try…*, *I would never try….* Present your ideas to the class.

☐ I CAN READ ABOUT THE PURSUIT OF HAPPINESS.

LESSON 5 WRITE AN ANALYTICAL ESSAY

SAM BENNETT
@SamB
There are so many famous quotes about happiness. Some of them I agree with, but others, not so much.

1 BEFORE YOU WRITE

A Read about analytical essays.

An analytical essay is used to analyze something, often a speech, a quote, or a piece of literature. It looks at several different aspects and may offer a point of view. The introductory paragraph introduces the piece to be analyzed and makes a thesis statement about the point of view that will be taken. The body paragraphs then offer an in-depth analysis, looking at several different angles in order to make critical judgments about the piece. The conclusion summarizes these points and restates the thesis.

B Read the model. What conclusion does the writer come to about the quotation?

Question: *Abraham Lincoln said, "Folks are usually about as happy as they make their minds up to be." Explain what the quote means. Do you agree or disagree? Why?*

The quote "Folks are usually about as happy as they make up their minds to be" indicates that people have a choice in how happy they are. The assumption is that if a person wants to be happy, he or she can be happy. By contrast, then, the quote also assumes that people who are unhappy have chosen to be unhappy. They are choosing to look only at the negative side of things. There may be some truth to the idea, but, fundamentally, the statement is overgeneralized and cannot work as a blanket concept covering all situations.

It seems likely that Lincoln was considering the ways in which people react to the small challenges that arise in daily life—for example, sickness. Some people who catch a cold or flu might complain and see only the negative side of it, worrying that they have to change their plans for the day. "Bad things always happen to me," they may think, ignoring the fact that everyone gets sick sometimes. Other people can maintain a positive outlook in the face of such challenges. They see sickness as just a part of life, and they understand that it will pass shortly. They might even see the bright side: "Well, I guess my body is telling me that I need a break."

However, this perspective neglects to look at the reality of how a challenge can affect people in different ways. For people who work at hourly wage jobs, the loss of money when they are sick may indeed be a significant hardship. People who live in poverty, people who have poor health, people who are discriminated against—these people all have genuine reasons to bemoan their situations. And indeed, revolutions throughout history may never have happened if everyone had simply decided to be happy with their situation.

Another important point that the quote overlooks is the role of mental illness. While in Lincoln's time, this was not something much discussed or understood, today it is a known fact that illnesses like depression and anxiety can affect how people experience their lives. It can no longer be considered acceptable to tell people that they just need to cheer up. Many people simply do not have the brain wiring to do this. They may need the help of medication or a therapist.

Perhaps these were the reasons that Lincoln added the word "usually." In circumstances where all else is equal, a positive outlook can certainly help people create the happiness they want. Nevertheless, it is important to keep in mind that usually not everything is equal. Taking these inequalities into consideration, the quotation simply does not hold true.

C PAIRS Discuss. Do you agree with the conclusion the writer comes to? Why or why not?

D PAIRS Read the model again. Complete the chart.

What the quote means: People can make themselves happy by ______________________________ .

Some people have a positive outlook when ______________________________ .

People are ______________ based on their circumstances; for example, hourly wage workers ______________ ______________________ .

Role of ______________ ; e.g., depression or anxiety. People might need medication or ______________ .

______________ only happen because people choose not to just be happy.

2 FOCUS ON WRITING

Read the Writing Skill. Then read the following informal sentences. Find sentences in the model that mean the same thing.

1. We have to consider how a challenge can affect each of us in different ways.
2. If you work at an hourly wage job, the loss of money when you are sick may be a hardship.
3. You can't just tell people to cheer up.

WRITING SKILL Use a formal style

Most analytical essays are written in a formal style. You can write more formally by avoiding personal pronouns like *I*, *you*, or *we* and instead use neutral words or structures like *one*, *people*, or the passive voice. Make your opinions strong and confident-sounding by eliminating phrases like *I believe* or *I feel*. Choose more academic vocabulary rather than common terms.

3 PLAN YOUR WRITING

A Choose one of the following quotes. What do you think the quote means? Do you agree or disagree with it? Create a chart like the one in 1D to organize your ideas.

- "Happiness is when what you think, what you say, and what you do are in harmony." –Mahatma Gandhi
- "Happiness is like a butterfly which appears and delights us for one brief moment, but soon flits away." –Anna Pavlova
- "Pain is inevitable. Suffering is optional." –Haruki Murakami

Writing tip

Create nuanced arguments. Analytical essays look at many different angles. You may agree with the quote in general but find some aspects of it problematic. The best essays are often not black and white but somewhere in between.

B PAIRS Discuss your ideas. *I'm going to use the Gandhi quote for my essay.*

4 WRITE

Write a first draft of an analytical essay about the quote you chose in 3A. Remember to use a formal style. Use the essay in 1B as a model.

5 AFTER YOUR FIRST DRAFT

A PEER REVIEW Read your partner's essay.

- Does the introductory paragraph explain the quote and provide a thesis statement?
- Do the body paragraphs analyze the quote from different angles?
- Is it written in a formal way, avoiding personal pronouns and using academic vocabulary?
- Does the conclusion summarize the points of analysis and restate the thesis?

B REVISE Write another draft, based on the feedback you got from your partner.

C PROOFREAD Check the spelling, grammar, and punctuation in your essay. Then read it again for overall sense.

☐ I CAN WRITE AN ANALYTICAL ESSAY.

PUT IT TOGETHER

1 PROBLEM SOLVING

A CONSIDER THE PROBLEM Carol Dweck, a professor of psychology, describes two mindsets that determine the ability to learn and deal with change: a *growth mindset* and a *fixed mindset*. Most people exhibit a combination of both. Review the chart and circle the correct answers.

Growth mindset traits	Fixed mindset traits
• recognize that abilities develop	• think people have talent or never will
• embrace challenges	• avoid challenges
• accept criticism and learn from it	• reject criticism as hurtful
• equate rewards with effort	• expect rewards without effort
• persist despite setbacks	• give up after setbacks
• never give up	• give up easily
• learn from failure	• see failing once as failing completely
• look to see what more can be done	• avoid doing more than necessary

1. **A growth / A fixed / Neither** mindset shows a belief that setbacks mean failure.
2. **A growth / A fixed / Neither** mindset shows a belief that people change.
3. Some people may not want to bother exerting more effort if it is not justified by **the costs / failure / the rewards**.

B THINK CRITICALLY Do you think people are born with or learn a particular mindset? Discuss with a partner.

C FIND A SOLUTION Consider the data, the problem, and possible solutions in small groups.

Step 1 **Brainstorm** Think of an important new project for which a team needs to work together. Choose 3-5 of the growth mindset traits and explain how you would convince a fixed mindset team to adopt them.

Step 2 **Evaluate** Choose the best approaches. Consider how each trait is important to the project and the team.

Step 3 **Present** Explain the best approach to the class.

2 REFLECT AND PLAN

A Look back through the unit. Check (✓) the things you learned. Highlight the things you need to learn.

Speaking Objectives
- ☐ Talk about emotions
- ☐ Talk about sadness
- ☐ Discuss happiness

Vocabulary
- ☐ Words related to emotions

Conversation
- ☐ Show empathy

Pronunciation
- ☐ Intensifiers and emphatic stress

Listening
- ☐ Listen for questions

Note-taking
- ☐ Use charts for organization

Language Choices
- ☐ Articles
- ☐ *Too* and *enough*
- ☐ Adverbs

Discussion
- ☐ Tell an anecdote

Reading
- ☐ Visualize a story

Writing
- ☐ Use formal style

B What will you do to learn the things you highlighted?

Notes Done

Review the Note-taking Skill in Lesson 3: Use charts for organization.

VOCABULARY PRACTICE ▶01-02 Listen. Complete the sentences with the correct form of the words from the box.

dependable	acknowledge	initiative	upbeat
brainstorming	~~skill set~~	collaboration	trait

1. Ana doesn't have the ___skill set___ for the position in the São Paulo office. She is honest enough to ________________ that she did not read the job description closely. Although she did not get the position, she was ________________ .
2. Fatma is a(n) ________________ employee, and she takes ________________ when it comes to problem solving. Commitment to the company is Fatma's strongest ________________ .
3. The managers are in a(n) ________________ meeting for a new project. They know ________________ is important for successful production of their training videos.

NOUN CLAUSES AS SUBJECTS, OBJECTS, AND COMPLEMENTS

A ▶01-03 Listen. Check (✓) the correct answers.

	True	False	Can't say
1. The manager is concerned that Lucas doesn't have enough goals.	☐	☑	☐
2. What is worrying Lena is her upcoming performance review.	☐	☐	☐
3. Omar thinks that he should have gotten a higher rating on his review.	☐	☐	☐
4. Ryan's poor track record is the reason why he won't get the promotion.	☐	☐	☐
5. Trudy isn't interested in what the other speaker is saying.	☐	☐	☐
6. Jamal always does what his manager expects of him.	☐	☐	☐

B Rewrite each pair of sentences as a single sentence with a noun clause. There may be more than one correct answer.

1. This challenge will be difficult. I realize that.
   I realize that this challenge will be difficult.
2. You're a high achiever. We recognize that.
   ____
3. He was promoted to manager. I'm happy about that.
   ____
4. What did she say? It wasn't clear.
   ____
5. How can we improve? We're thinking about that.
   ____
6. We don't have enough time to finish. That's the issue we're facing.
   ____

VOCABULARY PRACTICE Complete the sentences with the correct form of the words from the box.

the end is in sight	setback	build momentum
for one reason or another	not go (one's) way	temptation
~~take the plunge~~	map out	raise the bar

1. Always be willing to try something new. Go ahead and take the plunge.
2. Don't give up when things ______________. Remember that tomorrow is another day!
3. ______________, you may be unable to meet your goals. If you have a(n) ______________, don't give up.
4. The first week of a 30-day challenge will be hard. But eventually, you'll start to ______________.
5. Once you finish a basic challenge, you should ______________ and try something more difficult.
6. It's always important to plan. Be sure to ______________ each challenge carefully.
7. With a 30-day challenge, ______________. It doesn't require a lifetime commitment.
8. Don't eat that candy bar. Resist the ______________.

MORE WAYS TO EXPRESS FUTURE TIME

A ▶01-08 Listen. Circle the correct answers.

1. They're on the verge of **completing a project / going out to dinner**.
2. He is **about to / not about to** start a new 30-day challenge.
3. Her team is bound to **win / lose** the competition.
4. His gym membership is **due to / bound to** end soon.
5. She is not to **run twice a week / eat fast food**.
6. He is **on the brink of ending / due to end** the challenge early.
7. She is to **read / get outside** more.
8. She is **about to / not about to** face some new challenges.

B Rewrite the sentences. Use the verb form or expression in parentheses.

1. You'll see positive results soon.
   (bound to) You're bound to see positive results soon.
2. I'm going to live caffeine-free for the next 30 days.
   (about to) ______________
3. He'll finish his challenge very soon.
   (on the verge of) ______________
4. We have to submit our reports by the end of the week.
   (be to) ______________
5. The new gym equipment arrives this afternoon.
   (due to) ______________
6. We're not going to finish this project anytime soon.
   (bound to) ______________
7. There's no way I'm giving up chocolate.
   (about to) ______________
8. The system updates will not happen for another two weeks.
   (due to) ______________

VOCABULARY PRACTICE **Complete the sentences with the correct form of the words from the box.**

specialist expertise	norm	crowdsourcing	monumental effort
galvanize	small-scale initiative	innovation	renewable energy
vulnerable	tangible	breakthrough	~~spin-off~~

1. When it comes to sitcoms, ___spin-offs___ are never as good as the originals.
2. It's going to take a(n) ____________ to protect all of the endangered animals.
3. Her ____________ campaign worked great. She was able to fund her entire project.
4. There should be more ____________ to help local communities deal with plastic waste.
5. There will one day be a ____________ in finding a cure for cancer.
6. Teachers require more ____________ than police officers.
7. Protests too often fail to ____________ people; they tend to divide people even more.
8. ____________ is important for our future. Natural resources are becoming scarce.
9. ____________ in artificial intelligence is dangerous for the human race.
10. The government should do more to protect ____________ people in society.
11. Children must follow certain behavioral ____________ in school.
12. Scientists have discovered ____________ evidence that proves climate change is real.

PREPARATORY SUBJECTS: *IT*, *HERE*, AND *THERE*

A ▶01-14 **Listen. Write the preparatory subject you hear. Then circle the real subject of the sentence.**

	Preparatory subject	Real subject	
1.	there	(a.) breakthroughs	b. cancer research
2.		a. clear	b. that we must take action
3.		a. example	b. crowdsourcing platform
4.		a. firetruck	b. parking lot
5.		a. much time	b. funds
6.		a. new developments	b. challenge

B **Rewrite the sentences using a preparatory subject.**

1. Solving that problem would require a monumental effort.
   It would require/take a monumental effort to solve that problem.
2. More volunteer opportunities should exist in our community.
   ____
3. I have your application here.
   ____
4. Bringing attention to the issue is important.
   ____
5. The weather has been hot and humid this week.
   ____
6. Finding a specialist was a good idea.
   ____

UNIT 2, LESSON 1

VOCABULARY PRACTICE ▶02-02 **Listen. Complete the sentences with the correct form of the words from the box.**

objectively	drastic	commonplace	misconception	perpetuate
sensationalize	preconceived	generalization	~~absurd~~	

1. Debra and Mateo agree that the stereotype about women is ___absurd___. Debra claims it is ______________ for a stereotype to be the result of a(n) ______________.
2. Taka thinks that Gaby should not ______________ the recklessness of teen drivers. He says that she is making an unfair ______________ about teens as distracted drivers. He thinks Gaby should look at the situation ______________.
3. Sara and Nazir's students come to school with ______________ ideas about their classmates. They're worried that their students will ______________ stereotypes they've seen in movies. They plan to make ______________ changes to help their students.

PASSIVE VOICE: AGENT VERSUS NO AGENT

A ▶02-03 **Listen. Write the agent. When the agent is not clear, write *unknown*.**

1. ___Facebook___
2. ______________
3. ______________
4. ______________
5. ______________
6. ______________
7. ______________
8. ______________

B **Change the sentences from active to passive. Use the same verb tense and modal from the original sentence. Omit the *by*-phrase when possible.**

1. Someone should have finished the report last week.
   The report should have been finished last week.
2. Peter Merholz first coined the word *blog*.
   ____
3. The police have arrested the suspect.
   ____
4. People often characterize cats as less friendly than dogs.
   ____
5. People have sensationalized that story for the purposes of entertainment.
   ____
6. Why didn't anyone tell me about the meeting?
   ____
7. Dan gave me flowers for my birthday.
   ____
8. The media sometimes negatively portrays Millennials.
   ____

VOCABULARY PRACTICE **Circle the correct answers.**

1. When you have high self-esteem, you feel **ignored** / **successful** / **nervous**.
2. **Camaraderie** / **Alienation** / **Competition** is the result of the bond that people feel toward each other.
3. An example of a cathartic experience is **sleeping** / **studying** / **crying**.
4. Avid fans **are hooked on** / **sometimes like** / **usually avoid** watching their favorite athletes, musicians, or actors perform.
5. The cause of a visceral reaction is **scientific research** / **careful analysis** / **strong emotion**.
6. Scientists have found a correlation between being a fan and being in love. The **similarity** / **difference** / **comparison** is quite amazing.
7. Sports fans often live vicariously. Their excitement comes from their **own experiences** / **favorite athletes** / **love of sports**.
8. Research that provides telling information is **difficult** / **useful** / **time consuming**.
9. After years of **camaraderie** / **alienation** / **competition** from her family, the woman finally reconciled with them.
10. He wanted to get some exercise, so his inclination was to **walk** / **drive** / **take the bus**.

CAUSATIVE VERBS

A ▶02-08 **Listen. Circle the correct answers.**

1. The stadium doesn't **make** / **let** / **require** people bring food to the games.
2. Her roommate **helped** / **made** / **let** her watch the soccer games.
3. They can **help** / **have** / **let** their neighbor record the game for them.
4. Their manager **lets** / **makes** / **helps** them participate in team-building exercises.
5. The doctor is **helping** / **allowing** / **requiring** Caleb to follow a diet.
6. Amir **had** / **made** / **let** his favorite baseball player sign his ticket.
7. Pete may be able to **get** / **help** / **allow** them in the stadium.
8. The swim team is **required** / **getting** / **allowed** in the pool.

B **Write new sentences with the causative verbs in parentheses.**

1. The team's social media site is great. It gives fans an opportunity to bond.
   (allow) The team's social media site allows fans the opportunity to bond.
2. The coach is very tough on the players. They even practice on weekends.
   (make) ____________________
3. I don't have time to write the report. I'll ask Hao to do it.
   (get) ____________________
4. You can't bring your dog inside that restaurant. They won't allow it.
   (let) ____________________
5. Identifying with a team is a good way for people to build self-esteem.
   (help) ____________________
6. Artur doesn't cut the grass. He pays a lawn service to do it.
   (have) ____________________
7. You can't go on the court right now. There's a practice going on.
   (allow) ____________________
8. My boss couldn't finish the report. He asked me to finish it for him.
   (require) ____________________

VOCABULARY PRACTICE **Complete the sentences with the correct form of the words from the box.**

pay attention to	swayed into believing	prioritize	misinformation	tendency	filter
evolutionary trait	~~plagued with~~	ignorance	exploited by	reinforce	

1. Gross! This house is plagued with cockroaches! Look, there's another one!
2. Not all ________________, like having red hair, for example, are necessary for survival.
3. The mayor's ________________ about what's causing the rise in crime rates surprises me.
4. I think it's fair to say that politicians have a(n) ________________ to lie.
5. ________________ how he keeps his head still. That's the key to a good golf swing.
6. The masses are being ________________ the wealthy classes. It's time to rise up.
7. His success at diplomacy will ________________ his reputation as a great politician.
8. You should ________________ your work better. That project isn't due until next week.
9. I usually ________________ the comments made on my blog to check that they are not spam.
10. I was ________________ her lies about how she'd been hurt in the past. She made it all up.
11. This article says climate change is all a lie. It's filled with ________________.

ACTIVE VERSUS PASSIVE REPORTING

A ▶02-14 **Listen. Circle the sentence that correctly reports the information you hear.**

1. a. Specific populations have been reported by scientists to evolve.
   (b.) Some evolutionary traits have been reported to evolve only within certain populations.
2. a. Politicians are said to have a tendency to use social media.
   b. Social media users in the UK are reported to have a tendency to follow politicians.
3. a. It has been claimed that social media sites are being exploited to spread misinformation.
   b. Social media groups are claimed to be exploiting misinformation.
4. a. Fake news and swaying public opinion have been blamed by social media sites.
   b. Social media sites have been blamed for swaying public opinion with fake news.
5. a. Studies are shown to reinforce people's own beliefs.
   b. Many people are said to consume news that reinforces their beliefs.
6. a. It is expected that officials will plague the project with challenges and delays.
   b. The project is expected to be plagued with challenges and delays.

B **Rewrite the sentences using both passive reporting structures:** ***It*** **+ passive reporting verb + (*that*) clause and subject + passive reporting verb + infinitive.**

1. People say that actor has been plagued with bad luck.
   a. It is said that actor has been plagued with bad luck.
   b. That actor is said to have been plagued with bad luck.
2. Experts report that negative news stories are shared most often.
   a. ____
   b. ____
3. They say that young people read most of their news on their phones.
   a. ____
   b. ____
4. Doctors know that fake health news can spread like a virus.
   a. ____
   b. ____

VOCABULARY PRACTICE ▶03-02 Listen. Complete the sentences with the correct form of the words from the box.

hunch	~~gargantuan~~	fascination	baffling
evidence	enigma	conclusive	trivia

1. Hank says the Great Pyramid is __gargantuan__. Al says it's ________ to him how Hank knows so much ________ about the ancient pyramid.
2. Jean talks about her ________ with Khufu, the driving force behind the Great Pyramid. Khufu is a(n) ________ to her. Alicia has a(n) ________ that Jean is going to start reading more about Khufu.
3. The students say there was no ________ information to solve the mysteries of the Great Pyramid for centuries. The first breakthrough occurred with the introduction of a scientific approach to archaeology and the ________ it supplied.

MODALS FOR SPECULATION ABOUT THE PAST

A ▶03-03 Listen. Write the modal and verb you hear. How certain is the speaker? Check (✓) the correct answers.

		50% certain	> 90% certain
1.	might not have ever been	☑	☐
2.		☐	☐
3.		☐	☐
4.		☐	☐
5.		☐	☐
6.		☐	☐

B Rewrite the sentences using a modal for speculation. More than one answer may be possible.

1. According to experts, it's impossible that the Easter Island statues came from a different island.
   According to experts, the Easter Island statues couldn't have come from a different island.
2. Researchers are almost certain that the stones had a religious meaning.
   ____
3. It's possible that the stones were a monument to a tribal leader.
   ____
4. It is almost certain that construction of the pyramids took decades.
   ____
5. Some people believe it's possible that aliens built Stonehenge.
   ____
6. I don't think it's possible that aliens built Stonehenge.
   ____

UNIT 3, LESSON 2

VOCABULARY PRACTICE Complete the conversations with the correct form of the words from the box.

a sinking feeling	take (someone's) word for it	mind-blowing	~~skeptical~~	spitting image
the odds	not buy (something)	swear	gag	bogus

1. **Liz:** I'm a(n) ___skeptical___ person. I want cold hard facts to back up the information I get. I refuse to ________________ .
   Sue: I'll keep that in mind!
2. **Dimas:** You should see the new Earth exhibit at the Space Museum. It is ________________ .
   Eva: I saw that exhibit in California just last month. What are ________________ ?
3. **Hossam:** Some people believe in the existence of UFOs, but others will simply ________________ .
   Bella: I'm one those people. I think reports of UFO sightings are totally ________________ .
4. **Pablo:** I always have ________________ as soon as a professor announces a test.
   Camila: Professor Thompson's exams aren't difficult, so you can relax. I ________________ .
5. **Mom:** OK, you and Jon are twins. You're the ________________ of each other. But I'm your mother. Did you really think you could fool me with this prank?
   Joe: Ha ha. I guess not. But it was a funny ________________ , right?

MODALS FOR EXPECTATION

A ▶03-08 **Listen. Circle the correct statement based on what you hear.**

1. a. Ana's sister should have felt a pain in her leg.
   (b.) Ana's sister wasn't supposed to have known about the accident.
2. a. The man ought to have been in the picture.
   b. The man was supposed to be at the neighbor's house.
3. a. Diego was supposed to go kayaking that day.
   b. The tree should have been hit by lightning.
4. a. Our cat was supposed to have been lost.
   b. Our cat ought to have found its way back to our house.
5. a. Kate is supposed to love ghost towns.
   b. Kate is supposed to be a skeptical person.
6. a. A meteor ought to hit her hometown soon.
   b. A meteor wasn't supposed to fall over her hometown.

B **Rewrite the sentences using the words in parentheses.**

1. I wasn't expecting anyone to be in the building.
   (supposed to) There wasn't supposed to be anyone in the building.
2. It almost never snows in the summer.
   (should) ________________________________
3. I was expecting the ghost story to be a lot scarier.
   (ought to) ________________________________
4. Please don't touch anything in the museum.
   (supposed to) ________________________________
5. They say that my grandmother was the spitting image of her cousin.
   (supposed to) ________________________________

VOCABULARY PRACTICE Complete the quotes with the correct form of the words from the box.

armed with	worst-case scenario	reflection	cautionary tale
play up	sanitation	roam the streets	dissolve
thrive	plant	~~perceive~~	

1. "Because there is no sunlight at this depth, it is often ___perceived___ as inhospitable to life, but in fact, the angler fish ________________ here."
2. "The substance completely ________________ in the liquid after only a few seconds."
3. "The recent rise in crime is a(n) ________________ of how violent our society has become."
4. As far as I'm concerned, we have bigger issues than poor ________________ . The media tends to ________________ this issue just to get higher ratings."
5. "The drama, starring Hana Lee, is a(n) ________________ about the dangers of plastic surgery."
6. "He has a three-shot lead going into the final hole. The ________________ now is that he'll enter a play-off, but surely he can't lose."
7. "All units, all units: We've received reports of two individuals ________________ in the Westlake area. It is not clear whether the individuals are ________________ weapons. Over."
8. "In the news tonight, Simone Davies claims her innocence, suggesting that the letters were ________________ as a diversion."

PASSIVE MODALS

A ▶03-15 Listen. Write the passive modal that you hear. Circle the agent of the passive modal.

	Passive modal	Agent		
1.	might have been offered	a. Eric	(b.) a social media company	c. unknown
2.		a. the records	b. a fire	c. unknown
3.		a. urban legends	b. anyone	c. unknown
4.		a. consumers	b. car manufacturer	c. unknown
5.		a. Rina	b. a crocodile	c. unknown
6.		a. rats	b. the health department	c. unknown

B Complete the sentences with the active or passive form of the words in parentheses.

1. That story sounds like it ___could have been invented___ **(could + invent)** by some teenagers. You ___should check___ **(should + check)** the source.
2. The origins of urban legends ________________ **(should + explore)**. By studying urban legends, we ________________ **(can + gain)** insight into our own fears.
3. We ________________ **(may + make)** some big mistakes on our project last week, but I don't think it ________________ **(could + do)** any differently.
4. The monster story ________________ **(should + not + take)** seriously, but a lot of people actually believed it. It ________________ **(supposed to + be)** just a gag.

VOCABULARY PRACTICE ▶04-02 Listen. Complete the sentences with the correct form of the words from the box.

commercial value	~~tagging~~	covert	commentary
provoke	vandalism	phenomenal	

1. Rina tells Ben that ___tagging___ is a graffiti signature. She says it doesn't have the same level of social ________________ as a mural might.
2. Diego says there's ________________ to graffiti these days. However, it's still considered ________________ in many places, and as a result, this style of street art is ________________ .
3. Elena and Liz talk about various forms of street art. For example, flash mobs had ________________ popularity several years ago. People were able to capture the public's attention and ________________ discussion.

SUBSTITUTION WITH *SO* AND *NOT*

A ▶04-03 **Listen. Which clause or phrase is substituted? Circle the correct answers.**

1. *if not* =
   a. if you haven't seen the mural (circled)
   b. if the kids hadn't painted the building
2. *if so* =
   a. if you have other plans
   b. if you like street art
3. *by doing so* =
   a. attracting tourists and making the area beautiful
   b. working in cooperation with street artists to create murals
4. *did so* =
   a. had his own work shredded
   b. turned the auction into a work of art
5. *says so* =
   a. says that it's art
   b. says that it's a room full of balloons
6. *hope not* =
   a. hope the kids didn't say that
   b. hope the school wasn't vandalized

B **Part I. Rewrite the conditional sentence. Substitute the repeated information with *so, not,* or *do so.***

1. Does Jack like art? If he likes art, he should go to the auction with us.
   If so, he should go to the auction with us.
2. Do we still need these documents? If we don't need these documents, could you shred them?
   ____
3. Please let me know if I can help you out. I'm happy to help out.
   ____

Part II. Combine the sentences using *but*. In the second clause, substitute the repeated information with *so* or *not*.

4. I'm not sure everyone will attend the meeting. I expect they will attend the meeting.
   I'm not sure everyone will attend the meeting, but I expect so.
5. They might paint over the mural. I hope they don't paint over the mural.
   ____
6. People think his mural is a great work of art. I don't think it's a great work of art.
   ____

VOCABULARY PRACTICE Complete the conversations with the correct form of the words from the box.

endeavor	concept	blur	evoke	utilize
~~algorithm~~	depiction	emulate	compile	

1. A: What is a(n) ___algorithm___?
   B: It's what computer programmers ________________ as the basis of artificial intelligence.
2. A: Robots are not human, but they can learn to ________________ certain human behavior.
   B: That's a(n) ________________ that I can't begin to understand.
3. A: I have to stop driving. My vision is beginning to ________________.
   B: Pull over in this rest area. I can drive.
4. A: Listen to this book review. The ________________ of family relationships in the novel is perfect. The storyline ________________ true feelings of warmth and tenderness.
   B: Can you lend me that book when you finish reading it?
5. A: An important medical discovery was announced today. It was an expensive ________________, and it took years for researchers to ________________ all the data.
   B: I'm all ears. Can you tell me more?

PHRASAL VERBS

A ▶04-08 Listen. Write the phrasal verb you hear. Does it have a direct object? If so, is it separated or not separated? Check (✓) the correct answers.

	Phrasal verb	No object	Separated by object	Not separated by object
1.	catch on	☑	☐	☐
2.		☐	☐	☐
3.		☐	☐	☐
4.		☐	☐	☐
5.		☐	☐	☐
6.		☐	☐	☐

B Rewrite the sentences. Change the direct object to a pronoun (*it* or *them*).

1. Flavio is going to check out the new art exhibit.
   Flavio is going to check it out.
2. Why hasn't this issue been brought up yet?
   ____
3. We have to crank these reports out before 5:00.
   ____
4. Can you weed out some of these applications?
   ____
5. Is the algorithm written down somewhere?
   ____
6. Do you think machines will take over the art world?
   ____

UNIT 4, LESSON 3

VOCABULARY PRACTICE Complete the sentences with the correct form of the words from the box.

out of (your) comfort zone	empathy	mindset	checks all the boxes	conscious effort
~~daunting experience~~	on the spot	impartial	face (your) fears	

1. Presenting in front of so many people at the conference was a really daunting experience .
2. What are you so afraid of? It's only bungee jumping. It's time to ________________ .
3. She's the perfect partner. She's caring, funny, and independent. She ________________ .
4. You need to change your ________________ if you want to succeed in this role.
5. I couldn't connect with the characters in the book. I had no ________________ for them.
6. We shouldn't judge Fiona's new boyfriend until we get to know him. Let's stay ________________ .
7. She was late again! She needs to make a(n) ________________ to get to work on time.
8. It's time for a challenge. I'm going to step ________________ and move into management.
9. I can't give you a decision ________________ . I'll have to think about it.

PAST PERFECT AND PAST PERFECT CONTINUOUS WITH THE SIMPLE PAST

A ▶04-14 Listen. Check (✓) the correct answers.

	True	False	Can't say
1. They had been looking for a way to improve team-building when Jackson suggested an improv class.	☑	☐	☐
2. Kara had been drinking coffee when Sam called her.	☐	☐	☐
3. Gavin hadn't taught improv classes until he started working in sales.	☐	☐	☐
4. Amira had been studying French because she was planning a trip to Africa.	☐	☐	☐
5. Chris lost his job because he hadn't taken it seriously.	☐	☐	☐
6. The speaker had lost his favorite jacket years before he finally found it.	☐	☐	☐

B Complete the sentences with the simple past, past perfect, or past perfect continuous form of the verbs in parentheses.

1. We had been waiting (wait) for Ahmed for hours, so we were relieved when he finally showed up (show up) .
2. By the time we ________________ (make) it to the show, it ________________ (already, begin) .
3. Vinod ________________ (work) on a documentary film when he first ________________ (meet) his wife.
4. Everyone ________________ (go) home by the time we ________________ (arrive) .
5. The improv show ________________ (be) a lot more fun than I ________________ (expect) .
6. I ________________ (not, hear) of that comedy group until you ________________ (tell) me about them.

VOCABULARY PRACTICE ▶05-02 **Listen. Complete the sentences with the correct form of the words from the box.**

diplomatic	~~harsh~~	word	ultimatum
wording	wishy-washy	jargon	ambiguous

1. Peter's tone is a little too ___harsh___ . His co-worker suggests that he be more ______________ . He is worried that he will sound ______________ , but his co-worker assures him that his ______________ is completely clear. It is not at all ______________ .
2. The email sounds like a(n) ______________ .
3. The instructions are difficult to understand because they are full of ______________ . The customer wishes they would ______________ things in plain English.

THE SUBJUNCTIVE

A ▶05-03 **Listen. Circle the sentence that correctly restates the information you hear.**

1. (a.) I recommend you arrive on time to hear the keynote speaker.
   b. I recommend you attend the conference tomorrow.
2. a. Margo requested that she work next door.
   b. Margo asked that we not make so much noise.
3. a. It's important that you not park in that lot.
   b. It's not necessary that you park in that lot.
4. a. I suggest that you submit this report to our manager.
   b. Our manager insists we not submit reports before she reviews them.
5. a. Do you advise the article be sent to the editor?
   b. Is it important that the article be sent today?
6. a. How often do you recommend I change the password?
   b. Is it urgent that the password be changed right away?

B **Combine the sentences using the subjunctive.**

1. We need to finish this project on time. It's critical.
   It's critical that we finish this project on time.
2. You must wear your ID badge at all times. It's essential.
   ____
3. Please don't share this information with anyone. That's my request.
   ____
4. It's not a good idea to use a lot of jargon in your message. I don't recommend it.
   ____
5. You shouldn't be wishy-washy about your decisions. That's my suggestion.
   ____
6. He needs to tell the truth. It's crucial.
   ____
7. We need to schedule a meeting for next week. It's important.
   ____
8. Why are you rewriting the report? Did your manager insist on it?
   ____

VOCABULARY PRACTICE Complete the sentences with the correct form of the words from the box.

neglected	reflective	cultural gap	fill the silence
explicit	utterance	~~unsettled~~	counterpart

1. I am ___unsettled___ by conflict of any kind.
2. We don't understand each other very well because of the ______________ between us.
3. He is the director for the Middle East. His ______________ for North America is Joe Smith.
4. When Americans talk, there is usually only a second between ______________ .
5. I don't like being alone. I usually turn on the TV or listen to music to ______________ .
6. He is usually ______________ rather than reactive. He thinks carefully before he does something.
7. ______________ children whose parents don't pay enough attention to them sometimes grow up to be criminals.
8. Please be ______________ . If you don't tell me exactly what you need, I can't help you.

EMBEDDED *YES/NO* QUESTIONS

A ▶05-08 Listen. Circle the best response to the question you hear.

1. I'm not sure if **(that's enough time or not)** / **the deadline is in two weeks**.
2. I have no idea if **he seems unsettled** / **he's upset**.
3. I'm not 100% sure if **it's a holiday** / **the bank is closed**.
4. I've never met your audience, so I can't tell if **the instructions are clear enough** / **these are the instructions**.
5. I can't decide whether **I like it** / **it's culturally sensitive** or not. Let's ask our counterparts.
6. It's hard to say whether or not **we're merging with another company** / **there will be cultural gaps**.

B Rewrite the sentences as embedded *yes/no* questions. There is more than one correct answer.

Part I. Begin each sentence with *I don't know...*

1. Did they ever get our message?
   I don't know if they ever got our message.
2. Is the latest report ready?
   ____
3. Has the meeting started?
   ____
4. Will we be meeting our North American counterparts?
   ____

Part II. End each sentence with *is another question.*

5. Can we solve this problem?
   Whether or not we can solve this problem is another question.
6. Is it possible to translate silence?
   ____
7. Could this report cause cultural misunderstandings?
   ____

VOCABULARY PRACTICE **Complete the sentences with the correct form of the words from the box.**

cringeworthy	phenomenon	~~abbreviation~~	emoji	rebel	the status quo
no hard and fast rules	concise	downside	vulgar	hinder	solidarity

1. English addresses can be so confusing. They're full of abbreviations .
2. I thought her talk was really well-delivered. It was ______________ and to the point.
3. One ______________ to living in the city is the high pollution levels.
4. The students wore their own clothes to school today to ______________ against the new school uniform policy.
5. Some of the singers on this TV talent show are terrible. Their performances are so ______________ !
6. There are ______________ about the dress code, but most people dress business-casual.
7. Members of the public joined the miners in ______________ on their march for better working conditions.
8. The engine problems really ______________ his progress, but he still finished in the top three.
9. It's crazy that the idea of equal pay for women in sports is only a recent ______________ .
10. I hate it when someone sends a text message with lots of abbreviations and ______________ .
11. I can't believe how she talks to her parents. She must have picked up some of that ______________ language at school.
12. I don't think real change can occur in this country because the current government is only interested in maintaining ______________ .

EMBEDDED *WH-* QUESTIONS

A ▶05-14 **Listen. Circle the direct question equivalent of the embedded question you hear.**

1. a. Why do we have so many emojis? (b.) Why do people use emojis?
2. a. What does this word mean? b. How do you know this word?
3. a. Are you sure about this expression? b. How can I use this expression correctly?
4. a. How do you know about slang at work? b. When should I use slang in messages?
5. a. What do you know about this word? b. Why do people think that word is humorous?
6. a. Why is this phrase confusing? b. How can I reword this phrase?

B **Combine the sentences using an embedded *Wh-* question. Use an infinitive clause if the question contains *can* or *should*.**

1. What's the downside? I'm not sure.
   I'm not sure what the downside is.
2. Why do so many new words emerge on the internet? I've always wondered.
   ____
3. What does this emoji mean? It's anyone's guess.
   ____
4. How can we make this paragraph more concise? I have no idea.
   ____
5. When should I begin the next project? I'm not sure.
   ____
6. Why did you change the wording in this document? I don't understand.
   ____

VOCABULARY PRACTICE ▶06-02 Listen. Complete the sentences with the correct form of the words from the box.

~~charge~~	misappropriation of funds	scandal	internal audit
bribe	trace	inexcusable	

1. They're going to ____charge____ the mayor with bribery. They say he tried to ______________ a police officer. He was also involved in another ______________ earlier in the year.
2. The director has been charged with ______________ . He promised to get rid of corruption at the museum, but a(n) ______________ showed that he is most likely guilty of the crime. They were able to ______________ the money back to him. His behavior is ______________ .

RESTRICTIVE AND NON-RESTRICTIVE RELATIVE CLAUSES

A ▶06-03 **Listen. Circle the relative clause you hear. Is it restrictive or non-restrictive? Check (✓) the correct answers.**

	Relative clause	Restrictive	Non-restrictive
1.	a. that is an intentional misappropriation of funds (b.) that a person has been trusted to handle appropriately	☑	☐
2.	a. that get brought to court b. that involve the theft of government funds	☐	☐
3.	a. which tipped off law enforcement b. which led to a full investigation	☐	☐
4.	a. who finally solved the crime b. who is the detective	☐	☐
5.	a. who was the lead investigator b. who traced over ten years of financial transactions	☐	☐
6.	a. which is caught up in a corruption scandal b. which has slowed down progress on all projects	☐	☐

B **Combine the two sentences using the second sentence as a relative clause. Separate non-restrictive relative clauses with commas.**

1. An executive resigned yesterday. He was involved in the corruption scandal.
   An executive who was involved in the corruption scandal resigned yesterday.
2. Investigators combed through the company's financial records. It held clues to the crime.
   ____
3. Asep is the one. He'll conduct our internal audit.
   ____
4. The scandal destroyed the company's reputation. That was unfortunate.
   ____
5. He was accused of bribery. Bribery is a serious crime.
   ____
6. Mateo's wife wrote a book about corporate crime. She is a psychologist.
   ____

VOCABULARY PRACTICE Complete the sentences with the correct form of the words from the box.

random	eligible	have a say	~~restore~~	campaign	diversity
lobbyist	naïve	susceptible	on hold	employable	

1. After all the bad publicity, we need to ___restore___ people's trust in our company.
2. We couldn't choose our rooms. They were assigned at ________________ .
3. I may not have a lot of experience, but I'm not ________________ . I have a good idea of what's going on.
4. After the senator talked to a(n) ________________ , he changed his vote on an important law.
5. People without a degree are generally less ________________ than those who have one.
6. I was planning to go to university next year, but I've put my plans ________________ until I can save more money.
7. She has already made up her mind. I don't think she's ________________ to persuasion, no matter how good your arguments are.
8. Her ________________ for governor ended when it was discovered that she had bribed a government official.
9. In my small hometown, there is not much political ________________ . Most people vote the same way.
10. People who work for the company are not ________________ to win a prize in the contest.
11. I'm sorry to interrupt, but you've been talking a while and I'd like to ________________ .

RELATIVE CLAUSES AFTER PREPOSITIONS AND QUANTITY EXPRESSIONS

A ▶06-08 Listen. Circle the correct answers.

1. The campaign **highlights** / **doesn't highlight** diversity issues.
2. **Some** / **All** voting machines may be susceptible to fraudulent activity.
3. None of the **sales reps** / **executives** had a say.
4. Many of the **lobbyists** / **police officers** were accused of bribery.
5. **Job postings** / **Diversity statements** have become common these days.
6. The speaker discussed ways to **reduce** / **expose** corruption.

B **Combine the two sentences. Make the second sentence a relative clause. There may be more than one correct answer.**

1. I watched two new documentaries. Neither of them was very interesting.
   I watched two new documentaries, neither of which was very interesting.
2. Alma has two brothers. Both of them are politicians.
   ____
3. The conference room is not available today. We usually meet in that conference room.
   ____
4. Everyone applauded Demba's presentation on diversity. He won an award for his presentation.
   ____
5. We avoid conducting random surveys. Many of them are a waste of time.
   ____
6. I'm reading an article about voter fraud. Occurrences of voter fraud are rare.
   ____

UNIT 6, LESSON 3

VOCABULARY PRACTICE **Complete the sentences with the correct form of the words from the box.**

~~ubiquitous~~	coercion	adulation	idolize	barrier	liberating
ambivalent	dynamic	diminish	condemnation	aspire to	conformity

1. Avoid the tourist attractions unless you want to be held up by ___ubiquitous___ tour groups.
2. I don't think it's healthy to ________________ celebrities, especially pop stars. Why do you have so much ________________ for people who are that fake?
3. He used ________________ to force them into signing the agreement. They felt manipulated.
4. The ________________ between my partner and me has changed a lot since we became parents.
5. His parents strongly urged him to apply for college, but he was ________________ about it.
6. Sales at the fast-food chain ________________ after the health scare.
7. The judge's ________________ of the criminals' actions was very strong.
8. Camila found it ________________ to finally be done with exams.
9. She hid her feelings because she had been hurt in the past. She put up a(n) ________________ .
10. You should break away from ________________ and do your own thing.
11. She has ________________ be a doctor since she was a little girl.

REDUCING RELATIVE CLAUSES TO PHRASES

A ▶06-14 **Listen. Circle the correct meaning for each sentence you hear. Both answers may be correct.**

1. (a.) Harvard researchers conducted an experiment.
   (b.) The experiment was inconclusive.
2. a. Elena Lopez is the director of marketing.
   b. The sales team will deliver a presentation.
3. a. The talk will end early.
   b. People who do not want to attend the talk can leave early.
4. a. Some team members were ambivalent.
   b. Some team members were enthusiastic.
5. a. The study was designed to demonstrate the power of conformity.
   b. The participants designed the study.
6. a. The report contained mistakes.
   b. Dominic is responsible for the mistakes.

B **Rewrite the sentences. Change the relative clauses to adjective phrases.**

1. Those who show empathy towards others are more likely to become successful.
   Those showing empathy towards others are more likely to become successful.
2. He enjoyed a successful career that spanned four decades.
   ____
3. I spoke with the woman who sat next to me at the conference.
   ____
4. The books that are on my desk belong to Martin.
   ____
5. We should avoid aggression, which is a barrier to communication.
   ____
6. We can share resources that are ubiquitous.
   ____

VOCABULARY PRACTICE ▶07-02 Listen. Complete the sentences with the correct form of the words from the box.

~~talk (someone) into~~	dissuade	reconsider	top-notch
twist (someone's) arm	assure	make up (one's) mind	sweeten the pot

1. He tried to talk her into working for them, but was not successful. He even offered to ________________ to help her to ________________, but she had already decided. He couldn't ________________. It's too bad because she was a ________________ candidate.
2. At first, Yu was determined to apply to just one college. However, when they ________________ him that they would pay the extra application fees, he ________________. In the end, they managed to ________________ him from applying to just one college.

NEGATIVE GERUNDS AND INFINITIVES

A ▶07-03 Listen. Circle the negative form that you hear. Then check (✓) the correct answers.

Negative form		True	False
1. **working / (seeing)**	The speaker didn't like being far apart from family.	✓	☐
2. **listening / being**	The speaker recommends not twisting a client's arm.	☐	☐
3. **to make up / to rush**	The speaker suggests not waiting before making a decision.	☐	☐
4. **to reconsider / to find**	The speaker thinks the listener can find a better price.	☐	☐
5. **to pressure / to start**	The speaker wants to pressure the listener.	☐	☐
6. **returning / turning back**	Customers have a limited time in which they can return a car to that dealership.	☐	☐

B Combine each pair of sentences with a negative gerund or infinitive form of the underlined verb.

1. I don't have enough time. That is my biggest problem.
   Not having enough time is my biggest problem.
2. She's made up her mind. She will not buy a new house this year.
   ____
3. I didn't accept the job offer. I regret that now.
   ____
4. It's possible that we won't finish the project on time. We're worried about that.
   ____
5. You don't have to negotiate. Have you considered that?
   ____
6. I don't want to twist your arm. But I hope you'll reconsider my offer.
   ____

VOCABULARY PRACTICE Complete the sentences with the correct form of the words from the box.

let (someone) down easy	tons	~~figure~~	get back at (someone)
shoot (someone) a text	the perils of	romantic	dump
smash	hang out with	go for it	hideous

1. The trip is ten days long, so I ___figure___ I'll need to bring a good amount of a money.
2. He made me wait for an hour yesterday, so I'm going to ________________ and make him wait for me today.
3. I am so angry right now that I want to ________________ all the plates in the kitchen.
4. Last night we had a ________________ dinner at a nice restaurant—just the two of us, no kids.
5. That sweater is ________________ . I don't think I've ever seen an uglier piece of clothing!
6. If you really want to study art, you should ________________ . Don't let anyone talk you out of it.
7. Please, take some fresh tomatoes. I have ________________ of them in my garden this year.
8. If you're bored, why don't you go ________________ your friends?
9. She's decided to ________________ her boyfriend. He's too needy.
10. When you get home, ________________ so that I know you made it safely.
11. I really like him but just as a friend. I want to ________________ .
12. You're going to ruin your eyesight using that computer. Hasn't your doctor explained ________________ too much screen time?

PERFECT GERUNDS AND INFINITIVES

A 07-08 Listen. Circle the correct answers.

1. Eric is believed **to have upset** / **to be talking to** Min-ji.
2. Rita would prefer **to stay** / **to have stayed** home.
3. Jessica doesn't regret **having hurt Tim's feelings** / **having dated Tim**.
4. Omar resents **having been dumped by** / **having dumped** Heidi.
5. Sara would like **to travel** / **to have traveled** more in her university years.
6. Caleb is the third person **to have fired someone** / **to have been fired** this week.

B Complete the second sentence so that it has the same meaning as the first sentence. Use a perfect form of a gerund or infinitive.

1. She wishes she hadn't returned his call.
   She regrets ___having returned his call___ .
2. I think they were having a good time.
   They seemed ________________________________ .
3. He told us that he didn't smash his phone in anger.
   He denied ________________________________ .
4. He's angry because he was dumped.
   He's upset about ________________________________ .
5. We were invited to the wedding.
   We were delighted ________________________________ .
6. She broke up with him over the phone.
   It was wrong for her ________________________________ .

VOCABULARY PRACTICE **Complete the sentences with the correct form of the words from the box.**

innovation	~~stifle~~	clout	manipulative	distribute	start-up
harvest	monopolize	deter	exert	breach	patent

1. I wish we had more freedom at school. The curriculum ___stifles___ my creativity.
2. I didn't think his idea would take off, but he received ________________ for it.
3. The company was investigated after it allowed a third-party agency to ________________ the data of thousands of users.
4. His political campaign was helped by the ________________ of major investors from the oil industry.
5. He ________________ the terms of his bail, so he must return to prison.
6. The promotional leaflets were ________________ across the whole neighborhood.
7. Chatbots are one of the most important technological ________________ in the last decade.
8. The smoking area outside the entrance of the restaurant seems to ________________ potential customers.
9. He made her feel guilty for problems in their relationship. He was very ________________ .
10. The players ________________ their power by calling for the coach to be fired.
11. He got a business loan in order to establish his own tech ________________ .
12. If those two companies are allowed to merge, they will ________________ the entire industry.

REPORTED SPEECH

A ▶07-15 **Listen. Then circle the correct answers.**

1. She said that monopolies **could** / **might** raise prices.
2. He said that less competition **meant / might mean** less innovation and job growth.
3. She argued that the job market **hadn't / shouldn't have** grown much in certain fields the previous year.
4. He claimed that some companies **could / would** become monopolies without government intervention.
5. She wondered why the government **didn't take / hadn't taken** action to stop a monopoly.
6. He explained that sometimes monopolies **were** / **would be** a necessity.

B **Change the quotes to reported speech.**

1. She told me, "I have to work this afternoon."
   She said that she had to work that afternoon.
2. He said, "I don't want to shop at this giant retailer."
   ____
3. He said, "I'll bring the report tomorrow."
   ____
4. She told me, "I can finish it today."
   ____
5. She said, "I'll meet you here at two o'clock this afternoon."
   ____
6. He asked, "Why is this issue important?"
   ____

VOCABULARY PRACTICE ▶08-02 Listen. Complete the sentences with the correct form of the words from the box.

break the ice	fall flat	sarcastic	one-liner
punchline	~~crack up~~	hilarious	in hysterics

1. The woman always ___cracks up___ at the comedian's shows. The jokes are ________________ . By the end of the show, the whole audience is ________________ .
2. The man can never remember the ________________ . The woman's jokes always ________________ .
3. They don't appreciate Ming's humor because he is often ________________ .
4. The man wants to know what the woman does to ________________ on the first day of class.
5. Heidi is good at coming up with ________________ .

REDUCED ADVERB TIME CLAUSES

A ▶08-03 Listen. Check (✓) the correct answers.

	True	False	Can't say
1. Upon hearing the joke, everyone on the team cracked up.	☐	☑	☐
2. Hiro was laughing while telling a joke.	☐	☐	☐
3. The speakers feel entertained upon hearing Kevin's jokes.	☐	☐	☐
4. Mona laughs only when relaxed and in the company of good friends.	☐	☐	☐
5. Andre wants to read a review before going to the comedy show.	☐	☐	☐
6. Claire uses a lot of sarcasm when telling jokes.	☐	☐	☐

B Rewrite the sentences. Reduce the adverb clause to a phrase. If it is not possible to reduce the clause, write *not possible*.

1. When you're teaching a class, use humor to break the ice.
   When teaching a class, use humor to break the ice.
2. Before I started the presentation, I tried to joke around.
   ____
3. When the show started, someone's cell phone rang.
   ____
4. As I was driving to work, I heard a great podcast.
   ____
5. We can't complete this project until we are given instructions.
   ____
6. We felt inspired after we attended the conference in Bolivia.
   ____

VOCABULARY PRACTICE **Complete the sentences with the correct form of the words from the box.**

evolutionary	species	bonding	territory	exclude
~~alleviate~~	dominate	tickle	mammal	

1. To ____alleviate____ stress, I usually listen to music or watch TV. It helps me relax.
2. My older sister loves to ________________ me to make me laugh.
3. Boys, let your sister play, too. Don't ________________ her.
4. We have two ________________ of fish in our fish tank: angel fish and goldfish.
5. Due to ________________ changes, dogs and wolves are now two different species.
6. Teachers often start class with a fun activity to encourage ________________ among the students.
7. Don't go inside the fence or the dog will bite you. That's his ________________ .
8. He is a large-animal veterinarian. He only treats ________________ , not birds or snakes.
9. You need to let other students talk. You cannot always ________________ the discussion.

CAUSE AND EFFECT IN PARTICIPIAL PHRASES

A ▶08-08 **Listen. Circle the sentence that has the same meaning as what you hear.**

1. (a.) Wanting to be heard, Flora spoke in a loud, clear voice.
   b. Trying to be polite, Flora cleared her throat.
2. a. Shrugging, Ava gave the best answer she could think of.
   b. Not knowing the answer, Ava shrugged and shook her head.
3. a. Having put the design project on hold, we met our deadline.
   b. Given that our deadline is two days away, we should make the presentation our priority.
4. a. I've forgotten my classmate's name since running into him at a conference last week.
   b. Having forgotten my classmate's name, I felt embarrassed.
5. a. Having broken his arm, Taka is writing with his left hand.
   b. Given that Taka's note is really hard to read, I'm going to call him.
6. a. Unable to attend the meeting, Hana asked us to record it.
   b. Having recorded the meeting, Hana doesn't need to attend.

B **Rewrite the sentences with participial phrases.**

1. Because I realized how unprepared I was, I began to panic.
   Having realized how unprepared I was, I began to panic.
2. Because we always have meetings on Fridays, we shouldn't schedule anything else that day.
   ____
3. Because he realized that no one was listening to him, Ming stopped talking.
   ____
4. Because Nida didn't want to hurt our feelings, she laughed at all our jokes.
   ____
5. Since we were exhausted from a long day at work, we didn't go out last night.
   ____
6. Since I hadn't gone to the comedy show with everyone, I felt excluded.
   ____

VOCABULARY PRACTICE Complete the sentences with the correct form of the words from the box.

wish the ground would swallow (you) up	personalize	anecdote	current affairs
tailor	fit	vice-versa	signpost
hook	antiquated		

1. I can't stand to be in a room more than five minutes with her, and ___vice-versa___ !
2. I like hearing his __________ . It's just, well, they're supposed to be short.
3. You need to __________ the talk more. The main points aren't clear.
4. These tour companies help you __________ your trip to your own interests.
5. Her stand-up show was hilarious! She had us in __________ of laughter!
6. I usually do everything online. Paper forms are just __________ these days.
7. I buy newspapers to keep up with __________ .
8. The opening paragraph of the book describes a mysterious murder. It's a great __________ .
9. So I bent down to touch my toes, and my pants suddenly ripped right down the middle. It was so embarrassing! I __________ .
10. You can __________ the settings on your desktop and add your own background photo.

PARTICIPIAL ADJECTIVES AND NOUNS AS ADJECTIVES

A ▶08-15 Listen. Circle the noun as adjective and participial adjective in each sentence.

	Noun as adjective	Participial adjective
1.	lawyer / joke	tired / hearing
2.	birthday / toy	looking / personalized
3.	history / class	trying / opening
4.	Korean / restaurant	dropped / embarrassing
5.	anecdote / life	amusing / distracted
6.	paper / document	antiquated / digitized

B Complete the sentences with the words in parentheses. Change the verbs to participial adjectives and use the nouns as adjectives.

1. I was really ___embarrassed___ when I tripped and fell at a(n) ___job___ interview. It was one of the most ___embarrassing___ moments of my life. (job, embarrass, embarrass)
2. I saw a very __________ comedy show last night. It involved a lot of __________ participation. (audience, entertain)
3. It's __________ to call that movie a(n) __________ . It wasn't funny at all. Actually, it was pretty __________ . (comedy, depress, mislead)
4. Did you watch the __________ game last night? It wasn't a very __________ match. I was so __________ that I fell asleep before it ended. (bore, excite, soccer)
5. We went on a(n) __________ tour of the Grand Canyon. The __________ guide was very funny, and at the end of the day, we saw an awe-__________ sunset. (inspire, personalize, tour)

VOCABULARY PRACTICE ▶09-02 Listen. Complete the sentences with the correct form of the words from the box.

come down on	~~single (someone)~~ out	lay into	let bygones be bygones
point the finger at	be in the wrong	be short with	

1. The man was upset because his boss singled him out even though he was not the only one at fault. He didn't say anything though because he didn't want to ________________ others. He just wishes his boss hadn't ________________ him in front of everyone.
2. The girl thinks her father treats her unfairly. He ________________ her all the time, but he never yells at her brother. When she tries to talk to her father about it, he ________________ her. Her friend suggests that she speak honestly to her father, and perhaps he will see that he ________________. Then they can both ________________.

IMPLIED CONDITIONALS

A ▶09-03 Listen. What is the condition of the sentence? Circle the correct answers.

1. a. If the manager hadn't singled Taka out,
   (b.) If Taka hadn't done something wrong,
2. a. If I got on her nerves,
   b. If she didn't complain about everything,
3. a. If we made things easier,
   b. If he listened to us,
4. a. If they got along for more than five minutes,
   b. If they argued again,
5. a. If Kim hadn't intervened,
   b. If Kim had intervened sooner,
6. a. If we weren't at odds with him,
   b. If he had talked to us instead of our manager,

B Rewrite the conditional sentences using the words in parentheses.

1. If he hadn't been so short with me, I would have helped him out.
   (otherwise) He was short with me. Otherwise, I would have helped him out.
2. We would put the two brothers on the same team if they weren't always at odds with each other.
   (but) ________________
3. If it hadn't been for your help, I would never have solved the problem.
   (without) ________________
4. If you had called me, I would have answered.
   (Why didn't you) ________________
5. If she had wanted to patch things up, we would still be friends today.
   (or else) ________________
6. If he would apologize for the mistake, I could let bygones be bygones.
   (I wish) ________________

VOCABULARY PRACTICE **Complete the sentences with the correct form of the words from the box.**

intervention	down-to-earth	de-escalate	~~absorb~~	cool off
at hand	minimize	trivial	self-talk	food for thought

1. When I'm learning a new language, it takes time for me to use new vocabulary. I need time to ______absorb______ the lesson before I speak.
2. Don't waste your time on such a(n) ______________ matter. It's not even worth discussing.
3. Please don't ______________ my problems. I know they may not seem like a big deal to you, but they are very important to me.
4. She definitely gave me some ______________. I'm going to think seriously about what she said.
5. Using ______________ is a great way to build up your confidence. Look in the mirror and tell yourself that you can do whatever you set your mind to.
6. He and his boss were having trouble communicating, so he requested a(n) ______________ from the human resources department.
7. If someone yells at you, you should try to ______________ the situation by maintaining a calm, neutral tone of voice and not yell back.
8. I love this website because it contains so many ______________ suggestions about how to simplify your life.
9. After their argument, they decided to spend time apart so they could both ______________.
10. I'm sorry, but I'm afraid your question is off-topic. The topic ______________ is conflict resolution, not building self-confidence.

INVERTED CONDITIONALS

A ▶09-08 **Listen. What is the condition of the statement you hear? Circle the correct answers.**

1. a. if she could help us resolve the situation
   (b.) if she were here
2. a. if you find yourself in Quito
   b. if you visit me
3. a. if I had known then what I know now
   b. if I had done things differently
4. a. if I took the job offer in Japan
   b. if I were ten years younger
5. a. if we had given up
   b. if it had been any easier
6. a. if I had believed otherwise
   b. if we could finish the contract on time

B **Rewrite the sentence using an inverted conditional.**

1. If I had known how serious the conflict was, I would have intervened.
   Had I known how serious the conflict was, I would have intervened.
2. If you find yourself in a hostile situation, try to leave.
   ____
3. If we had de-escalated the argument sooner, things wouldn't have gotten so ugly.
   ____
4. I wouldn't have to read this report again if I had absorbed the information the first time.
   ____
5. If he were more down to earth, we could relate to our manager better.
   ____
6. I wouldn't have gone to the meeting if I had known how trivial it would be.
   ____

UNIT 9, LESSON 3

VOCABULARY PRACTICE Complete the sentences with the correct form of the words from the box.

captivate	resolution	fundamental	~~circumstance~~	confrontation	woes
premise	triumph	literary heritage	escapism	insurmountable	

1. He withdrew from the course due to personal __circumstances__ .
2. It's important that we talk about this issue, but I don't want a(n) ________________ . I can tell you're upset.
3. The decision to legalize gay marriage is a(n) ________________ for equality.
4. I don't think fantasy novels are just about ________________ . There's more substance to them for sure.
5. If sales don't increase, then the company's problems will be ________________ and the company will probably go bankrupt.
6. The film is based on the ________________ that Earth is run by apes, and humans are subordinate.
7. I thought the fireworks display was amazing. I was ________________ by it.
8. Japan has a strong ________________ . Famous authors from the country include Haruki Murakami and Banana Yoshimoto.
9. A(n) ________________ skill for any golfer is hand-eye coordination.
10. After two decades of fighting, there was a peaceful ________________ to the conflict between the two countries.
11. Despite finding a better paid job, his financial ________________ continued for some time.

HOPE AND *WISH*

A ▶09-14 Listen. Circle the correct answers.

1. He **wishes they hadn't dismissed / hopes they won't dismiss** the problem as trivial.
2. She **wishes the café were / hopes the café is** open.
3. He **wishes he had stayed / hopes he can stay** home.
4. She **wishes they could / hopes they can** go hiking today.
5. He **wishes the director were / hopes the director is** down to earth.
6. She **wishes her co-worker had taken / hopes her co-worker took** notes at the meeting.

B Rewrite the *if*-clause as a separate sentence with *hope* or *wish*.

1. If I can come up with a resolution, I'll let you know.
   I hope I can come up with a resolution.
2. I'd be willing to help if it weren't an insurmountable challenge.
   ____
3. If the conflict ends soon, there may still be a peaceful solution.
   ____
4. You'll be able to calm down and cool off a bit if you take a break.
   ____
5. If I could speak Japanese, this project would be a lot easier.
   ____
6. Maybe things would have turned out better if we hadn't intervened.
   ____

VOCABULARY PRACTICE ▶10-02 Listen. Complete the sentences with the correct form of the words from the box.

compassion	gratifying	condolences	~~down in the dumps~~	console	uplifting

1. Chris is _down in the dumps_. Iris tries to ____________ him by offering advice.
2. The woman thinks the man's books are ____________. He finds it ____________ to hear that she likes his books so much.
3. Peter offers Julie his ____________. She thanks him and his family for their ____________.

ARTICLES

A ▶10-03 Listen. Circle the article you hear. Circle Ø if there is no article. Why does the speaker use or not use an article? Check (✓) the correct answers.

	Article	Non-specific, singular count noun	Non-specific, plural or noncount noun	Specific noun	Proper noun	Previously mentioned noun
1.	a / (an) / the / Ø accident	☑	☐	☐	☐	☐
2.	a / an / the / Ø accident	☐	☐	☐	☐	☐
3.	a / an / the / Ø psychologist	☐	☐	☐	☐	☐
4.	a / an / the / Ø psychologist	☐	☐	☐	☐	☐
5.	a / an / the / Ø doctor	☐	☐	☐	☐	☐
6.	a / an / the / Ø compassion	☐	☐	☐	☐	☐

B Complete the paragraph with articles. Write Ø for no article.

What do _the_ (1) United States, ______ (2) United Kingdom, ______ (3) Germany, ______ (4) France, and ______ (5) Sweden have in common? They are ______ (6) top five countries with ______ (7) most Nobel Prize winners. They are also some of ______ (8) countries with ______ (9) highest rates of chocolate consumption. Is that just ______ (10) coincidence? Probably. But ______ (11) recent study found that ______ (12) chocolate consumption may actually improve ______ (13) brain function. Moreover, ______ (14) chocolate has been shown to be ______ (15) natural mood lifter. Researchers say ______ (16) key to getting the brain and mood-boosting effects of ______ (17) chocolate is to choose dark chocolate with ______ (18) high percentage of cocoa. Dark chocolate contains ______ (19) nutrients called flavanols, which are believed to reduce ______ (20) stress, ______ (21) anxiety, and ______ (22) depression. So, ______ (23) next time you're feeling down in ______ (24) dumps, ______ (25) piece of dark chocolate might help you feel better.

VOCABULARY PRACTICE Complete the sentences with the correct form of the words from the box.

intriguing	dull	~~documentary~~	suppress	subjective
fellow	boost	enhance	preliminary	illuminating

1. I watched an interesting documentary last night about how the invention of the automobile changed American life forever.
2. I'm going to drop my history class. I thought it would be interesting, but it's really ________________ .
3. It's not good to ________________ your feelings. It is better to express them.
4. Good evening and a warm welcome to my ________________ classmates! It has been a privilege to get to know you over the past year.
5. The doctors haven't finished all the tests yet, but the ________________ results are good.
6. If you want to ________________ your chances of getting the job, you should dress appropriately for the interview.
7. Thank you for your ________________ talk. I thought I already knew a lot about the subject, but now I understand things on a far deeper level than before.
8. What a(n) ________________ possibility. I had never considered it before, but I find it very interesting.
9. If you want to graduate from university, you will need a(n) ________________ in your grades.
10. You shouldn't take everything he says as the absolute truth. He is just expressing his opinion, which is quite ________________ .

TOO AND *ENOUGH*

A ▶10-08 **Listen. Circle the correct answers.**

1. Carlos **can** / **can't** drive.
2. The doctors **had** / **didn't have** enough information to make a diagnosis.
3. They **don't have enough** / **have too much** paper.
4. The box **is** / **isn't** too heavy to lift alone.
5. The packages **are** / **aren't** too heavy to lift alone.
6. There's **plenty** / **not enough** for everyone.

B **Rewrite the sentences using *too* or *enough*.**

1. The movie was sad, but it didn't make me cry.
   The movie wasn't sad enough to make me cry.
2. We can't make any definite conclusions. It's very early.
   ____
3. We can't fit 100 people in this room. There isn't space.
   ____
4. I couldn't learn Arabic. It was very difficult.
   ____
5. Let's finish this project today. We have plenty of time.
   ____
6. We can't rely on that report. It's very subjective.
   ____

VOCABULARY PRACTICE Complete the questions with the correct form of the words from the box.

trauma	obstacle	synthetic	relative
miscalculate	overestimate	paraplegic	~~coping mechanism~~
be confined to	contribution	immune system	tedious

1. Do you have any ___coping mechanisms___ for dealing with difficult situations?
2. Are there any duties in your job that you find ______________________?
3. Do you think it is fair when pets ______________________ small spaces?
4. Do you know of any illnesses or diseases that attack our ______________________?
5. Have you ever achieved success after overcoming a(n) ______________________?
6. I'm stuffed! I ______________________ how hungry I was.
7. Which scientist has made the biggest ______________________ in the last 100 years?
8. How is a(n) ______________________ material like nylon made?
9. Has an employer ever ______________________ your monthly salary?
10. Have you, or someone you know, ever survived a serious ______________________?
11. Do you know anyone who is ______________________? What difficulties, if any, does the person face?
12. What are the ______________________ strengths and weaknesses of education in your country?

ADVERBS

A ▶10-14 Listen. Write the adverb that you hear. Then circle the item that it modifies.

	Adverb	Modifies
1.	easily	(agree) / the whole sentence
2.		needs / the whole sentence
3.		bitter / the whole sentence
4.		a child / the whole sentence
5.		the sales team / the whole sentence
6.		she / the whole sentence

B Rewrite each sentence twice with the adverbs in parentheses. Change the position of the adverb.

1. Exercise is a coping mechanism for her. (obviously)
   Exercise is obviously a coping mechanism for her.
   Obviously, exercise is a coping mechanism for her.
2. He overestimated his abilities. (basically)
   ____
   ____
3. It took a long time to fix a small problem. (relatively)
   ____
   ____
4. Luis doesn't like to do tedious tasks. (even)
   ____
   ____

GLOSSARY

UNIT 1, LESSON 1, page 6

initiative: the ability to do things without waiting for someone to tell you what to do
a high achiever: someone who is successful and achieves more than the average person in school or at work
oversight: the action of overseeing or supervising something
dependable: when someone always does what is needed or wanted
a track record: all the things that a person or organization has done in the past that show how well he, she, or it is likely to do in the future
upbeat: cheerful and confident that good things will happen
a trait: a characteristic
acknowledge: to accept or admit that something is true or correct
collaboration: the act of people working together to create or achieve the same thing
brainstorming: trying to think of different ways of doing something in order to solve a problem
a skill set: a list of things that someone is good at
juggle: to try to do two or more jobs or activities at the same time

UNIT 1, LESSON 2, page 8

for one reason or another: because of any of a number of reasons
take the plunge: to finally do something momentous or challenging after thinking about it for a while
the end is in sight: something is coming to an end soon
build momentum: to gather speed and strength
not go (one's) way: to proceed in a way that is against one's plans or wishes
raise the bar: to set a higher standard for people to follow
a setback: a problem that makes progress or success less likely
a temptation: a strong feeling of wanting to have or do something that you should not
map out: to plan the details of something

UNIT 1, LESSON 3, page 10

a monumental effort: a serious and determined attempt to do something requiring a vast amount of strength and determination
galvanize: to shock or excite someone into taking action
an innovation: a new idea, invention, or way of doing something
specialist expertise: special skills or knowledge needed for a particular job
a breakthrough: an important achievement by someone who is trying to make, find, or do something new
renewable energy: energy from a source that is naturally replenished, such as wind or solar power
a spin-off: a product that develops from another, more important product
crowdsourcing: the practice of obtaining input, money, or services by enlisting the help of a large group of people, often online
a small-scale initiative: a new plan or attempt for solving a problem that impacts only a small area or number of people
vulnerable: easy to harm, hurt, or attack
a norm: an accepted way of behaving in society
tangible: able to be seen, touched, or felt

GLOSSARY

UNIT 1, LESSON 4, page 12

innocuous: not harmful or offensive
blindfold: to cover someone's eyes with a piece of cloth
in the wake of: happening after an event or as a result of an event
beg the question: to raise a question or point that has not been dealt with
alluring: very attractive or tempting; enticing
be predisposed to: to be more likely than others to behave in a particular way
hardwired: automatically thinking or behaving in a particular way
inhibition: an inability to act in a natural, relaxed way
bragging rights: the presumed right to brag or boast, often associated with winning a contest
kudos: (informal) praise for doing something well
daredevil antics: risky or dangerous behavior
inherent: existing as a natural and permanent quality of someone or something

UNIT 2, LESSON 1, page 18

debunk: to show or prove that something is not true
an assumption: something that you think is probably true
absurd: completely silly
preconceived: an idea or opinion that is formed too early, often without enough thought or knowledge
commonplace: the usual; ordinary
perpetuate: to cause something to continue
a misconception: a wrong or inaccurate idea, often based on the failure to understand a situation
characterize: to describe the character or quality of something
sensationalize: to present information in such a way in order to excite or shock people
objectively: in a way that is based on facts and not influenced by personal beliefs or feelings
a generalization: a statement in which you say or write that something is always true when it is actually only true some of the time
drastic: sudden and severe

UNIT 2, LESSON 2, page 20

visceral: based on an emotional reaction rather than reason or thought
telling: having a significant or revealing effect
cathartic: the relief of emotional tension, especially through different kinds of art
self-esteem: the feeling that you are a good person and that you deserve to be liked and respected
live vicariously: to live or experience something through watching, listening to, or reading about the activities of other people, rather than by doing them yourself
a correlation: a connection between two or more things
an inclination: a feeling that you want to do something
a bond: a strong feeling of love or trust that people have for each other
camaraderie: a friendly feeling toward people with whom you share an experience
alienation: the feeling of being disconnected from or disliked by the people around you
avid: showing a lot of interest in something, and eagerness to do it
hooked: fascinated by or devoted to something

UNIT 2, LESSON 3, page 22

plagued with (something): to have problems that are widespread and cause wide-ranging damage
misinformation: incorrect information intended to trick people
filter: to process information before displaying it, or to prevent it from being seen through the use of a computer program
reinforce: to make someone's beliefs, opinions, or behavior stronger and more definite
pay attention to (something): to focus on or think carefully about something
an evolutionary trait: a quality or characteristic that has evolved over time
prioritize: to decide what is most important, so that you can do it first
exploited by (something): to be treated unfairly, often asked to do too much (e.g. work)
ignorance: the state of not knowing something, especially something you should know
swayed into believing: to be influenced by somebody so that you change your opinion
a tendency: a likelihood to do or think something

UNIT 2, LESSON 4, page 24

popularize: to make something become popular, or liked by a lot of people
the advent of: the introduction of a new product, idea, etc.
a drop in the ocean: a small amount of something (especially when compared to a larger amount)
intimate: having a very close relationship with someone
correlate: to have a mutual connection, in which one thing affects or depends on another
an underlying issue: a big problem that is not obvious or easily noticeable
crucial: extremely important
replicate: make an exact copy of; reproduce
trigger: to make something happen

UNIT 3, LESSON 1, page 30

baffling: impossible to understand
shrouded: concealed or hidden from view; unknown
gargantuan: very large; enormous
a fascination: a very strong interest in something or someone
an enigma: a person or thing that is mysterious or difficult to understand
evidence: things that you see, hear, or learn that make you believe that something exists or is true
a scroll: a long piece of paper that can be written on and rolled up; used often in the past
a hunch: a feeling that something is true or will happen, which is not based on any facts
conclusive: proving that something is true
intrigue: to arouse curiosity or interest; to fascinate
trivia: unimportant facts

UNIT 3, LESSON 2, page 32

a sinking feeling: a feeling of dread or that something bad is going to happen
mind-blowing: surprising and often difficult to understand or imagine
swear: to say firmly that what you are saying is true
skeptical: not believing that something is true or right
take (someone's) word for it: to believe what someone says without checking for oneself
not buy (something): to not accept something as the truth
the odds: how likely it is that something will or will not happen
a gag: a joke
a spitting image: an exact double of someone or something
bogus: not real, true, or honest

GLOSSARY

UNIT 3, LESSON 3, page 34

thrive: to become very successful, strong or healthy
sanitation: the process of keeping places clean and healthy
armed with (a weapon): to have or carry (a weapon)
perceive: to think of something in a particular way
a reflection: a sign of something
play (something) up: to exaggerate or highlight a feeling or a fact
a worst-case scenario: the worst thing could happen in a situation
dissolve: to be absorbed or to cause a substance to be absorbed by a liquid
plant: to secretly put something somewhere, especially in order to deceive
a cautionary tale: a story that warns others of danger or risk
roam the streets: to walk around the streets, usually negative

UNIT 3, LESSON 4, page 36

dim: not bright, so that you cannot see well
a neuron: a cell that sends and receives messages from the brain
a contour: the curved shape or edge of something
an illusion: something that seems to be real or true but is not
an arthropod: an animal with no spine and a segmented body (like a spider, crab, or insect)
segmented: divided into separate parts
advantageous: giving an advantage; useful; beneficial
anatomy: the structure of the body of a person or animal
stability: the ability to stay in position; being stable
plausible: seeming reasonable or probable
consciousness: the state of being and thinking

UNIT 4, LESSON 1, page 42

graffiti: writing and pictures that people draw illegally on buildings, fences, signs, etc.
tagging: the writing of a mark or nickname on a surface; usually done by a graffiti artist
self-expression: the expression of one's thoughts or ideas; usually through writing, art, music, or dance
a mural: a large painting that someone has done on a wall
covert: hidden or secret
vandalism: the crime of deliberately damaging property
phenomenal: extremely impressive or good
commercial value: the expected value of an item should it be put up for sale
provoke: to deliberately make someone angry
commentary: an expression of opinions or explanations about an event or situation
auction off: to sell something at an auction

UNIT 4, LESSON 2, page 44

a concept: a general idea of something
an endeavor: an attempt to do something
blur: to become unclear
compile: to collect information from a variety of sources and combine it together into a list, report, etc.
an algorithm: a set of rules or mathematical guidelines that will help to calculate an answer to a problem, especially by a computer
utilize: to use something
a depiction: the way in which something is represented or shown
emulate: to copy something achieved by someone else
evoke: to make someone remember a feeling or emotion

UNIT 4, LESSON 3, page 46

on the spot: without any delay; immediately
checks all the boxes: meets all the needs or requirements for something
a daunting experience: a situation that is difficult, frightening, or overwhelming
out of (your) comfort zone: to feel uncomfortable in an unfamiliar situation
face (your) fears: to accept and overcome what you are afraid of
a mindset: a person's way of thinking
empathy: the ability to understand how someone feels
impartial: fair and balanced; not supporting any person or group
a conscious effort: an effort that is deliberate or intended

UNIT 4, LESSON 4, page 48

a gathering: a meeting of a group of people
descend on (a place): to arrive at a place, usually a lot of people at once
a pop-up: appearing for a short time, often in a surprising location
a vast array: a large and impressive group of people or collection of things
communal: shared by all members of a community
radical: new or very different from the usual way
unconditional: without limits or conditions
culminate: to end, especially to reach a final or climactic stage
an effigy: a roughly made model of someone or something, made in order to be damaged or destroyed.
humble: ordinary; not special or very important
a bucket list: a list of things you want to do before you die

UNIT 5, LESSON 1, page 54

diplomatic: dealing with people politely in a sensitive and effective way
harsh: critical, cruel, or not nice
tactful: careful not to do or say anything that will upset or embarrass other people
word: to use carefully chosen words to express something
an ultimatum: a statement saying that if someone does not do what you want, he or she will be punished
ambiguous: having more than one meaning, so that it is not clear which meaning is intended
wording: the words and phrases used to express something
vague: not clear in your mind because of not having enough details
wishy-washy: not having firm or clear ideas and seeming unable to decide what you want
not mince (one's) words: to say exactly what you think, even if this may offend people
jargon: technical words and phrases that people doing the same type of work use, which other people find difficult to understand

UNIT 5, LESSON 2, page 56

neglected: not taken care of very well
explicit: expressed in a way that is very clear
reflective: thinking carefully and deeply about things
an utterance: something that someone says
a cultural gap: a big difference between two cultures
unsettled: slightly worried, upset, or nervous
fill the silence: to replace quietness with conversation, music, or noise
a counterpart: someone or something that has the same job or purpose as someone or something else in a separate place

GLOSSARY

UNIT 5, LESSON 3, page 58

cringeworthy: causing embarrassment or awkwardness
a phenomenon: something that happens in society or nature, usually something unusual
an abbreviation: the short way of writing a word or phrase
an emoji: an image, such as a smiley face, made by using a combination of letters on the keyboard; usually expresses the writer's emotions
rebel: to disobey or fight against someone who has power over you, such as parents or the government
the status quo: the present situation, one that is considered the normal situation
solidarity: mutual support within a group
no hard and fast rules: no fixed guidelines to follow, but there may be a traditional way to do things
concise: short and not containing too many words
a downside: a negative aspect of something
vulgar: rude and often inappropriate for a situation
hinder: to make it difficult for someone to do something

UNIT 5, LESSON 4, page 60

decipher: to discover the meaning of something that is hard to understand or that contains a hidden message
divided on: to have different, opposing opinions on a topic
on the premise (that): based on a theory, argument, or idea
render (something) unnecessary: make or cause something to be unimportant or no longer needed
interstellar: happening or situated between the stars
a cultural construct: a shared understanding or practice among a certain cultural group
a long way off: a long time in the future
a boundary: the limit of what is possible or acceptable

UNIT 6, LESSON 1, page 66

charge: to accuse someone of something, especially to officially accuse someone of a crime
bribe: to illegally pay money or offer gifts to someone in order to persuade the person to do something for you
fraud: the crime of deceiving people in order to gain money, power, etc.
embezzlement: the act of stealing money from the place where you work
misappropriation of funds: the dishonest act of taking money that you have been trusted to keep safe for a particular purpose
a scandal: behavior or events, often involving famous people, that are considered to be shocking or not moral
tip off: to give someone, such as the police, a secret warning or piece of information, especially about illegal activities
an internal audit: the official examination of a company's financial records, conducted by someone within the company in order to check that they are correct
trace: to find someone or something that has disappeared by searching for them carefully
an accusation: a statement saying that someone has done something wrong
inexcusable: too bad to be forgiven

UNIT 6, LESSON 2, page 68

random: happening or chosen without any plan, aim, or pattern
eligible: officially allowed to have or do something
have a say: to have the opportunity to give your opinion about something
restore: to make something return to its former level or condition
a campaign: a series of things that you do in order to persuade people to do something
a lobbyist: someone who tries to persuade the government to do something
naïve: believing that people are nicer and things are easier than they really are because you do not have much experience in life
susceptible: easily influenced or affected by something
on hold: delayed from starting or happening
employable: having skills or qualities that are necessary to get a job
diversity: the quality of being made up of a range of different people, ideas, or things

UNIT 6, LESSON 3, page 70

ubiquitous: seeming to be everywhere
a dynamic: the way that people behave with each other because of a particular situation
idolize (someone): to admire someone so much that you think of that person as perfect
aspire to (something): to have a strong wish or desire to do or have something
ambivalent: to have two opposing feelings at the same time
adulation: praise or admiration for someone, perhaps more than the person deserves
condemnation: the act of criticizing someone or something in a very strong way
liberating: freeing; allowing you to behave as you like
coercion: the use of force to persuade someone to do something the person is unwilling to do
diminish: to become smaller or weaker
a barrier: a rule or problem that prevents people from doing something
conformity: behavior that follows the accepted rules of society or a group

UNIT 6, LESSON 4, page 72

stunted: not developing properly or to full size
an isolated occurrence: something that happens only once, and is not connected to other events
overexposure: the experience of being affected by something for too long, especially something harmful
armed with (something): having the knowledge, skills, or equipment needed to do something
cognitive impairment: a condition where part of a person's mind is damaged and doesn't work well
fall on deaf ears: to be completely ignored, especially in the case of advice
dispel: to make something go away, especially a belief or fear
unearth (something): to find something hidden, lost, or kept secret
afflict: to cause pain or suffering to someone or something
the tipping point: the moment when a lot of small incidents become big enough to prompt change
an accolade: an expression of praise, often a prize or award

UNIT 7, LESSON 1, page 78

talk (someone) into: to persuade someone to do something
dissuade: to persuade someone not to do something
far apart: to have very different opinions or positions on something
reconsider: to think again about something in order to decide if you should change your opinion
out of (one's) hands: out of one's control
coax: to persuade someone to do something by talking gently and calmly
wiggle room: room for negotiation or operation, especially in order to change a previous statement or decision
top-notch: having the highest quality or standard
twist (someone's) arm: to force someone to do something that he or she does not want to do
assure: to tell someone that something will definitely happen or is true so that he or she is less worried
make up (one's) mind: to decide something or become very determined to do something
sweeten the pot: to make a deal seem more acceptable, usually by offering more money or a special perk

UNIT 7, LESSON 2, page 80

let (someone) down easy: to give someone news in a gentle and kind way
tons: a lot
figure: to think that something is probably true
go for it: to do something difficult without worrying about potential problems
shoot (someone) a text: to send someone a text message, usually quickly
the perils of: the dangers or problems relating to a particular activity or situation
get back at (someone): to do something to hurt or embarrass someone who has hurt or embarrassed you; to get revenge
hideous: extremely ugly or bad
smash: to break into many small pieces violently or loudly, or to make something do this by dropping, throwing, or hitting it
hang out with: to spend a lot of time with particular people, doing a variety of activities together
romantic: showing strong feelings of love
dump: to end a romantic relationship, especially in a sudden way

UNIT 7, LESSON 3, page 82

an innovation: a new idea, invention, or way of doing something
distribute: to share things among a group of people, usually in an organized way
monopolize: to have complete control of a business activity
stifle: to stop something from happening or developing
a start-up: a new company that has been recently started
deter: to stop someone from doing something by making it difficult
clout: power and influence, especially in politics
a patent: a legal document that gives you the right to make and sell a new product
exert: to use power and influence to make something happen
manipulative: good at controlling or deceiving people to get what you want
harvest: to collect large amounts of information, especially automatically
breach: to break a law, rule, or agreement

GLOSSARY

UNIT 7, LESSON 4, page 84

outweigh: to be more important or have more effect than something else
debris: the pieces of something that are left after an accident or explosion
profound: having a strong influence or effect
viable: a plan or idea that is capable of being successful
mitigate: to make something less harmful or unpleasant
derive: to develop or come from something else
a raw material: a substance such as coal, oil, or iron that is in its natural state
dispose of: to get rid of something, especially something that is hard to get rid of or might cause a problem

UNIT 8, LESSON 1, page 90

break the ice: to do or say something to relieve tension and make someone more willing to talk
crack a smile: to smile
fall flat: to fail to produce the intended or expected effect
sarcastic: saying things that are the opposite of what you mean in order to make a joke that is not nice, or to show that you are annoyed
bomb: to be unsuccessful, often in the entertainment business
a one-liner: a very short joke or humorous remark
a punchline: the last few words of a joke or story that make it funny or surprising
pull off: to succeed in doing something difficult
crack up: to laugh a lot at something
slapstick: humorous physical acting in which the performers fall down, throw things at each other, etc.
hilarious: extremely funny
in hysterics: to laugh so hard that you are unable to stop

UNIT 8, LESSON 2, page 92

evolutionary: connected with the scientific theory that plants and animals develop and change gradually over a very long period of time
a species: a group of animals or plants of the same kind, that breed to produce young animals or plants
bonding: a process in which a strong feeling of love or trust develops between two or more people
a territory: an area that an animal, person, or group thinks belongs to them and tries to control
exclude: to not allow someone to enter a place or to do an activity
alleviate: to make something less bad, painful, severe, or difficult
dominate: to have control over someone or something or to have more power or importance than them
tickle: to move your fingers lightly over someone's body in order to make them laugh
a mammal: an animal that drinks its mother's milk when it is young, for example a cow, lion, or person

UNIT 8, LESSON 3, page 94

wish the ground would swallow (you) up: to wish that you could escape from a very embarrassing situation
a fit: a sudden outbreak of intense emotion, laughter, coughing, etc.
vice-versa: the opposite of a situation you have just described
tailor: to adjust something to fit someone's particular needs or situation
antiquated: old-fashioned
current affairs: important political or social events that are happening now
personalize: to design, change, or make something suitable for a particular person
a hook: something that is designed to attract people's attention
an anecdote: a short story that you tell people, based on your personal experience
signpost: to clearly show how something is organized and how it's going to develop

UNIT 8, LESSON 4, page 96

set out (to do something): to start doing something, or to make plans in order to achieve a result
cast a vote: to vote in an election
glazed (over): showing no expression with your eyes, usually because you are bored or tired
incongruity: when something is strange, unusual, or unsuitable for a certain situation
a respondent: a person who replies to something, especially a survey
offbeat: unconventional; unusual
yield: to produce something
dying to know: eager and excited to learn something

UNIT 9, LESSON 1, page 102

come down on: to punish or criticize someone severely
single (someone) out: to choose someone from among a group of similar people, especially in order to praise or criticize the person
lay into: to attack someone with words
be at odds: to disagree
be short with: to speak to someone using very few words, in a way that seems impolite or unfriendly
point the finger at: to blame
be in the wrong: to be responsible for something bad, such as a quarrel or mistake
make amends: to say you are sorry for something you did to someone, and try to make things better
patch up: to end an argument because you want to stay friendly with someone
do (someone) a disservice: to do something unkind to someone, causing others to have a bad opinion about the person
let bygones be bygones: to forget something bad that someone has done to you and forgive the person

UNIT 9, LESSON 2, page 104

an intervention: the act of getting involved in something such as an argument or activity to influence what happens
down-to-earth: practical, sensible, and honest
de-escalate: to stop something such as an argument or an attack from becoming worse
absorb: to take in new information and understand it
cool off: to become calm, especially after a fight or disagreement
at hand: present and current
minimize: to make something seem less serious or important than it really is
trivial: unimportant or of little value
self-talk: the act of talking to yourself, especially in order to encourage yourself
food for thought: something that makes you think carefully

UNIT 9, LESSON 3, page 106

captivate: to hold the attention of someone by being attractive, charming, interesting, etc.
a resolution: the ending of a problem or difficulty
fundamental: relating to the most basic or important part of something
a circumstance: a condition or fact that is involved in an event or situation
a confrontation: an angry argument or fight
a premise: a theory on which a statement or action is based
a triumph: a victory or success
literary heritage: the beliefs, values, or customs of society as expressed through literature
escapism: the activity of avoiding reality with entertainment
woes: the problems and troubles affecting someone
insurmountable: problematic to the degree that it is too large or difficult to deal with

UNIT 9, LESSON 4, page 108

a genre: a particular type of movie, art, music, or literature
a guise: an external presentation of something, typically concealing its true nature
a hijacking: the use of violence or threats to take control of an airplane, vehicle, or ship
a franchise: a title used for creating or marketing a series of products, typically movies or television shows
cheesy: silly; cheap; not new or interesting
hard-hitting: strong, serious, and effective
retaliation: action against someone who has done something bad to you
substance: importance or significance
a conspiracy: a secret plan that people make together to do something bad
vast: extremely large
emotive: causing strong feelings
oppression: a state of being in which people are treated badly and not allowed to do what they want

UNIT 10, LESSON 1, page 114

grief: extreme sadness, especially because someone you love has died
heartbroken: very sad because you have lost someone you love, or because someone has disappointed you
devastated: extremely shocked and sad
compassion: a strong feeling of sympathy for people who are suffering and of wanting to help them
condolences: an expression of sympathy for someone, especially when someone has died
console: to make someone feel better when the person is feeling sad or disappointed
uplifting: making you feel more cheerful
gratifying: pleasing and satisfying
savor: to enjoy an activity or experience slowly so that you can appreciate every moment of it
be down in the dumps: to feel very sad or depressed

UNIT 10, LESSON 2, page 116

intriguing: very interesting because of the strange, mysterious, or unexpected nature of someone or something
dull: not interesting or exciting
a documentary: a movie or television program that gives facts and information about something
suppress: to stop yourself from showing your feelings or from doing an action
subjective: influenced by personal opinion and therefore possibly unfair
fellow: belonging to the same class, school, or group as you
a boost: an act of increasing or improving something
enhance: to improve the quality or strength of something
preliminary: happening before something that is more important, often to get ready for it
illuminating: making things much clearer and easier to understand

UNIT 10, LESSON 3, page 118

a trauma: an unpleasant and upsetting experience
an obstacle: something that stops you from doing or achieving something successfully
synthetic: not naturally produced; artificial
an immune system: a system that helps the body fight illness or disease
a coping mechanism: a strategy or technique people use to help them deal with stress or difficulty
miscalculate: to make a wrong judgement about a situation
overestimate: to think something is bigger, longer, better, or more important than it really is
a paraplegic: someone who is unable to move the lower part of his or her body, including the legs
relative: having a particular value or quality when compared with something else
tedious: boring and continuing for a long time
be confined to: to be restricted to a particular place or area
a contribution: something you give or do that helps something be successful

UNIT 10, LESSON 4, page 120

tremendous: very large in size, amount, or power; very good
death-defying: very dangerous, possibly resulting in death
sheer: used to emphasize the size or amount of something
a memoir: a piece of writing written by a person having intimate knowledge of the subject; based on personal observation
a turning point: the time when an important change happens, normally one that makes a situation better
throw caution to the wind: to do something without worrying about risks or potential problems
spirituality: the quality of being interested in the human spirit or soul
strive: to try very hard to get or do something
relentlessly: without stopping, usually negative in meaning
rags-to-riches: from very poor to very rich

UNIT 5, LESSON 1, TRY IT YOURSELF, page 55

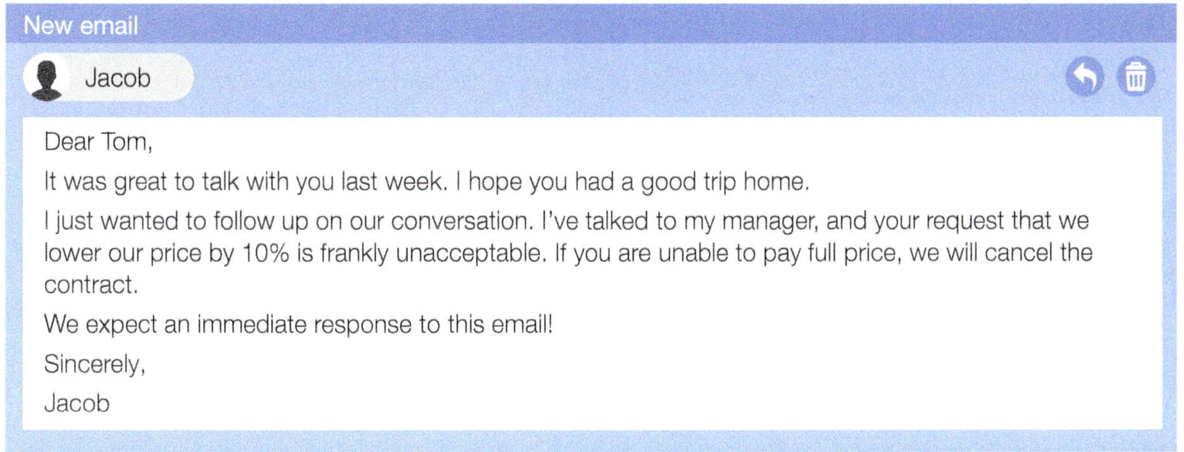
New email

Jacob

Dear Tom,

It was great to talk with you last week. I hope you had a good trip home.

I just wanted to follow up on our conversation. I've talked to my manager, and your request that we lower our price by 10% is frankly unacceptable. If you are unable to pay full price, we will cancel the contract.

We expect an immediate response to this email!

Sincerely,

Jacob

Photo Credits

Cover

Yusuke Shimazu/EyeEm/Getty Images; Tovovan/Shutterstock.

To The Teacher

Page viii: Ulla Lohmann/National Geographic Image Collection/Getty Images; ix (p. 82): Kite_rin/Shutterstock; ix (p. 83): Sergii Gnatiuk/Shutterstock; ix (p.5 chapter opener): Ulla Lohmann/National Geographic Image Collection/Getty Images; ix (p. 5 bottom right): Ranta Images/Shutterstock; ix (video talk): Robert Adrian Hillman/Shutterstock; ix (video talk, girl): Pearson Education; ix (bottom): G-Stock Studio/Shutterstock.

Welcome Unit

Page 2: Shutterstock; 3 (front cover image): Yusuke Shimazu/EyeEm/Getty Images; 3 (Image on cell phone): Ulla Lohmann/National Geographic Image Collection/Getty Images; 4 (Sam Bennett): Ranta Images/Shutterstock; 4 (Camila Rivas): Shutterstock; 4 (Edgar Vela): Ranta Images/Shutterstock; 4 (Iris Lin): Fotogenicstudio/Shutterstock; 4 (Artur Tavaras): Kite_rin/Shutterstock; 4 (Ariya Suksuay): Ekkamai Chaikanta/Shutterstock; 4 (Adriana Lopez): Pearson Education; 4 (Kendrick Scott): Pearson Education; 4 (David Cruz): Pearson Education.

Unit 1

Page 5: Ulla Lohmann/National Geographic Image Collection/Getty Images; 5 (Sam Bennett): Ranta Images/Shutterstock; 6: Ranta Images/Shutterstock; 7: Rawpixel.com/Shutterstock; 8: Ranta Images/Shutterstock; 10: Ranta Images/Shutterstock; 11: Robert Adrian Hillman/Shutterstock; 12 (Sam Bennett): Ranta Images/Shutterstock; 12 (center): Izf/Shutterstock; 14 (Sam Bennett): Ranta Images/Shutterstock; 14 (background): Sklo Studio/Shutterstock.

Unit 2

Page 17: Flashpop/DigitalVision/Getty Images; 17 (Edgar Vela): Ranta Images/Shutterstock; 18: Ranta Images/Shutterstock; 19: M-SUR/Shutterstock; 20: Ranta Images/Shutterstock; 22 (Edgar Vela): Ranta Images/Shutterstock; 22 (middle, right): Kuliperko/Shutterstock; 23: Desdemona72/Shutterstock; 24: Ranta Images/Shutterstock; 26 (Edgar Vela): Ranta Images/Shutterstock; 26 (sports fans): Juri Pozzi/Shutterstock.

Unit 3

Page 29: Mopic/Shutterstock; 29 (Artur Tavares): Kite_rin/Shutterstock; 30 (Artur Tavares): Kite_rin/Shutterstock; 30 (great pyramid): Jeremy Red/Shutterstock; 31: Guenter Albers/Shutterstock; 32: Kite_rin/Shutterstock; 34: Kite_rin/Shutterstock; 35: Clara/Shutterstock; 36 (Artur Tavares): Kite_rin/Shutterstock; 36 (center): Michaeljung/Shutterstock; 38 (Artur Tavares): Kite_rin/Shutterstock; 38 (center): Tom Tom/Shutterstock.

Unit 4

Page 41: Jaki Good Photography - Celebrating the art of life/Moment/Getty Images; 41 (Camila Rivas): Shutterstock; 42 (Camila Rivas): Shutterstock; 42 (ancient latin graffiti): Karl Allen Lugmayer/Shutterstock; 42 (graffiti tag): Banana Republic Images/Shutterstock; 42 (graffiti mural): Zarya Maxim Alexandrovich/Shutterstock; 42 (hip hop): STREET STYLE/Shutterstock; 42 (auction): Hxdbzxy/123RF; 43: Sam Cornwell/Shutterstock; 44: Shutterstock; 46 (Camila Rivas): Shutterstock; 46 (center): Shutterstock; 47: Shutterstock; 48 (Camila Rivas): Shutterstock; 48-49 (background): Sunshine Seeds/Shutterstock; 50 (Camila Rivas): Shutterstock; 50 (center): Pealiku/Shutterstock.

Unit 5

Page 53: PeopleImages/E+/Getty Images; 53 (Iris Lin): Fotogenicstudio/Shutterstock; 54: Fotogenicstudio/Shutterstock; 55: Who is Danny/Shutterstock; 56 (Iris Lin): Fotogenicstudio/Shutterstock; 56 (center): Mythja/Shutterstock. 58 (Iris Lin): Fotogenicstudio/Shutterstock; 58 (center): Josie Elias/Shutterstock; Page 59: ARENA Creative/Shutterstock; 60 (Iris Lin): Fotogenicstudio/Shutterstock; 60 (alien): Adike/Shutterstock; 61: Vchal/Shutterstock; 62 (Iris Lin): Fotogenicstudio/Shutterstock; 62 (athlete jumping hurdle): Sirtravelalot/Shutterstock.

Unit 6

Page 65: Rawpixel.com/Shutterstock; 65 (Ariya Suksuay): Ekkamai Chaikanta/Shutterstock; 66: Ekkamai Chaikanta/Shutterstock; 67: Motortion Films/Shutterstock; 68 (top, right): Ekkamai Chaikanta/Shutterstock; 68 (middle, right): Alexandru Nika/Shutterstock; 70: Ekkamai Chaikanta/Shutterstock; 71: BigAlBaloo/Shutterstock; 72 (Ariya Suksuay): Ekkamai Chaikanta/Shutterstock; 72 (Flint water plant): Geoff Robins/AFP/Getty Images; 74 (top, right): Ekkamai Chaikanta/Shutterstock; 74 (copy/paste key): Jurgenfr/Shutterstock.

Unit 7

Page 77: Porstocker/Shutterstock; 77 (Artur Tavares): Kite_rin/Shutterstock; 78 (Artur Tavares): Kite_rin/Shutterstock; 78 (center): Rido/Shutterstock; 79: Kite_rin/Shutterstock; 80: Kite_rin/Shutterstock; 82: Kite_rin/Shutterstock; 83: Sergii Gnatiuk/Shutterstock; 84 (Artur Tavares): Kite_rin/Shutterstock; 84 (center): Jag_cz/Shutterstock; 86 (Artur Tavares): Kite_rin/Shutterstock; 86 (center): Krissikunterbunt/Shutterstock.

Unit 8

Page 89: Joe Regan/Moment/Getty Images; 89 (Edgar Vela): Ranta Images/Shutterstock; 90: Ranta Images/Shutterstock; 91: Ntkris/Shutterstock; 92: Ranta Images/Shutterstock; 94: Ranta Images/Shutterstock; 95: Kzenon/Shutterstock; 96 (Edgar Vela): Ranta Images/Shutterstock; 96 (bottom): WAYHOME studio/Shutterstock; 98 (Edgar Vela): Ranta Images/Shutterstock; 98 (bottom): Sirtravelalot/Shutterstock.

Unit 9

Page 101: Gregobagel/E+/Getty Images; 101 (Camila Rivas): Shutterstock; 102: Shutterstock; Page 103: Victoria 1/Shutterstock; 104 (Camila Rivas): Shutterstock; 104 (center): Michal Kowalski/Shutterstock; 106 (Camila Rivas): Shutterstock; 106 (center): Romolo Tavani/Shutterstock; 107: GoodStudio/Shutterstock; 108 (Camila Rivas): Shutterstock; 108 (center): © DreamWorks/courtesy Everett Collection; 110 (Camila Rivas): Shutterstock; 110 (background): Sean Pavone/Shutterstock.

Unit 10

Page 113: Francesco Carta fotografo/Moment/Getty Images; 113 (Sam Bennett): Ranta Images/Shutterstock; 114 (Sam Bennett): Ranta Images/Shutterstock; 115: Pimchawee/Shutterstock; 116 (Sam Bennett): Ranta Images/Shutterstock; 116 (bottom): Aslysun/Shutterstock; 118 (Sam Bennett): Ranta Images/Shutterstock; 119: Arun P Sidharthan/Shutterstock; 120 (Sam Bennett): Ranta Images/Shutterstock; 120 (hiker on cliff): Michael Carni/Shutterstock; 120 (canoe): Mooshny/Shutterstock. Page 121: Mungkhood Studio/Shutterstock; 122 (Sam Bennett): Ranta Images/Shutterstock; 122 (Abraham Lincoln): Everett Historical/Shutterstock.